GROSSKONZERN

Deutsch für den Ausländer

Ein famoses Lehrbuch

Florian Lamp
&
Heldrich Johannes

Inhalt

Chapter 5

Chapter 6:

Chapter 7

Chapter 8

Chapter 9

Chapter 10

Chapter 11

Chapter 12

Chapter 13

Chapter 14

Vocabulary

Präambel

Wieso, weshalb, warum?

Lehrbücher sind in der Regel todlangweilig. Sprachlehrbücher gehen meistens noch, weil man sie zeichnerisch verschönern kann, indem man beispielsweise allen Personen in den Zeichnungen und Fotografien Pistolen und Maschinengewehre in die Hand malen kann. Das war in den 90er Jahren noch möglich, ohne dass man direkt zum Schulpsychologen geschleift wurde, wenn die so entstandenen Bilder entdeckt wurden.

Aber wir wollen nicht der guten alten Zeit nachtrauern. Das vorliegende Buch ist ein Sprachehrbuch. Richtig schrecklich waren – und sie sind es bestimmt immer noch – Mathebücher. Da aber keiner von uns Mathe richtig toll kann, geschweige denn mag, haben wir uns mit diesem Werk vorerst nur auf die Deutsche Sprache konzentriert, weil wo wir die gut verstehen tun. Das Ganze haben wir mit Englisch vermischt, da wir das auch noch können.

Der Ausländer, der dieses Buch erwirbt, um damit die schöne deutsche Sprache zu erlernen, soll ein ungeschöntes und vor allem unverfälschtes Bild von Deutschland, seinen Einwohnern, seinen Sitten und Bräuchen erhalten. Er soll feststellen, dass wir Deutschen wirklich richtig hässlich sein können, dass wir keinerlei Humor haben und nicht mal die Perfektionisten sind, als die wir im Ausland immer gern gesehen werden.

Trotzdem soll ihm, dem Ausländer, bewusst werden, wie wichtig Deutschland und die Deutschen sind, wenn dieser Planet die Finanzkrise und dann irgendwann auch andere Krisen wie die globale Erwärmung, die Geburtenkrise oder den Einschlag eines kilometergroßen Meteoriten kurz vor der französischen Atlantikküste, überwinden will.

Der deutsche Erfindergeist ist ungebrochen groß. Vor kurzem erst wurde die Abwrackprämie erfunden, vor gut 100 Jahren das Automobil und nur wenig früher das Rad – alles urdeutsche Erfindungen wie der Weltkrieg, der Nationalsozialismus und die Kehrwoche. Wir, die Erfinder dieses Buches, wollen dazu beitragen, dass am deutschen Wesen die Welt genesen möge, haben aber keinerlei Invasionspläne für Polen vorliegen und können nur immer wieder darauf hinweisen, dass es keinen Heldrich-Putin-Pakt gibt.

Wir sind friedliche Pazifisten, die keiner Fliege was zu leide tun können, sofern sie außerhalb unserer Reichweite ist und wir keine Mückenklatsche zur Hand haben. Bisher gibt es nur eine universelle Sprache – die Sprache der Liebe. Mit Hilfe dieses Buches soll Deutsch der Sprache der Liebe ebenbürtig werden. Da ist es dann egal, dass weltweit und bisher noch andere Sprachen wie Englisch, Russisch, Portugiesisch oder Französisch von mehr Menschen gesprochen werden als Deutsch.

Wir planen mit diesem Buch erfolgreicher zu sein als Charlotte Roche mit Feuchtgebiete oder Gott mit der Bibel. Sollte dies nicht der Fall sein, wird der Großkonzern so lange weiter Fortsetzungen dieses Buches drucken lassen, bis das eintritt, was bei der schönen Matheaufgabe, bei denen ein Schachbrett und Reiskörner eine große Rolle spielen, passiert. Ihr kennt die Aufgabe bestimmt, oder? Ihr habt ein Schachbrett und legt auf das erste Feld 1 Reiskorn, dann auf das nächste 2, dann 4, dann 16, dann 256 usw. Am Ende würden auf dem Schachbrett so viele Reiskörner liegen, dass man damit die ganze Welt mit Reis bedecken könnte.

Wenn man jetzt das Wort „Reiskorn" gegen „Deutsch für den Ausländer" austauscht, dann wäre die gesamte Erdoberfläche (inklusive der Weltmeere) 8,8 Zentimeter hoch mit Exemplaren von „Deutsch für den Ausländer" bedeckt. Kaufen Sie dieses Buch, lernen Sie mit diesem Buch und verschenken Sie dieses Buch an den Ausländer und die Ausländerin. Sie werden Ihnen dankbar sein.

Chapter 1

Die Schmidts

Das sind die Schmidts. Die Schmidts sind eine typisch deutsche Familie.

Reporter: *„Hallo, Familie Schmidt!"*

Vater: *„Ach halten Sie doch die Fresse!"*

Reporter: *„Herr Schmidt, kommen Sie aus Deutschland?"*

Vater: *„Woher soll ich sonst kommen? Vom Mond?"*

Helmut Schmidt ist arbeitslos. Er hat eine Ausbildung als Fallschirmspringer und Inoffizieller Mitarbeiter und trinkt sehr gerne sehr viel Alkohol.

Reporter: *„Prost, Herr Schmidt!"*

Tochter: *„Hallo! Ich bin die Doreen Schmidt! Ich bin 14 Jahre alt und gehe nicht zur Schule. Schule ist doof!"*

Mutter: *„Du gehst nicht zur Schule, Doreen? Egal. Mein Name ist Eve und ich arbeite in einem Imbiss. Ich liebe Ketwurst, meinen Mann und das Leben. Wo ist unser Sohn, der Sven?"*

Sohn: *„Hier bin ich. Ich bin der Svengster, ein großer Gangster und wenn es nicht hart ist, ist es nicht mein Prozess, yo!"*

Mutter: *„Nachts nässt sich der Sven oft ein. Sven tut nur so böse. In Wirklichkeit ist er ein ganz Lieber."*

Grammar stuff – Chapter 1

Personal Pronouns / Personalpronomina:

SINGULAR	PLURAL
ich *(I)*	wir *(we)*
du *(you)*	ihr *(you)*
Sie *(you)*	Sie *(you)*
er / sie / es *(he / she / it)*	sie *(they)*

Present Tense / Das Präsens

Regular verbs on the example of "*gehen*" (go)

SINGULAR		PLURAL	
ich	gehe	wir	gehen
du	gehst	ihr	geht
Sie	gehen	Sie	gehen
er / sie / es	geht	sie	gehen

Sein / Haben (be / have)

Sein

SINGULAR		PLURAL	
ich	bin	wir	sind
du	bist	ihr	seid
Sie	sind	Sie	sind
er / sie / es	ist	sie	sind

Haben

SINGULAR		PLURAL	
ich	habe	wir	haben
du	hast	ihr	habt
Sie	haben	Sie	haben
er / sie / es	hat	sie	haben

Word order in different kinds of sentences

Affirmative Statement

Er	ist	der Svengster.
He	*is*	*the Svengster.*
(Subject)	(Verb)	(Object)

Question including question word

Wer	ist	der Svengster?
Who	*is*	*the Svengster?*
(Question word)	(Verb)	(Subject)

Question without question word

Ist	er	der Svengster?
Is	*he*	*the Svengster?*
(Verb)	(Subject)	(Object)

Das ist das Haus von Familie Schmidt.
This is the Schmidt's house.

Exercises – Chapter 1

Complete these incomplete sentences with the correct pronouns.

.... ist der Svengster. (Masculine)

.... hält die Fresse. (Feminine)

.... arbeitet in einem Imbiss. (Feminine)

.... kommt vom Mond. (Masculine)

.... lieben den Alkohol. (Plural)

.... ist doof. (Feminine)

Complete these sentences. Right! They are lacking a verb in the correct form.

Wir .... Menschenfleisch. (essen)

Ihr .... Blut. (trinken)

Eve .... Ketwurst und ungeschützten Sex. (lieben)

Der Svengster .... in die Hose. (machen)

Drogen .... gut. (schmecken)

Would you be so kind and complete these sentences.

Du .... blöd. (sein)

Ihr .... behindert. (sein)

Ich .... der Größte. (sein)

Wir .... kein Gehirn. (haben)

Er .... ein Maschinengewehr. (haben)

Complete these sentences and have fun with two verbs.

Ich.................... ein Schlachtermesser und.................... schwarze Katzen. (haben / töten)

Wir.................... Gangstarapper und....................kurze Schwänze. (sein / haben)

Du....................ein Opfer und .... wie ein schwuler Hund. (sein / klingen)

Sie.................... die Atombombe und ....die Welt in die Luft. (haben / sprengen)

Ihr ....erbärmlich und....................nicht meine Homies. (stinken / sein)

Ich.................... deine Mutter und du....................ein Bastard. (ficken / sein)

Questions and answers – Match the sentences

Wo wohnen die Schmidts?	Sie liebt Ketwurst.
Was liebt Eve Schmidt?	Ja. Sie ist doof.
Nässt sich Sven am Tag ein?	Nein. Sie ist nicht vom Mond.
Ist Schule doof?	Sie wohnen in Deutschland.
Ist Helmut Fallschirmjäger?	Er ist ein Gangster.
Ist die Familie Schmidt vom Mond?	Nein, Sven nässt nachts ein.
Wer trinkt gerne sehr viel Alkohol?	Helmut trinkt gerne Alkohol.
Was ist der Svengster?	Ja. Er ist Fallschirmjäger.

Bonus-Track – Chapter 1

The Germans – Who they are and why they could be

The Schmidts are one of 10.000.000 German families that need financial help from the government because they neither have money nor a job – or they don't feel like having a job would be useful for them. In Germany, there are a lot of alcoholics. This is an old tradition and being an alcoholic in the third generation even gets you lower rates in public transport or a cheaper entry fee in museums. It does not matter if it is early morning or late in the afternoon: When you wake up, you eat breakfast starting with a beer. Supper naturally consists of at least two large beers and when it's dinner time you first order a bottle of schnapps before you eat some raw bacon or grilled fat cat.

In case all this does not sound very appealing to you, be careful. People, even foreigners from other countries, are expected to join in and become "honorary Germans" for the longevity of their stay in the country. If you fail to take part in this traditional behaviour, you are stigmatised as a "Spaßbremse" which means you are a completely retarded failure that others are allowed to spit or even urinate on. Very seldomly rumors have been reported of foreign tourists who eagerly refused the German customs and did not survive.

Other foreigners have eagerly become more German than the Germans themselves. One of the best examples is called Roberto Blanco (*07.06.1937). He was born as the son of an African Cuban couple in Tunis / Tunisia and raised in Beirut and Madrid. First he studied medicine in Madrid and then decided it was much more fun to "heal the world" by singing German "Schlager"-music. His first hits were "Ein bisschen Spaß muß sein" and "Der Puppenspieler von Mexiko".

In his first hit he pleaded that "A little fun has to be" and described in a socio-critical way that one should drink until 4 o' clock in the morning and everything would be fine, because "a little bit of fun" was fine. The second hit single about a puppeteer from Mexico proved to be even more socially aware of the current situation in Germany 1972 and told a story about a puppeteer that was sometimes happy and sometimes sad. However, the audience of that puppeteer didn't care too much because they were drunk most of the time – although they were not German but Mexican.

Blanco followed his path of success with more happy drinking songs. Amongst these songs were anthems like "Samba si! Arbeit no!" (1976) and later with his German born brother in spirit, Tony Marshall, "Resi bring Bier". "Resi" must be seen as the best song to show the proverbial "German Gemütlichkeit". In this song Tony and Roberto order beer after beer from waitress Resi and conclude that at a real party in Germany everyone is happy and funny and wets him- or herself while laughing until the doctor comes. But until then everyone is shouting for more beer: Resi, bring beer! (See also the imperative lesson in Chapter 8, pages 85–86). By the way: "Resi bring Bier!" is a German cover version of Mr. David Hasselhoff's German hit-single "Crazy for you" – but we don't want to talk about German taste in music now.

Chapter 2

Der Svengster beim Dealer

Svengster: *„Mahlzeit, Hoschi! Ich bin der Svengster! Ein real Gangster...“*

Dealer: *„Ach, halt doch die Fresse! Komm rein in die gute Stube. Was brauchst du?“*

Svengster: *„Dickes Danke!“*

Dealer: *„Hier sind meine Verkaufsräume. Setz dich da in den Sitzsack! Möchtest du Speed, Koks, Heroin, Hasch oder doch lieber erst eine Fassbrause?“*

Svengster: *„Eine Fassbrause? Habt ihr auch eine Fanta?“*

Dealer: *„Das da hinten ist mein Labor. Hier stellen wir Crystal Meth her. Das da ist das Bad. Da kannst du dir gern was drücken. Und das Zimmer dort ist unser fettes Waffenlager.“*

Svengster: *„Wow! Ihr verkauft auch Waffen? Habt ihr auch einen Flammenwerfer und ein Maschinengewehr?“*

Dealer: *„Sicher doch. Wir haben auch guten Flüssigsprengstoff.“*

Svengster: *„Und wer ist das da oben auf dem Poster?“*

Dealer: *„Das sind die No Angels. Wenn ich eine Line gezogen habe, dann wichs...“*

Svengster: *„Ach so. Schon gut. Ich stehe total auf Bushido. Kennst du den?“*

Dealer: *„Ist das der Tempelhofgangster? Von der Skyline zum Bordstein? Alles Gute kommt von hinten? Ist das der mit der Autobiografie?“*

Svengster: *„Ja genau! Das ist er!“*

Dealer: *„Neeee. Den kenn ic h n i c h t*

Grammar Stuff – Chapter 2

Nouns and articles

der = MASCULINE **die = FEMININE** **das = NEUTER**

Some hints:
Typically feminine: female persons, female jobs, animals
Examples: die Mutter *(mother)*, die Nutte *(whore)*, die Schlampe *(slut)*, die Hündin *(bitch)*

Typically male: male persons, male jobs, male animals, all weekdays
Examples: der Rapper, der Zuhälter *(pimp)*, der Papst *(pope)*, der Hengst *(stallion)*

Typically neuter: words with suffixes* "chen" *or* "o" *as last letter
Examples: das Mädchen *(girl)*, das Lotto *(lottery)*, das Häschen *(bunny)*, das Pornofilmchen *(diminuitive form of porno movie)*

Indefinite and definite article

ein Papst / **der** Papst **eine** Nutte / **die** Nutte **ein** Pferd / **das** Pferd

"ein" *or* "eine" *are usually used when something is unknown or new*
"der", "die" *and* "das" *shows that something is known*

NOMINATIVE & ACCUSATIVE

It depends on the verb which case of the noun you have to use.
The verb* "sein" *(to be) = always with the NOMINATIVE
=> Das ist eine Nutte. *(This is a whore.)*

Typical verbs used with the accusative:
nehmen, trinken, mögen, kaufen, klauen, brauchen, haben

Examples:	Ich klaue ein Pornoheftchen.	*I steal a porno magazine.*
	Du trinkst 2 Flaschen Schnaps.	*You drink 2 bottles of schnapps.*

Indefinite and definite article in the NOMINATIVE and in the ACCUSATIVE			
	MASCULINE	**NEUTER**	**FEMININE**
NOMINATIVE	der / ein	das / ein	die / eine
ACCUSATIVE	den / einen	das / ein	die / eine

Question words for things and persons – NOMINATIVE and ACCUSATIVE		
Person NOMINATIVE SG.	Das ist Sven.	**Wer** ist das?
Persons NOMINATIVE PL.	Das sind Sven und Bushido.	**Wer** sind die Nulpen?
Person ACCUSATIVE SG.	Ich sehe Eve.	**Wen** sehe ich?
Persons ACCUSATIVE PL.	Ich sehe Eve und Doreen.	**Wen** sehe ich?
Thing NOMINATIVE SG.	Das ist eine Bombe.	**Was** ist das?
Things NOMINATIVE PL.	Das sind 3 Bomben.	**Was** ist das?
Thing ACCUSATIVE SG.	Ich sehe ein Kondom.	**Was** siehst du?
Things ACCUSATIVE PL.	Ich sehe 3 Kondome.	**Was** siehst du?

Modal verbs *"können" "dürfen"* and *"möchten"*				
können ***can***	ich	kann	wir	könn**en**
	du	kann**st**	ihr	könn**t**
	Sie	könn**en**	Sie	könn**en**
	er, sie, es	kann	sie	könn**en**
dürfen ***may***	ich	darf	wir	dürf**en**
	du	darf**st**	ihr	Dürf**t**
	Sie	dürf**en**	Sie	dürf**en**
	er, sie, es	darf	sie	dürf**en**
möchten would like *(Subjonctive II of* mögen*)*	ich	möcht**e**	wir	möcht**en**
	du	möcht**est**	ihr	möcht**et**
	Sie	möcht**en**	Sie	möcht**en**
	er, sie, es	möcht**e**	sie	möcht**en**

Exercises – Chapter 2

Nouns and articles

***Complete the sentences with* "der", "die" *or* "das"**

.... Waffenlager ist groß.
.... Ausländer lernt Deutsch.
.... Sex ist gut.
.... Frau heißt Schacklihn
.... Koch kocht Essen.

Indefinite and definite articles

Fill in the correct indefinite article then the correct definite article.

Das ist	....	Penis.	....	Penis gehört Helmut.
Das ist	....	Rapper.	....	Rapper heißt Svengster.
Das ist	....	Brust.	....	Brust ist aus Silikon.
Das ist	....	Kampfjet.	....	Kampfjet tötet Menschen.

***Fill in the right form:* "ein", "eine" *or* "einen"**

Hoschi hat	....	Sitzsack.
Svengster hat	....	nasse Hose.
Helmut hat	....	Alkoholproblem.
Eve hat	....	dicken Hintern.

NOMINATIVE & ACCUSATIVE

***Fill in the right question word:* "wer", "wen" *or* "was"**

....	ist das?	Das sind die No Angels.
....	sehen wir da?	Das ist der Svengster.
....	sehen Sie?	Ich sehe Kokain.
....	liebt Helmut?	Helmut liebt Eve.
....	ist grün und stinkt nach Fisch?	Das ist Werder Bremen.

Modal verbs

***Fill in the right forms of* "können", "dürfen" *and* "möchten"**

(Möchten)	....	du Flüssigsprengstoff, Svengster?
(Dürfen)	Ihr	hier gerne fixen.
(Können)	Wir.............................	euch gleich töten.
(Dürfen)	Sie	die Braut küssen.
(Möchten)	Er	kotzen.
(Können)	....	du mal die Waffe halten?

Was ist das? Das ist .... Haus in Deutschland.

Wer ist das? Das sind .... 88 Zwerge.

Was ist das? Das ist .... Kokain.

Was ist das? Das ist .... gegrillte fette Katze.

B Bonus-Track – Chapter 2

Drugs in Germany

Marihuana, speed, ecstasy, crystal meth, cocaine and heroin and several other drugs are completely legalized in the big cities in Germany like Berlin, Frankfurt, Hamburg, Cologne and Munich but also in Rothenburg ob der Tauber, Heidelberg and Bonn. So feel free to buy as many drugs as possible over here in Germany. However: where do you get these drugs? And, can you really trust those people who sell the drugs? Do not worry about such things. As everything is legal, the German police are the main drug dealers in Germany.

Just walk into any local police office and ask the friendly officer behind the desk which kind of drug is on the menu that day. If you are lucky he may be as nice as to recommend his favourite drug or even mix you some special drug cocktail.

BUT!!! Be careful! Keep in mind that you, as a tourist you need some special extraordinary document of the German custom service if you want to buy Fanta or bitter chocolate. You have to apply for this document beforehand – at least three months before you travel to Germany. Also remember that Fanta and bitter chocolate are not allowed to be eaten in public outside on the streets. The use of one of these articles of food in public will have severe consequences ranging from deportation to Guantanamo to revocation of your permission to live.

Bonus Bonus

The publishing house "DER GROSSKONZERN" is cooperating with a lot of health insurances and the pharma lobby. Thanks to our great friends in this beautiful industry we were able to pimp this book with an exclusive bonus: A feel-free-to-cut-out drug test.

Here is what to do with the test.

1. Cut it out.
2. Pee on it.
3. Wait up to 15 minutes.
4. Check which of the colours shines the brightest?
5. Find out who your perfect drug buddy is.

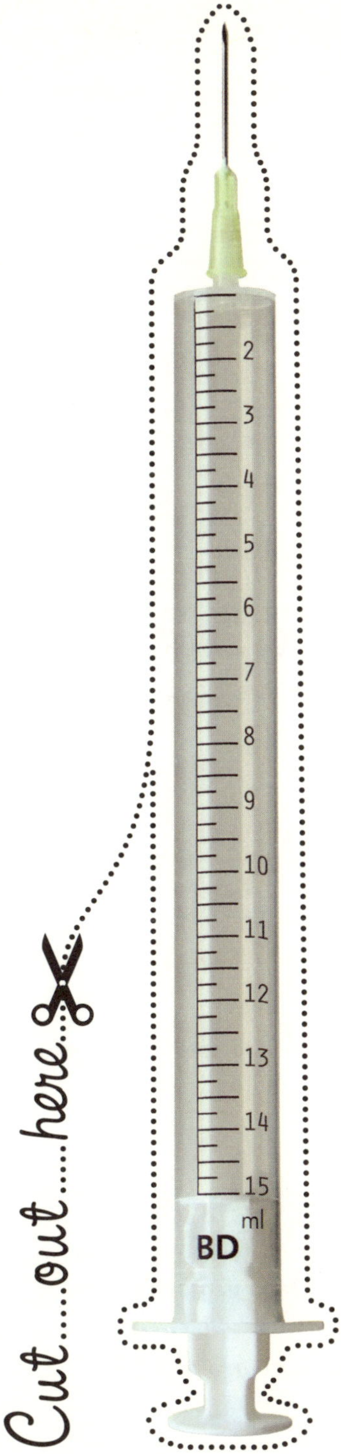

MATCH YOUR COLOUR TO THE SCALE.

Harald Juhnke
Amy Winehouse
Pete Doherty
Ben Becker
Slash
Steven Adler
Xavier Naidoo
Boy George
George Michael
Michel Friedman
Jörg Immendorff
Boris Jelzin
Sid Vicious
Ralf Richter
Keith Richards

Note: You as the person, who owns this book, are also allowed to pee all over the book without cutting out the drug test. But we advice you to buy another book then because the old one will be wet and smelly.

Chapter 3

Der Svengster in der Schule

Sven, der Svengster, fährt in die Schule. Dort trifft er He-Man Müller, She-Do und MC Feuermelder. Alle drei mögen den Svengster nicht gerne.

Svengster: *„Hallo Leute! Sollen wir ein wenig batteln?“*

He-Man: *„Ach halt doch die Fresse, Svengster! Geh selber betteln!“*

She-Do: *„Ich kann dir auch ins Gesicht schlagen!“*

MC Feuermelder: *„Wie oft müssen wir dir noch sagen, dass wir dich nicht mögen?“*

Svengster: *„Ihr sollt doch nicht immer so gemein sein! Wir können uns doch schön unterhalten. Ich habe auch Drogen gekauft!“*

She-Do: *„Wir dürfen Drogen nicht mehr nehmen.“*

MC Feuermelder: *„Man hat es uns in der Schule verboten.“*

Svengster: *„Und jetzt nehmt ihr nicht mehr Drogen?“*

He-Man: *„Neeee! Wir sind jetzt gegen Drogen. Denn Drogen sind verlogen! ...Kannst Du mir nach der Schule trotzdem welche geben?“*

Svengster: *„Ich kann dir Drogen verkaufen.“*

He-Man, She-Do und MC Feuermelder: *„Verkaufen?! Dann sprechen wir jetzt Klartext: Gib uns alle deine Drogen! Sofort!“*

Svengster: *„Nein! Nur gegen Geld!“*

He-Man und seine Freunde möchten nicht warten und auch nicht zahlen und schlagen den Svengster zusammen. She-Do tritt den Svengster in die Eier, He-Man haut Svengster „in die dumme Fresse“ und MC Feuermelder sticht dem Svengster mit dem Messer durch die Kniescheibe. Dann nehmen sie ihm die Drogen ab.

Svengster: *„AUA! Menno! Man sagt: Drei gegen einen ist unfair!“*

He-Man: *„Ich kenne nur ‚Dreimal ist Bremer Recht‘.“*

MC Feuermelder: *„Wer dreimal mit derselben pennt, gehört schon zum Establishment!"*

She-Do: *„Und ich sag immer 3 und 3 ist 9!"*

Svengster möchte widersprechen, aber der Krankenwagen ist schon da. Die Sanitäter bringen ihn direkt ins Krankenhaus.

Grammar Stuff – Chapter 3

Irregular verbs in the PRESENT TENSE:

nehmen = ***to take***	
ich nehm**e**	wir nehm**en**
du nimm**st**	ihr nehm**t**
Sie nehm**en**	Sie nehm**en**
er / sie / es nimm**t**	sie nehm**en**

fahren = ***to drive***	
ich fahr**e**	wir fahr**en**
du fähr**st**	ihr fahr**t**
Sie fahr**en**	Sie fahr**en**
er / sie / es fähr**t**	sie fahr**en**

sprechen = ***to speak***	
ich sprech**e**	wir sprech**en**
du sprich**st**	ihr sprech**t**
Sie sprech**en**	Sie sprech**en**
er / sie / es sprich**t**	sie sprech**en**

Modal verbs in the PRESENT TENSE

wollen = ***to want***	
ich **will**	wir **wollen**
du **willst**	ihr **wollt**
Sie **wollen**	Sie **wollen**
er / sie / es **will**	sie **wollen**

sollen = *shall / should*	
ich **soll**	wir **sollen**
du **sollst**	ihr **sollt**
Sie **sollen**	Sie **sollen**
er / sie / es **soll**	sie **sollen**

Müssen = *to must*	
ich **muss**	wir **müssen**
du **musst**	ihr **müsst**
Sie **müssen**	Sie **müssen**
er / sie / es **muss**	sie **müssen**

Word order: Modal verb + verb

a) Statement:

Svengster muss im Wohnzimmer kiffen.
Svengster must smoke pot in the living room.

Helmut kann auf der Toilette schlafen.
Helmut can sleep on the toilet.

b) Question Word:

Wo muss ich das Heroin hinspritzen?
Where do I have to inject the heroin?

Wie lange soll ich denn noch bettnässen?
How much longer shall I wet my bed anymore?

c) Question:

Muss ich doof sterben?
Must I die as an idiot?

***Note:* THE INFINITIVE is always at the end of the sentence! If the context is completely evident you can kick out the infinitive completely which leads you to sentences like:**

Ich möchte 30 Gramm Koks ~~kaufen.~~ = *I would like to have 30g of cocaine.*
Helmut will nach Kolumbien ~~fliegen.~~ = *Helmut wants to go to Colombia.*

What is all that stuff about?

Sollen
= Svengster soll nicht so viele Drogen nehmen.
= *Svengster shouldn't take so many drugs.* => recommendation / piece of advice.

Wollen
= Ich will etwas Kokain.
= *I want some cocaine.* => *"wollen"* is most often used by children. As an adult, you are much nicer and this is why you use the subjunctive of *"mögen"* which is in the ICH-FORM: *Ich möchte einen Joint.* (= I would like a joint.)

Müssen
= Helmut muss wenigstens 15 Bier trinken, bis sein Tremor aufhört.
= *Helmut must drink at least 15 beers to stop his tremor.* => necessity / compulsion

Dürfen
= Helmut darf nicht auf die Straße pissen.
= *Helmut is not allowed to pee on the street.* => permission / prohibition

= Darf ich mit einem Pferd Sex haben?
= *May I have sex with a horse?* => polite question

Können
= Svengster kann sich Drogen bei seinem Dealer zuhause kaufen.
= *Svengster can buy drugs at his dealer's home.* => possibility

= Doreen kann singen und rappen.
= *Doreen can sing and rap.* => ability

= Helmut kann sowohl in seinem Bad als auch in seinem Bett trinken.
= *Helmut can drink in his bathroom and in bed.* => permission

The pronoun *"man" (= one / you)*

If there is a generalization, you can use "man".

Hier darf man Leute schlagen.
It is allowed to beat up other people here.

Hier darf man nicht sitzen.
It is not allowed to sit down here.

Say "not" – Negation with *"nicht"*

"nicht" makes verbs negative. And to do so it comes right after the verb.

Bist du schwul? Nein, ich bin nicht schwul.	*Are you gay?* *No, I am not gay.*
Dein Penis ist klein. Nein, mein Penis ist nicht klein, Arschloch!	*Your penis is small.* *No, my penis is not small, asshole!*

In case there is a modal verb and INFINITIVE construction,* "nicht" *is just between these two verbs – the same as in English.

Ich kann nicht sprechen. Man soll nicht lügen!	*I cannot speak.* *You shall not lie!*

Prepositions with the ACCUSATIVE

***Usually prepositions are found before a noun and require a particular case like ACCUSATIVE, DATIVE or GENITIVE. Here, we present you some often used* ACCUSATIVE*-only prepositions:* "bis", "durch", "gegen", "für", "ohne", "um"**

Das Medikament ist **gegen die Syphilis.**	*The medicine is against Syphilis.*
Ich bin **für die Todesstrafe.**	*I'm for the death penalty.*
Ich krieche **durch die Gosse.**	*I crawl through the gutter.*
Ohne Drogen kann Svengster nicht leben.	*Svengster can't live without drugs.*
Um die Ecke liegt eine Psychiatrie.	*Around the corner there is a psychiatry.*
Ich verfolge dich **bis Timbuktu.**	*I'll trail you to Timbuktu.*

A special case: The preposition *"in"*

"in" *is used with THE ACCUSATIVE when you can ask* "wohin?" *(where… to?)*

Eve tritt in den Hundehaufen. Wohin tritt Eve?	*Eve steps into poo.* *Where is she stepping into?*
Der Zug fährt in das Zentrum der Hölle. Wohin fährt der Zug?	*The train goes straight into hell.* *Where does the train go to?*

Exercises – Chapter 3

***Fill the gaps with the correct form of* "wollen"**

Ich	....	eine Million Euro in kleinen Scheinen.
Ihr	....	eine in die Fresse haben?
Wir	....	euer Leben!
Sie	....	mich nicht töten.
Svengster und Helmut	....	komasaufen.

Now take your pens and write some fantastic sentences with verbs + verbs in THE INFINITIVE!

Doreen singt Englisch. (können)	=>	....
Du bist blöd. (müssen)	=>	....
Wir fahren Ferrari. (wollen)	=>	....
Helmut liebt keine Ausländer. (können)	=>	....

"Können", "dürfen", "müssen" *or* "sollen". *Find out and fill in.*

.... ich mich hier ausziehen?

Sven .... gleichzeitig wichsen und trinken.

.... wir dich gleich verhauen?

Doreen .... auch Französisch.

Fill in können, dürfen _or_ müssen.

Hier.......................... /.......................... man auf Toilette gehen.

Hier........................ man nicht kotzen.

Hier........................ man gleich Schokolade essen.

Hier........................ man nicht schnell sterben.

Hier........................ man nicht Jesus sein.

Hier........................ man nackt sein.

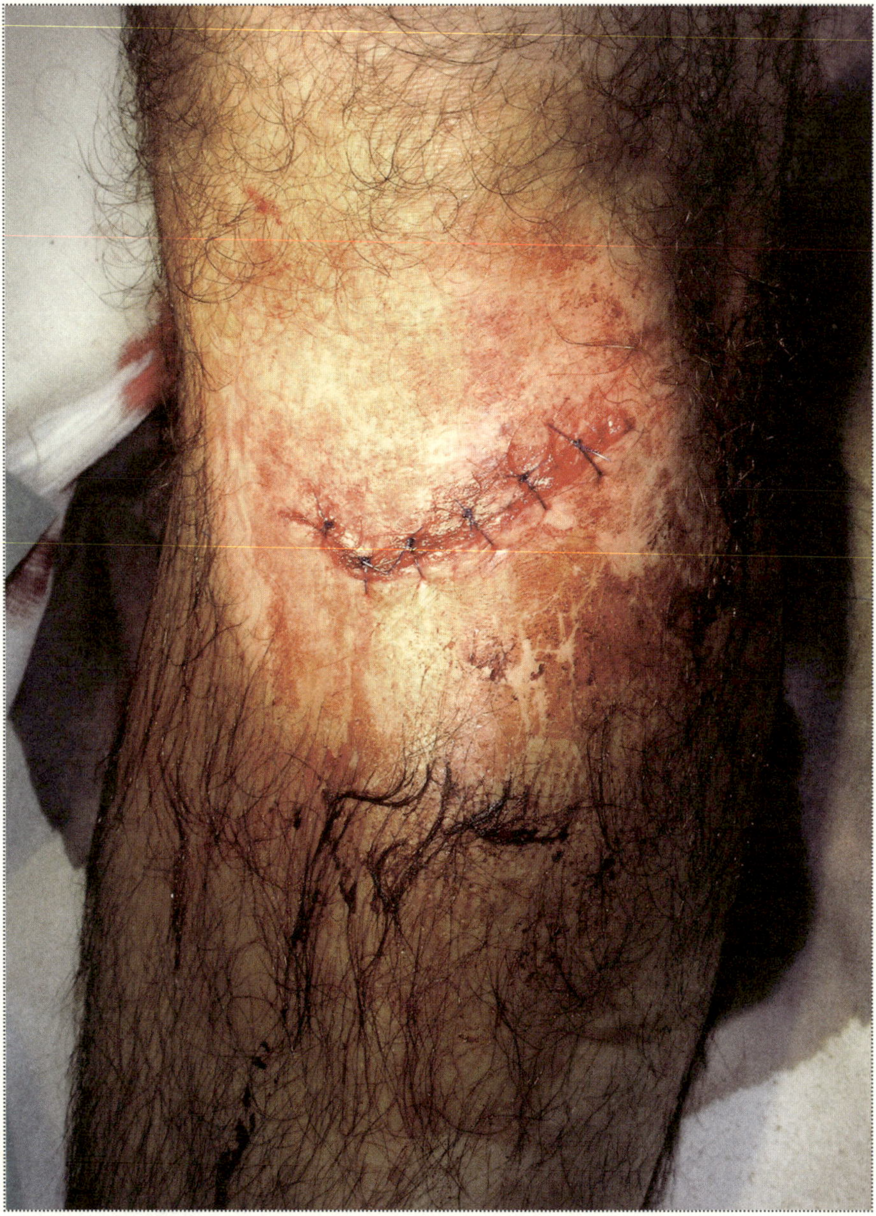

Be a negative creep and say "nicht"

Svengster geht in den Puff.

....

Wir zerstören die Bundesrepublik Deutschland.

....

Die Bombe explodiert im Reichstag.

....

Doreen singt wie ein Superstar.

....

Dieses Buch verkauft 100.000 Exemplare.

....

Die Autoren sind genial und gut aussehend.

....

***If you are clever, you will know where to put* "durch", "gegen", "ohne", "für", "um" *and* "in".**

.... Kondome fickt Doreen nicht.

.... böse Menschen hilft nur Gewalt.

Helmut haut Svengster .... die Fresse.

Der Panzer fährt .... die Menschenmenge.

Der Attentäter flüchtet .... die Ecke.

.... einen Ausländer sprichst du gut Deutsch.

Bonus-Track – Chapter 3

The weather in Germany

The German weather is mostly fine but very often quite bad. There are times when the sun is shining, but sometimes there might also be a lot of rain. Very seldomly it happens that the sun shines while it is raining. The result of this strange weather is what you call a *"Regenbogen"* or "rainbow". This is a phenomenon which has never ever been seen or documented outside of Germany and this is also the reason why Germany is known to the world as the "Rainbow-Country". Other weather conditions that have recently been seen in Germany are, in loose order: hurricanes, tornados, thunderstorms, sandstorms and the impact of meteorites and comets – the last two of them mainly in the southern part of Saxony and in winter.

If for more than 3 weeks there is a very strong polar southern wind, it is also possible that snow leopards, polar bears and frozen ready-to-make-pizzas are falling from the skies. So always wear a gun and an oven when you are out alone in the German wilderness.

In summer it is very warm because it is summer and in winter it is also warm because one wears corduroy or warmer clothes or sits inside at a tiled stove. In case you are dressed in fur and sit at the stove it might even get really hot in winter and you might become physically ill if you are not already mentally ill because you sit at a stove dressed in fur. Anyway, you should see a doctor, I guess.

Last but not least: There are no such seasons as "spring" or "fall" or "autumn" in Germany. In former times Germany still had 4 seasons like any other country but when the Nazis lost the war, Germany had to give away two of its four seasons as reparation payments to Canada and the Easter Islands. In a popular vote summer and winter were voted the most favourite seasons with spring running in on rank 3 with only 1,2 % less than winter. The final result of this plebiscite was:

Summer:	27,6 %
Winter:	25,3 %
Spring:	24,1 %
Autumn:	22,0 %

In the following riots in 1968 the spring fans united and revolted against the vote. They lost and huge parts of them left Germany to settle down on the Easter Islands.

Chapter 4

Ein Tag im Leben des Helmut Schmidt

11:00 Uhr: Helmut erwacht und steht auf. Zuerst trinkt er ein Aufwach-Bier. Er geht in die Küche und zündet sich eine Zigarette an. Dann schaut er aus dem Fenster und hetzt gegen Ausländer.

Helmut: *„Der Russe ist gemeingefährlich und frisst Kinder! Der Chinese ist gelb und riecht streng! Der Iraner hat Recht. Italiener sind feige. Der Ami hat sie nicht mehr alle und ist doof. Der Somalier ist auch nicht besser. Der Spanier ist ein Paellafresser…"*

14:00 Uhr: Helmut ist müde vom Hetzen. Er zündet sich eine Zigarette an und legt sich ins Bett.

14:15 Uhr: Es klingelt an der Tür. Helmut ist stinkwütend und öffnet. Es ist Ivo. Ivo ist ein Drogenfreund von Svengster. Er möchte ein Zeitungsabo verkaufen.

Ivo: *„Hallo! Ich bin Ivo und ich komme aus dem Kosovo."*

Helmut: *„Lüg nicht! Du kommst aus dem Knast, Ivo. Schwere Körperverletzung!"*

Ivo: *„Ja. Ist ja gut. Ich brauche Geld. Möchten sie ein Zeitungsabo?"*

Helmut: *„Nein. Ich besitze Zeitungsabos von der BILD und der Nationalzeitung."*

Ivo: *„Vielleicht möchte ihre Frau eine Brigitte?"*

Helmut: *„Nein. Sie kann nicht lesen. Aber ich gebe dir Geld, wenn du dann in den Kosovo, die Schweiz oder den Irak fährst."*

Ivo: *„Danke, Herr Schmidt."*

Helmut gibt Ivo 10.000 Euro und schließt die Tür. Dann sagt er: *„Diese Ausländer! Kennst du einen, kennst du alle. Der Ausländer ist faul, arbeitet nicht und klaut unser Geld. Arbeitsscheues Gesindel."* Helmut setzt sich auf das Sofa, holt den Schnaps aus der Küche und schaut Richter Alexander Holt. Heute möchte er nicht duschen.

17:00 Uhr: Es ist kalt. Helmut bemerkt, dass er nur eine Unterhose trägt.

17:35 Uhr: Helmut trinkt Schnaps und raucht. Jetzt trägt er eine Jogginghose.

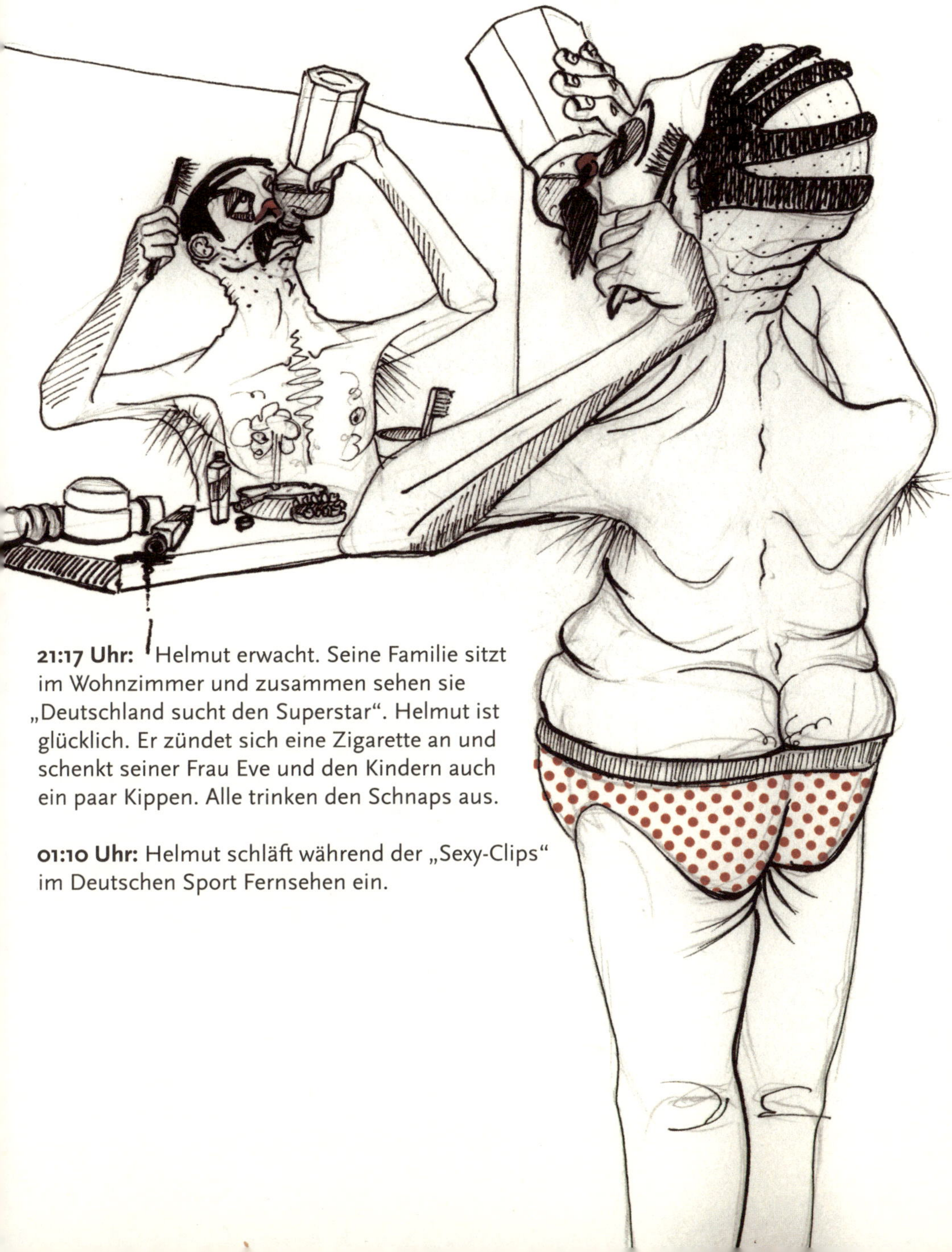

21:17 Uhr: Helmut erwacht. Seine Familie sitzt im Wohnzimmer und zusammen sehen sie „Deutschland sucht den Superstar“. Helmut ist glücklich. Er zündet sich eine Zigarette an und schenkt seiner Frau Eve und den Kindern auch ein paar Kippen. Alle trinken den Schnaps aus.

01:10 Uhr: Helmut schläft während der „Sexy-Clips“ im Deutschen Sport Fernsehen ein.

Grammar – Chapter 4

Compounds – how to form words in German

It is very easy to make up new German words by just putting together two German nouns. Here are some examples.

die Schwangerschaft	+	der Abbruch	=	der Schwangerschaftsabbruch
pregnancy	+	*abort*	=	*induced abortion*
die Drogen	+	die Überdosis	=	die Drogenüberdosis
drugs	+	*overdose*	=	*drug overdose*
die Kinder	+	der Schänder	=	der Kinderschänder
children	+	*molestor*	=	*child molestor*

Zahlen – German numbers

There are a few things that make it easier for you to memorize how to pronounce the German numbers.

a) From 20 onwards you read the 2nd digit first,
then add *"und"* and then the 1st digit.
b) Three-digit numbers: Always read the hundreds first
c) Four-digit-numbers: Always read the thousands first

0 = null	10 = zehn	20 = zwanzig	30 = dreißig
1 = eins	11 = elf	21 = einundzwanzig	40 = vierzig
2 = zwei	12 = zwölf	22 = zweiundzwanzig	50 = fünfzig
3 = drei	13 = dreizehn	23 = dreiundzwanzig	60 = sechzig
4 = vier	14 = vierzehn	24 = vierundzwanzig	70 = siebzig
5 = fünf	15 = fünfzehn	25 = fünfundzwanzig	80 = achtzig
6 = sechs	16 = sechzehn	26 = sechsundzwanzig	90 = neunzig
7 = sieben	17 = siebzehn	27 = siebenundzwanzig	
8 = acht	18 = achtzehn	28 = achtundzwanzig	
9 = neun	19 = neunzehn	29 = neunundzwanzig	

100 = (ein)hundert
200 = zweihundert
300 = dreihundert
400 = vierhundert
500 = fünfhundert
600 = sechshundert
700 = siebenhundert
800 = achthundert
900 = neunhundert

1.000 = (ein)tausend
2.000 = zweitausend
3.000 = dreitausend
4.000 = viertausend
5.000 = fünftausend
6.000 = sechstausend
7.000 = siebentausend
8.000 = achttausend
9.000 = neuntausend

10.000 = zehntausend
20.000 = zwanzigtausend
30.000 = dreißigtausend
40.000 = vierzigtausend
50.000 = fünfzigtausend
60.000 = sechzigtausend
70.000 = siebzigtausend
80.000 = achtzigtausend
90.000 = neunzigtausend

100.000 = (ein)hunderttausend
200.000 = zweihunderttausend
1.000.000 = eine Million

Die Zeit – Time in German

The most important questions in Germany are:* "Wie spät ist es?" *and* "Wie viel Uhr ist es?" *Both have the same meaning which is: "What time is it?"

There are differences in formal and informal speech and if you are jobless, you do not even talk about time except when the time is concerns your early afternoon TV schedule.

TIME	FORMAL	INFORMAL
12:00	zwölf Uhr	zwölf Uhr
12:15	zwölf Uhr fünfzehn	Viertel nach zwölf / Viertel eins
12:20	zwölf Uhr zwanzig	zwanzig nach zwölf
12:30	zwölf Uhr dreißig	halb eins* / Halber
12:40	zwölf Uhr vierzig	zehn nach halb eins / zwanzig vor eins
12:45	zwölf Uhr fünfundvierzig	Viertel vor eins / Dreiviertel eins

* You say *"ein Uhr"* if it is straight 1pm but as you see *"halb eins"* and *"viertel vor eins"*.

Second	=	die Sekunde	PLURAL: die Sekunden
Minute	=	die Minute	PLURAL: die Minuten
Hour	=	die Stunde	PLURAL: die Stunden

Day times

Note that there is one really funny statement if someone is asking you about the time in Germany. Even if you know the correct time, just smile and say* "Viertel vor Muck! Geh' heim und guck!"** ***which might be translated as "A quarter to fuck! Go home, good luck!" Some people probably will not understand your kind of humor, but do not take it personally if they don't start laughing with you.

Even in Germany there are day times. Here are the most important of them.

heute Nacht	=	this night
heute Abend	=	this evening
heute Nachmittag	=	this afternoon
heute Mittag	=	this early afternoon
heute Vormittag	=	this morning
heute Morgen	=	this morning
nachts	=	every night
abends	=	every evening
nachmittags	=	every afternoon
mittags	=	every early afternoon
vormittags	=	every morning
morgens	=	every morning
in der Nacht	=	in the night
am Abend	=	in the evening
am Nachmittag	=	in the afternoon
am Mittag	=	in the early afternoon
am Vormittag	=	in the morning
am Morgen	=	in the morning

The days of the week

Montag	=	Monday
Dienstag	=	Tuesday
Mittwoch	=	Wednesday
Donnerstag	=	Thursday
Freitag	=	Friday
Samstag or Sonnabend	=	Saturday
Sonntag	=	Sunday

Just like with the times of the day you say for example "montags" if you speak about something you do every Monday. You say "am Montag" if you have a special date or something on that particular day.

Remember: All days of the week and all day times are masculine except *"die Nacht" (= night)*

The months

Januar	*January*	Juli	*July*
Februar	*February*	August	*August*
März	*March*	September	*September*
April	*April*	Oktober	*October*
Mai	*May*	November	*November*
Juni	*June*	Dezember	*December*

Note: All German months are masculine and have the article "der"

The singular and plural article in THE NOMINATIVE

	DEFINITE ARTICLE	INDEFINITE ARTICLE
SINGULAR MASCULINE	**der** Triebtäter	ein Triebtäter
	the sex maniac	*a sex maniac*
SINGULAR FEMININE	**die** Prostituierte	eine Prostituierte
	the prostitute	*a prostitute*
SINGULAR NEUTER	**das** Arschloch	ein Arschloch
	the asshole	*an asshole*
PLURAL MASCULINE	***die*** Triebtäter	Triebtäter
	the sex maniacs	*sex maniacs*
PLURAL FEMININE	***die*** Prostituierten	Prostituierte
	the prostitues	*Prostitutes*
PLURAL NEUTER	***die*** Arschlöcher	Arschlöcher
	the assholes	*assholes*

The singular and plural article in the ACCUSATIVE

	DEFINITE ARTICLE	INDEFINITE ARTICLE
SINGULAR MASCULINE	***den*** Triebtäter	ein***en*** Triebtäter
	the sex maniac	*a sex maniac*
SINGULAR FEMININE	**die** Prostituierte	eine Prostituierte
	the prostitute	*a prostitute*
SINGULAR NEUTER	**das** Arschloch	ein Arschloch
	the asshole	*an asshole*
PLURAL MASCULINE	***die*** Triebtäter	Triebtäter
	the sex maniacs	*sex maniacs*
PLURAL FEMININE	***die*** Prostituierten	Prostituierte
	the prostitutes	*Prostitutes*
PLURAL NEUTER	***die*** Arschlöcher	Arschlöcher
	the assholes	*assholes*

Attention: The plural of the definite article in the nominative AND the accusative is always *"die"* and there is no article in the indefinite article!

The nouns in singular and plural

There is no logic at all in the German language. Sorry! There is in fact a lot of logic in the German language, but concerning the plural of nouns there are no quality-rules on how to form the plural. The only advice which makes any sense: When you learn a new word, always also learn the plural of it. Anyway, here you will get some smart hints on how to learn typical signs of the plural.

If there is an *"a", an "o" or an "u"* in the singular, it sometimes might become an *"ä"*, *"ö"* or *"ü"*.

Example: der Vater *(the father)* => die Väter *(the fathers)*
die Mutter *(the mother)* => die Mütter *(the mothers)*

You will love German nouns that end with "-er", "-en", "-el", "-chen" or "-lein". Why? The reason is they do not change their ending in the plural and stay the same. So you only have to take care about the correct article in front of the word.

SINGULAR	PLURAL
der / ein Penner *the / a bum*	die / – Penner *the / – bums*
das / ein Wettwichsen *the / a wanking*	die / – Wettwichsen *the / – wankings*
der / ein Prügel *the / a stick*	die / – Prügel *the / – sticks*
das / ein Schweinchen *the / a little pig*	die / – Schweinchen *the / – little pigs*

Also quite easy are many other words that just hang an "-e" on the end of themselves in the plural.

SINGULAR	PLURAL
der / ein Hund the / a dog	die / – Hund***e*** the / – dogs
der / ein Tisch the / a table	die / – Tisch***e*** the / – tables
der / ein Nachmittag the / an afternoon	die / – Nachmittag***e*** the / – afternoons
der / ein Kredit the / a credit	die / – Kredit***e*** the / – credits

Let's have a look at the feminine words. Close to 100% of them ending on "-e" in the singular have the plural ending "-n". And all feminine nouns ending on a consonant, have the plural ending "-en".

SINGULAR	PLURAL
die / eine Nutte *the / a whore*	die / – Nutte***n*** *the / – whores*

SINGULAR	PLURAL
die / eine Küche *the / a kitchen*	die / – Küche***n*** *the / – kitchens*
die / eine Schussverletzung *the / a drive by shooting injury*	die / – Schussverletzung***en*** *the / – drive by shooting injuries*

***Neuter words with only one syllable and also some masculine nouns have the plural ending* "-er".**

SINGULAR	PLURAL
das / ein Buch *the / a book*	die / – Büch***er**** *the / – books*
der / ein Mann *the / a man*	die / – Männ***er**** *the / – men*
das / ein Kind *the / a Kid*	die / – Kind***er**** *the / – kids*

***Note: Some words containing an *"-a"*, *"-o"* or *"-u"* do change to *"-ä"*, *"-ö"* or *"-ü"* in the plural. E.g.: *Mutter* (mother) => *Mütter* (mothers), *Apfel* (apple) => *Äpfel* (apples)...**

Most foreign words and all nouns with "*-a*", "*-o*" and "*-i*"-ending have the plural ending "*-s*".

SINGULAR	PLURAL
das / ein Koma	die / – Koma**s**
der / ein Opa	die / – Opa**s**
das / ein Handy	die / – Handy**s**
der / ein Hallodri	die / – Hallodri**s**
das / ein Restaurant	die / – Restaurant**s**
das / ein Foto	die / – Foto**s**
der / ein Porno	die / – Porno**s**

Exercises – Chapter 4

Now you are allowed to be creative and make up your own German words. Take out your dictionary, find yourself some words and put them together. Here are some examples for you to get an impression.

der Terror *terror*	+	der Anschlag *attack*	=	....
der Killer *killer*	+	die Maschine *maschine*	=	....
der Krieg *war*	+	der Verbrecher *criminal*	=	....
der Holocaust *holocaust*	+	der Leugner *denier*	=	....
der Fick *fuck*	+	die Gesichter *faces*	=	....

Now it is your turn!

....	+	....	=	....
....	+	....	=	....
....	+	....	=	....
....	+	....	=	....

What's that number?

a) sechshundertsechsundsechzig = ...

b) sechshundertsechsundsechzig Millionen sechshundertsechsundsechzig-tausendsechshundertsechsundsechzig = ...

c) siebenhundertachtzigtausend und sieben = ...

d) dreiundzwanzig = ...

e) siebzehn und vier = ...

What is your lucky number? Write it down in German!

....

What is your least favourite number? Write it down in German!

....

The times they are a-changin! But how to spell them in German?

16:17 = ...

23:23 = ...

21:45 = ...

00:00 = ...

03:30 = ...

16:55 = ...

At what time were you born? Tell it to this book: ....

Fill in the gaps and trust us: There is a gap for every word we wrote down in this book!

Mittags, montags, dienstags, mittwochs, donnerstags, freitags, samstags, sonntags, nachts, nachmittags

Helmut steht ...., ..., ..., ..., ..., ... und .... immer um 11 Uhr auf. Gleich danach macht er .... Pause. .... schaut er „Richter Alexander Holt". Bei den „*Sexy Clips*" im Deutschen Sport Fernsehen, spät ...., schläft Helmut schon.

One is the loneliest number. So put the following nouns in the plural.

Helmut hat drei (Hoden)

....

Svengster will eine Ménage-à-trois mit zwei (Mädchen)

....

Eve kauft in Russland zwölf (Auto)

....

Doreen liebt dumme (Mann)

....

Bonus-Track – Chapter 4

German Sayings

The Germans really like to speak in proverbial sayings. There is a saying for every situation, as strange as it may be. Below, there are some of the most common sayings, including the English translation and the situation in which you can cunningly make use of them.

ORIGINAL SAYING IN GERMAN	ENGLISH TRANSLATION	WHAT DOES IT MEAN AND WHEN TO USE IT
Morgenstund hat Gold im Mund.	*Morning hour has gold in the mouth.*	*Brush your teeth.*
Wie die Nase des Mannes, so sein Johannes.	*Like the nose of the man, so his John.*	*A nice compliment for big nosed men.*
Dumm fickt gut.	*Stupid fucks well.*	*Pick up line for boys.*
Grün und blau trägt die Sau.	*Green and blue wears the pig.*	*Fashion advice for policemen.*
Lügen haben kurze Beine.	*Lies have short legs.*	*Beware of short people!*
Nach dem Essen sollst du ruhn, oder 1.000 Schritte tun.	*After eating, thou shall rest or walk a 1.000 steps.*	*Fitness advice from the German branch of the Weight Watchers.*
Je später der Abend, desto schöner die Gäste.	*The later the evening, the better-looking are the guests.*	*Don't be early at a German party if you're beautiful.*
Hände hoch. Das ist ein Überfall.	*Hands up. How are you.*	*Special greeting phrase often used in gas stations or banks.*
Mädchen, die pfeifen, und Hühnern, die krähen, soll man beizeiten den Hals umdrehen.	*Girls that whistle and chicken that crow should be killed immediately.*	*Pro-Emancipation slogan invented in the late 70s.*
Wer nicht hören will, muss fühlen.	*Whoever doesn't want to listen, has to feel.*	*Feeling is better than listening anyways. Feel free to feel.*

Wer anderen eine Grube gräbt, fällt selbst hinein.	*Whoever digs a ditch, falls in it himself.*	*Pay attention while gardening.*
Die Axt im Haus erspart den Zimmermann.	*The axe in the house saves the carpenter.*	*DIY is nice.*
Wer zuletzt lacht, lacht am besten.	*Whoever laughs last, laughs best.*	*Spare your laughing for the last chance.*
Einem geschenkten Gaul schaut man nicht ins Maul.	*Do not look into the mouth of a gifted stallion.*	*Be happy when someone gives you a stallion as a present – no matter how you feel about horses.*
Zicke zacke, Hühnerkacke.	*Zigzag, chicken shit.*	*Equivalent of Hey! Ho! Let's go!*
Trete nicht ins Fettnäpfchen.	*Do not step into fat.*	*"fat" is another word for "mental dookie".*
Jemanden auf den Zahn fühlen.	*To touch someone's tooth.*	*German expression for French kissing.*
Die Flinte ins Korn werfen.	*To throw the shotgun in the corn.*	*If you own an illegal gun, hide it wisely.*
Von der Hand in den Mund leben.	*To live from the hand in the mouth.*	*Bad advice for bulimics.*
Er / Sie hat den Löffel abgegeben.	*He / she gave away the spoon.*	*Say that to show condolence at a funeral.*
Da liegt der Hund begraben.	*There the dog lies buried.*	*Point your finger to the grave on a funeral of a friend an say it out loud to show condolence.*
Jemanden Würmer aus der Nase ziehen.	*To pull worms out of your nose.*	*Metaphorical expression for fishing for snot in your nose.*
Wo man singt, da laß dich ruhig nieder. Böse Menschen kennen keine Lieder.	*Thou shall sit down whe-re people sing, because evil people do not know any songs.*	*Naive statement because there is no real death metal scene in Germany with bands like Slayer.*

Chapter 5

Eve kauft und verkauft

Eve besitzt einen Imbiss. Dort verkauft sie Ketwurst. Ketwurst besteht aus Ket und aus Wurst. Niemand weiß, was Ket ist, und niemand weiß, woraus die Wurst ist. Aber das ist auch egal, denn es gibt ja Glutamat. Heute kauft Eve im Großmarkt vor der Stadt ein. Dort gibt es alles, aber manchmal muss sie auch nach Polen auf den Schwarzmarkt fahren. Eve hat 500 Euro in kleinen unmarkierten Scheinen dabei. Das Geld hat sie dem Svengster abgenommen. Jetzt steht Eve beim Ketwurst-Regal und spricht mit dem Ketwurst-Regal-Fachverkäufer.

Eve: *„Was kostet diese leicht grünliche Ketwurst-Großpackung?"*

Verkäufer: *„57 Euro und 13 Cent."*

Eve: *„Aber die sind doch schon schimmlig!"*

Verkäufer: *„Das ist gut für das Ketwurst-Aroma."*

Eve: *„Ich gebe Ihnen 56 Euro 87 Cent."*

Verkäufer: *„Aber ich muss doch auch von was leben!"*

Eve: *„Ich habe zwei Kinder und einen Mann und die Schulden aus dem Nagelstudio am Hals. Bitte, Herr Verkäufer!"*

Verkäufer: *„Vielleicht kann ich am Preis was machen. Aber Sie müssen mir schon entgegenkommen."*

Eve: *„Alles! Alles, was Sie wollen!"*

10 Minuten später. Eve verlässt den Großmarkt. Zusätzlich zur Großpackung hat sie noch einen Zentnersack Milchpulver aus Minsker Produktion, 27 von Hand abgezählte Brötchenpulverbrötchen und zwei Freikarten für ein neues Musical von Michael Flatley über den Genozid der Türken an den Armeniern bekommen. Eve ist glücklich und fährt zu ihrem Ketwurst-Imbiss.

Sie schabt den gröbsten Schimmel von den Würsten, erwärmt sie in altem Fett, zieht sich ihre Schürze an und beginnt mit dem Verkauf.

Kunde: *„Guten Tag! Keine Ketwurst! Ich will eine Cola und Geld umtauschen!"*

Eve: *„Sehe ich aus wie eine Bank?"*

Kunde: *„Nein, eher wie ein großer breiter Hocker. Oder ein fetter, bequemer Ledersessel."*

Eve: *„Sie Komiker. Wie viel Geld möchten Sie denn umtauschen?"*

Kunde: *„Hier den 300-Euro-Schein. Tut mir leid. Kleiner hab ich es nicht."*

Eve: *„Na gut. 300 Ocken, also Euronen minus die Cola, das macht dann 292 Euro und 50 Cent!"*

Kunde: *„Aber ist das nicht ein bisschen teuer für eine Cola. 7 Euro Fuffzich!"*

Eve: *„Inklusive Umsatzsteuer und Service-Pauschale! Schließlich muss ich ja auch von was leben!"*

Kunde: *„Ich habe zwei Kinder und einen Mann und die Schulden aus dem Nagelstudio am Hals."*

Eve: *„Sind Sie schwul?"*

Kunde: *„Nein. Nur mein Mann ist schwul. Ich war völlig überrascht, als er es mir nach 3 Jahren Beziehung erzählte. Aber wir haben uns selten gesehen, weil er blind ist und ich LKW-Fahrer."*

Eve: *„Ich liebe LKWs!"*

Kunde: *„Ich glaube, das ist der Beginn einer wunderbaren Freundschaft."*

Grammar Stuff – Chapter 5

Demonstrative Nouns – NOMINATIVE and ACCUSATIVE

"Dieser" ***is a demonstrative noun which is used to refer to a particular or special object. That word is declined in the same way as the definite article.***

	SINGULAR MASCULINE	SINGULAR NEUTER	SINGULAR FEMININE	PLURAL
NOMINATIVE	dieser (vgl. der)	dieses (vgl. das)	diese (vgl. die)	diese (vgl. die)
ACCUSATIVE	diesen (vgl. den)	dieses (vgl. das)	diese (vgl. die)	diese (vgl. die)

Keep in your memory:

a) In the ACCUSATIVE SG. only the masculine form changes.

Eve möchte diesen 300-Euro-Schein, dieses alte Fett und diese Ketwurst-Packung.
Eve likes this 300-euro-note, that old piece of fat and this pack of Ketwurst.

b) In the NOMINATIVE and ACCUSATIVE PL. the forms all stay the same.

Eve möchte diese Euroscheine, diese Nagelstudios und diese Colas besitzen.
Eve likes to obtain these euro-notes, these nail studios and these Cokes.

Personal Pronoun: NOMINATIVE and ACCUSATIVE

Essen Sie diesen Scheiß?
Do you eat that shit?

Ja, ich esse ihn.
Yes, I do eat it.

Trinken Sie diese Plörre?
Do you drink that juice?

Ja, ich trinke sie.
Yes, I do drink it.

Kennen Sie dieses Kondom?
Do you know that rubber?

Ja, ich kenne es.
Yes, I know it.

SG. NOMINATIVE	SG. ACCUSATIVE	PL. NOMINATIVE	PL. ACCUSATIVE
ich	mich	wir	uns
du / Sie	dich / Sie	ihr / Sie	euch / Sie
er	ihn	sie	sie
sie	sie	sie	sie
es	es	sie	sie

Zahlen bitte!
Numbers and numbers in different situations

a) Jahreszahlen *(Years)*

Written: 1794	Spoken: siebzehnhundertvierundneunzig
Written: 1936	Spoken: neunzehnhundertsechsundreißig
Written: 2009	Spoken: zweitausendneun

b) Geldscheine *(Money notes)*

It is possible to say *50-euro-Schein,* but for all of the notes there are more common and shorter equivalents. Here they are:

ein Fünfhunderter	= ein 500- Euro-Schein
ein Zweihunderter	= ein 200- Euro-Schein
ein Hundertfünfundsiebziger	= ein 175- Euro-Schein
ein Hunderter / ein Hunni	= ein 100- Euro-Schein
ein Fünfziger / ein Fuffi	= ein 50- Euro-Schein
ein Zwanziger /ein Zwanni	= ein 20- Euro-Schein
ein Zehner	= ein 10- Euro-Schein
ein Fünfer	= ein 5- Euro-Schein

Two special forms which are often used but do actually not exist in correct German

2 = zwei is often spoken like *"zwo"*. Mostly, to better differentiate between the similar sounding *"eins"* (1) and *"drei"* (3).

50 = Fünfzig is also very often spoken like *"Fuffzig"* without the Umlaut. That's why a *50-Euro-Schein* is also called *"ein Fuffi"*.

Exercises – Chapter 5

Helmut is insulting people and things

Example:
Angela Merkel

Ich hasse	diese	Angela Merkel.
Ich ekele mich vor	....	Klaus Wowereit.
Ich verachte	....	Gesellschaft.
Ich hasse	....	Olympiastadion.

.... Italiener, die kann ich nicht abhaben.

Ich hasse	....	Scheißwetter.

Fill in the right personal pronouns and be happy when you're right

Example:

Ich möchte dieses Heroin.	Ich möchte es.
Svengster trifft Hoschi.	....
Wohin fährt die Polizei?	....
Wo leben die Schmidts?	....
Wie viel kostet die Welt?	....

Replacing time again!

Put in personal pronouns instead of the underlined words

Example:

Wohin geht <u>Mutter Eve</u>?	Wohin geht sie?
Ich treffe den <u>Drogendealer</u>.	....
Ich möchte <u>diesen Totschläger</u>.	....
Wo wohnt <u>der Kinderschänder</u>?	....

Peter verkloppt Svengster. ....

Ida kennt Adam und Eva. ....

Warum tötet der Serienkiller? ....

B Bonus-Track – Chapter 5

Paying, money and finance in Germany

One euro consists of 100 Cents. There are several Cent-Coins ranging from 1 Cent to 2 Cents, 5 Cents, 10 Cents, 20 Cents, 27 Cents, to 50 Cents and also two euro-coins of 1 euro and 2 euros. However, you don't have to pay attention to any of these coins if you are in big business and only cherish the expensive euro-notes like 100-euro and above.

If you do not have any money, feel free to steal it from the rich and give it to the poor. In case you are poor, keep it. In case you are neither poor nor rich be satisfied with what you have or haven't got and live a boring life watching the entertainment of the rich and the poor stealing from each other. Take yourself a soft cushion, lean on that cushion watching out of your window and cheer and / or applaud for the party you fancy.

In Germany there is a saying: *Nur der Tod ist umsonst – und der kostet das Leben.* (Only death is for free and that costs your life.) This saying is complete bullshit, because in this very short and simple-minded saying the payments for the funeral, the coffin, the New-Orleans-Blues-and-Gospel-Choir running in front of your coffin playing their trumpets, the *"Totenkaffee"* (death-coffee) for all the people who take part in your funeral and pretend to howl about you, the *"Schnittchen"* (= Sandwiches with egg and bacon, sandwiches with bacon and egg, sandwiches with egg and egg and sandwiches with bacon and bacon and so on) are not included. Finally, the priest of the Church of Satan has to be paid. If you are ever buried in Germany, you should not be astonished about the priest of the Church of Satan

The German Government declared the Church of Satan *"National Religion"* in 1967 and since then a priest of this church has to be present whenever someone is buried, christened, crucified, baptized, sacrificed or married. Two more facts that you may never have heard of but which are really interesting in the sense of really being interesting and not just pretending to be really interesting:

a) The idea of money was invented in Germany. The patent for money is in possession of the Deutsche Bank. The Deutsche Bank earns gazillions of money by allowing other minor countries like the US, Russia or the UK to print money notes with funny names like "dollar", "dound" or "rubel".

b) If you are familiar with origami, it is possible to fold a 500 euro-note into a German *"Königstiger"*.

To fold a terrifying German "Königstieger" you'll need:

1 500 euro-note (smaller notes create smaller rinky-dink tanks like the M1 Abrams, Merkava IV or the T 84

2 slender hands (preferably with glaring red nails)

1 8.8 cm KwK 43 L/71

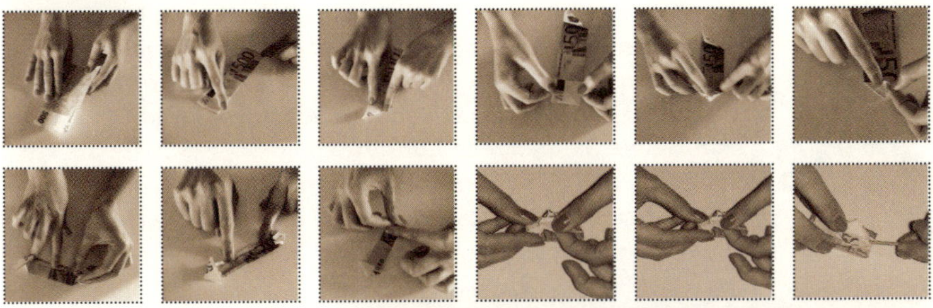

1. Start by folding the bill in half (hot dog style).
2. Then take one of the corners from the end and fold it down. Crease and unfold. (Repeat with the other 3 corners).
3. Now pinch in, along the creased guidelines to make a triangle-shape (Rotate the sheet and repeat at the other end).
4. Now choose one end and fold the flaps up and in, towards the centre. Don't fold exactly to the middle. You'll need a gap between the two flaps.
5. Fold the sides, so that they fit underneath the triangle-flaps. Make a good crease and then fold it back on itself. This'll become the tracks of the tank. (Repeat on the other side).
6. Flip the bill over and fold the end up and back. Then take the opposite end and fold it towards the flaps that you just created (if you haven't failed so far).
7. Fit the flaps of the front underneath the flaps from the back.
8. Next tuck these hanging flaps underneath to create the "Porsche turret".
9. Slide a finger underneath here and pop the tracks out gently (both sides).
10. Go and find a formidable 88 cannon made of "Kruppstahl" (a bamboo-twig will also do a good job) and stick it up to the turret.

And now, go ahead for some armoured ground warfare – blow stuff up!

Chapter 6

Doreen und das Casting

Doreen und ihre beste Freundin Schacklihn sind 14 Jahre alt und möchten Superstars werden. Leider sehen Doreen und Schacklihn nicht aus wie Superstars. Aber das wollen sie jetzt ändern. Gemeinsam sparen sie auf eine Brust-Operation. Sie sind sich nur noch nicht einig, wem zuerst die eine von zwei Brüsten vergrößert wird. Heute gehen Doreen und Schacklihn einkaufen. Sie möchten hübsch sein für das „Superstar"-Casting in einer Großraumdiskothek am Ende der Stadt. Tolle Kleider gibt es bei „Restposten aus Birmingham – Mode aus Brest" am Kottbusser Damm.

Doreen: *„Ich liebe R.A.B.M.A.B.! Hier gibt es geile Klamotten. Findest Du auch?"*

Schacklihn: *„Ja. Ich liebe goldene Miniröcke und auch rosa und auch pink."*

Doreen: *„Und dann die tollen Sachen von Et Hertie!"*

Schacklihn: *„Ja! Et Hertie hat voll den Geschmack und den Style."*

Doreen: *„Gehen wir in die Et Hertie-Abteilung, Schacklihn."*

Verkäuferin zum Verkäufer: *„Guck mal da! Schon wieder so ein paar Gangstarapvideobabystricherinnen!"*

Verkäufer zur Verkäuferin: *„Ach Mensch, wäre ich doch nur Bundesverfassungsrichter geblieben!"*

Schacklihn: *„Hallo Verkäuferin! Haben Sie dieses T-Shirt auch in XXL? Das fällt irgendwie sehr klein aus in XL!"*

Verkäuferin: *„Kauf doch zwei und näh sie zusammen. Mit ein bisschen Glück passt es dann."*

Doreen: *„Ich sage es dir ja immer, Schacklihn. Seit du nicht mehr ess-brech-süchtig,* *sondern nur noch esssüchtig bist, solltest du mehr Sport treiben."*

Schacklihn: *„Stimmt doch gar nicht. Die Farbe ist unglaublich schön. Pink und gold! Und mit diesen glitzernden Applikationen drauf. Und der Totenkopf ist auch fantastisch."*

Doreen: *„Dann nehme ich diesen Rock hier! Er ist genau richtig, spannt schön eng über meinem Intimbereich. Außerdem schmückt er mein Bauchnabelpiercing!"*

Schacklihn: *„Ich weiß ja nicht ..."*

Doreen: *„Ey! Der ist auch von Et Hertie!"*

Verkäuferin: *„Dieser Rock ist ein Gürtel, Mädchen!"*

Doreen: *„Sie sind doch nur neidisch, weil Sie so was nicht mehr tragen können."*

Schaclihn: *„Stimmt! Sie sollten überhaupt nicht mehr raus auf die Straße gehen!"*

Doreen: *„Nee! Bleiben Sie daheim und schließen Sie sich ein."*

Verkäuferin: *„Bitte hört auf! Die Kasse ist im Erdgeschoss."*

Schacklihn zu Doreen: *„Als ob wir zahlen wollen!"*

Doreen und Schacklihn laufen auf ihren Pumps aus dem „Restposten aus Brest". Beide stolpern und fallen auf ihre Gesichter. Der Ladendetektiv nimmt sie fest und erteilt ihnen Hausverbot. Doreen und Schacklihn sind sehr traurig. Jetzt können sie keine Klamotten mehr von Et Hertie kaufen.

Doreen: *„Menno! Wie soll ich jetzt Superstar werden?"*

Schacklihn: *„Warum ‚ich'? Wir wollten doch zusammen Superstar werden!"*

Doreen: *„Wenn ich ‚ich' sag, mein ich ‚wir'!"*

Schacklihn: *„Manchmal bist du echt philosophisch."*

Famous German brand No. 1: *Et Hertie*

Et Hertie was founded by Ernst Thomas Hertie, one of the many relatives of the famous German department store founders. Ernst Thomas was always kind of an outsider who was known for his extremely bizarre, weird bad taste. No one ever believed that this strange looking guy in rags would ever manage to stay rich and become a successful entrepreneur in the haute couture department store business. Especially when he presented his first collection of clothes to the public. It looked so trashy, so bizarre and so bad that all German people with any sense of taste had to puke. However, there were only 10 or 12 people in Germany with taste at all. So very soon Ernst Thomas Hertie shortened his name to Et Hertie and sold and sold and sold his trashy clothes. Below this text you will find exclusive material, showing how a typical Et-Hertie-T-Shirt is produced.

Inuit chewing on the fluffy white seal fur to make it even more fluffy with his saliva.

Chinese PhDs sewing together the seal fur into T-Shirts. Students must at least be 12 before they are hired.

Hired far-left autonomous people from "Der Schwarze Block" smash the glass out of telephone boxes, destroy the indicators of bigwig SUVs and set these cars on fire from time to time even getting the chance to trash the flashing lights of police cars.

The ruins of the mayhem are collected by the dustmen and delivered to the Et Hertie-production centre (EHPC).

Indian PhDs glue the broken pieces of glass and plastic on the T-Shirts and try to make it look like art showing everyday commodities like cars, washing machines or dead bodies.

Et Hertie himself puts the prize tags on the T-shirts and wipes his ass with every single one of them to make them even more posh and unaffordable.

KEHRPAKET

Grammar Stuff – Chapter 6

Adjectives

Adjectives after *"sein"*:
To describe a noun and specify the kind of it you can use adjectives.

Example: Das Maschinengewehr ist tödlich. *(The machine gun is deadly.)*

Attention: The adjectiv after the verb *"sein"* is not declined!

NOMINATIVE and ACCUSATIVE of the adjective following the definite article

SINGULAR NOMINATIVE		
MASCULINE	der doof***e*** Arsch	dieser doof***e*** Arsch
NEUTER	das blöd***e*** Schwein	dieses blöd***e*** Schwein
FEMININE	die bekloppt***e*** Kuh	diese bekloppt***e*** Kuh
SINGULAR ACCUSATIVE		
MASCULINE	den doof***en*** Arsch	diesen doof***en*** Arsch
NEUTER	das blöd***e*** Schwein	dieses blöd***e*** Schwein
FEMININE	die bekloppt***e*** Kuh	diese bekloppt***e*** Kuh
PLURAL NOMINATIVE		
MASCULINE	die doof***en*** Ärsche	diese doof***en*** Ärsche
NEUTER	die blöd***en*** Schweine	diese blöd***en*** Schweine
FEMININE	die bekloppt***en*** Kühe	diese bekloppt***en*** Kühe
PLURAL ACCUSATIVE		
MASCULINE	die doof***en*** Ärsche	diese doof***en*** Ärsche
NEUTER	die blöd***en*** Schweine	diese blöd***en*** Schweine
FEMININE	die bekloppt***en*** Kühe	diese bekloppt***en*** Kühe

Always keep in your mind: In the PLURAL all the endings are the same: "-en". The ending "-e" is correct for all forms of SINGULAR NOMINATIVE and ACCUSATIVE, except the MASCULINE SINGULAR ACCUSATIVE. There, the correct ending is "-en".

NOMINATIVE and ACCUSATIVE of the adjective following the indefinite article

SINGULAR NOMINATIVE		
MASCULINE	ein / kein	doof***er*** Arsch
NEUTER	ein / kein	blöd***es*** Schwein
FEMININE	eine / keine	bekloppt***e*** Kuh
SINGULAR ACCUSATIVE		
MASCULINE	einen / keinen	doof***en*** Arsch
NEUTER	ein / kein	blöd***es*** Schwein
FEMININE	eine / keine	bekloppt***e*** Kuh
PLURAL NOMINATIVE		
MASCULINE	– / keine	doof***e*** Ärsche
NEUTER	– / keine	blöd***e*** Schweine
FEMININE	– / keine	bekloppt***e*** Kühe
PLURAL ACCUSATIVE		
MASCULINE	– / keine	doof***e*** Ärsche
NEUTER	– / keine	blöd***e*** Schweine
FEMININE	– / keine	bekloppt***e*** Kühe

Always remember!

No definite article in the PLURAL! And also all adjectives have *"-e"* as ending in the PLURAL.

Note: In the SINGULAR NOMINATIVE and ACCUSATIVE the NEUTER ending is always *"-es"* and the feminine ending is always *"-e"*.

Attention: Only the masculine ending of the adjective following the indefinite article changes from the NOMINATIVE ending *"-er"* to *"-en"* in the SINGULAR ACCUSATIVE.

Remember: *"Kein"*, the negative of *"ein"* is also declined like an indefinite article and in contrast to *"ein"* also exists in the PLURAL.

Exercises – Chapter 6

Enough with the dry stuff... it's exercise time!

Build sentences and learn more about the German language and probably yourself! Here are some words. Fill the gaps with them, because no one else will do so!

(häßlich), (tot), (senil), (rechtsradikal), (asozial), (dumm)

Example: Helmut: Helmut ist asozial.

Svengster: ....

Gott: ....

Nazis: ....

VW Beetles: ....

Der Papst: ....

And here are some more possibilities for you to show that you have understood everything so far. Do not forget the definite or indefinite articles!

(böse), (gemeingefährlich), (schlimm), (betrügerisch), (schlecht), (ekelhaft)

Pitbull: ....

Essen: ....

Hitler: ....

Bank: ....

Pest: ....

Deutscher Gangstarap: ....

As always: It is getting worse or more difficult: Two words and you have to combine them and make sentences. And above all: GERMAN sentences.

Example: Al Quaida will *(eine Atombombe)* *(französisch)*

Al Quaida will eine französische Atombombe.

(eine Droge) *(billige)*

Svengster möchte ....

(ein Pilz) *(juckend)*

Eve hat ....

(ein Opfer) *(neu)*

Helmut sucht ....

(ein Rock) *(kurz)*

Doreen braucht ....

(keine Hose) *(trocken)*

Svengster hat ....

(ein 300-Mrd-Kredit) (frisch)

Die Bank braucht ....

(kein Zeitungsabo) (beschissen)

Herr Siebenhoden will ....

Bonus-Track – Chapter 6

Biology: Body parts of German men and women

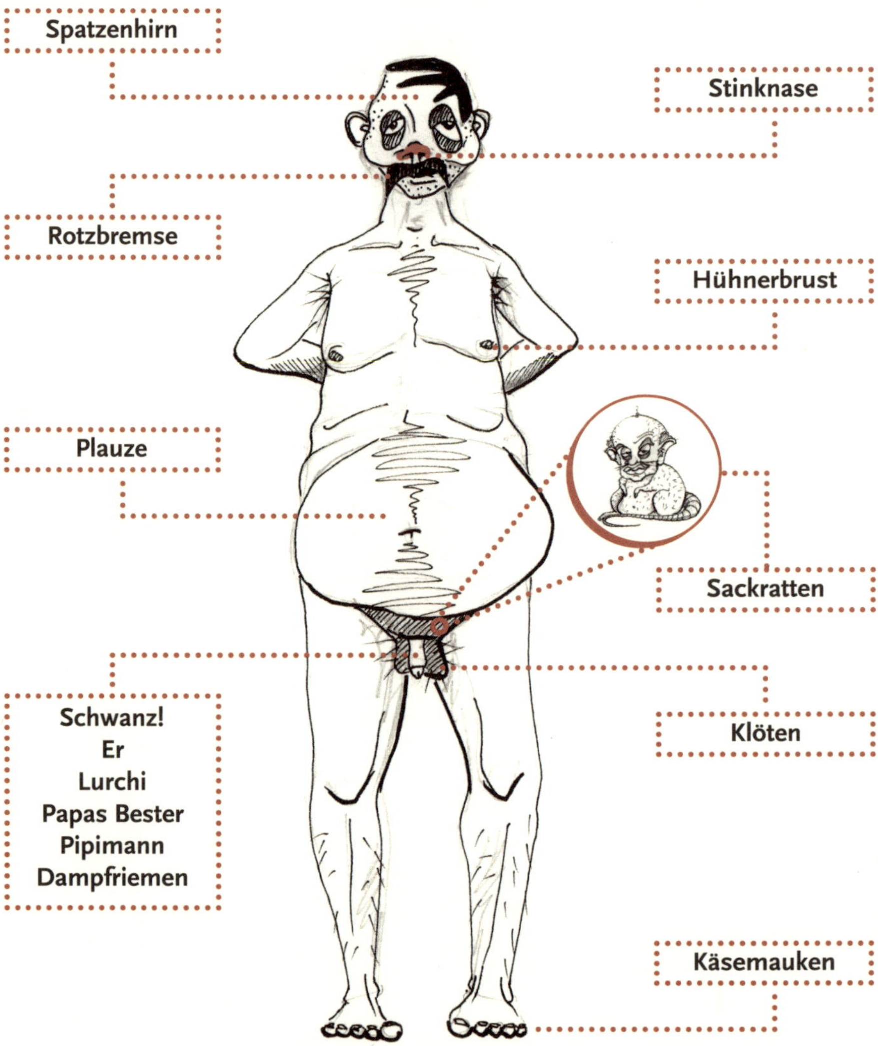

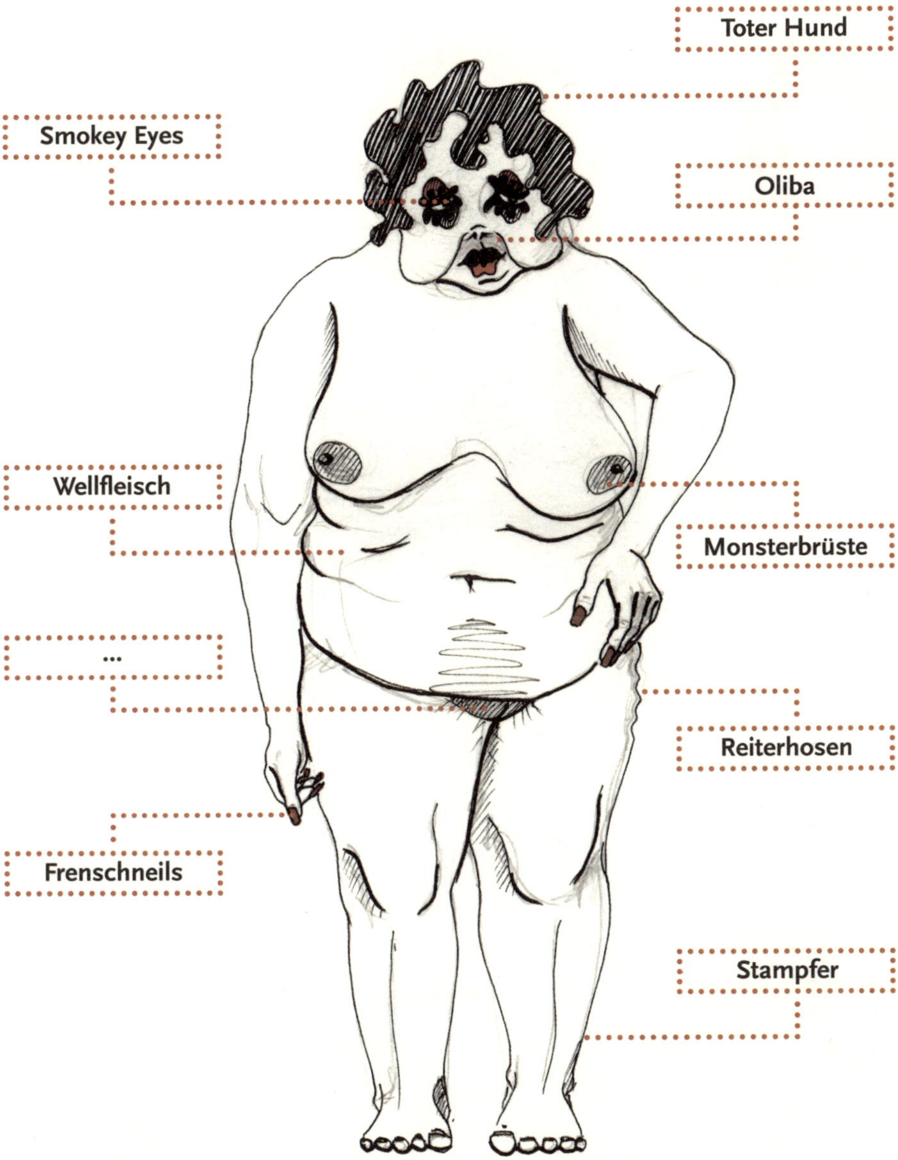
Toter Hund
Smokey Eyes
Oliba
Wellfleisch
Monsterbrüste
...
Reiterhosen
Frenschneils
Stampfer

Chapter 7

Frühstück bei den Schmidts

Die Familie Schmidt ist heute früh um 10 Uhr aufgestanden. Gemeinsam sitzen alle um den Frühstückstisch, als Helmut Eve etwas fragt:

Helmut zu Eve: „*Was gibt es denn zu essen, Eve?*"

Eve: „*Bitte? Was soll es schon geben? Erdbeeren mit Scheiße!*"

Svengster: „*Lecker! Erdbeeren! Ich liebe Erdbeeren!*"

Helmut: „*Bitte rede nicht so mit mir, Eve. Ich liebe dich doch. Ich bringe dir auch nachher noch was vom Kiosk mit!*"

Eve: „*Ach Helmut! Wirklich? Entschuldigung! Dann bring mir doch einen Nordhäuser Doppelkorn mit. Eine Magnumflasche.*"

Svengster: „*Vater! Mutter! Doreen! Ich muss euch etwas sagen.*"

Doreen: „*Sieh mal einer an. Mein Bruder hat was mitzuteilen!*"

Eve: „*Svennie! Du musst uns doch nicht wieder erzählen, dass du dein Bett eingenässt hast. Irgendwann wächst sich das aus.*"

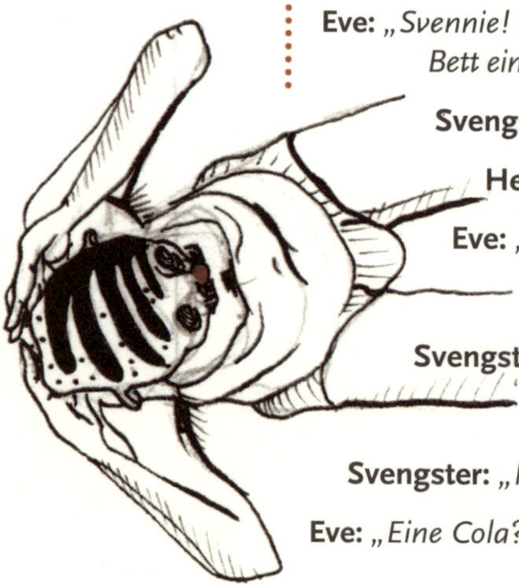

Svengster: „*Aber das ist es nicht...*"

Helmut: „*Und was gibt es jetzt zu essen?*"

Eve: „*Ich reich dir erst einmal ein Bier rüber.*"

Doreen: „*Ich will auch ein Bier.*"

Svengster: „*Ich...*"

Eve: „*Du möchtest auch ein Bier, Svennie?*"

Svengster: „*Nein, ich möchte doch nur...*"

Eve: „*Eine Cola?*"

Helmut: *„Das ist mein Sohn! Gleich möchte er noch eine Cola Light und dann am Ende noch einen schwulen Strohhalm."*

Doreen: *„Voll schwul, ey. Du, Sven! Weißt du, wie ich dich von jetzt an nenne? Svenja!"*

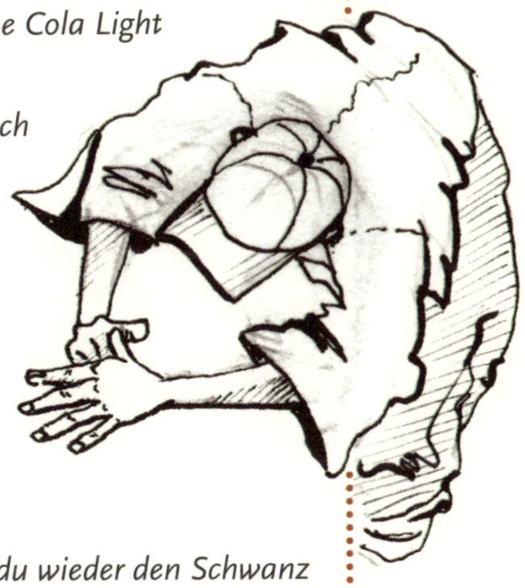

Eve: *„Warum seid ihr seid so gemein zu Svennie?"*

Helmut: *„Und was gibt es jetzt zu essen?"*

Eve: *„Warte noch kurz!"*

Helmut zu Svengster: *„Svennie, du wolltest doch noch was Wichtiges mitteilen, nicht wahr?"*

Svengster: *„Och, ist nicht so wichtig."*

Doreen: *„Ey bitte! Erst tust du so groß und dann ziehst du wieder den Schwanz ein wie ein schwules Mädchen!"*

Helmut: *„Ich möchte noch ein Bier, Eve! Bier ist die beste Mahlzeit! Findet ihr nicht auch, Kinder?"*

Eve: *„Mist! Jetzt ist mir die Tiefkühlpizza im Backofen verbrannt."*

Doreen: *„Menno, Mama!"*

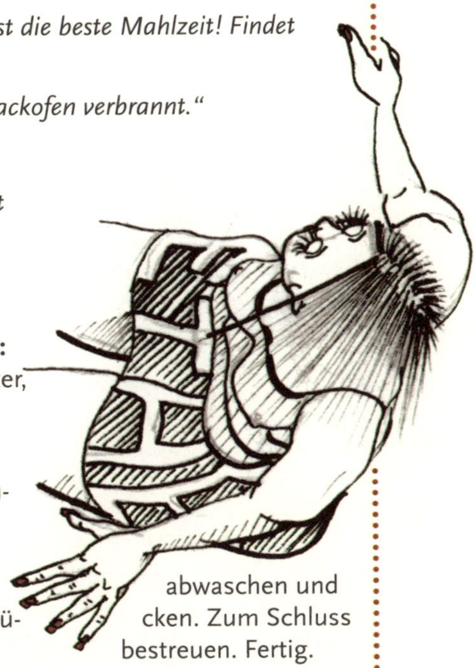

Svengster: *„Ist nicht so schlimm. Doreen wiegt sowieso schon zuviel."*

Doreen: *„Halt dein Maul, Svenja!"*

REZEPT: **Erdbeeren mit Scheiße (4 Pers.):**

500 g frische oder alte Erdbeeren, Salz, Zucker, zwei Löffel frischen Rinderkot (gibt es beim Metzger), 2 / 3 Zitrone (ungespritzt)

Zubereitung: Den Kot mit der Zitrone beträufeln. Dann mit einem Fleischhauer zermanschen bis es fluffig wird. Masse in einer Glasschale verteilen, Erdbeeren vierteln und abwaschen und vorsichtig in die Zitronenscheißematsche drücken. Zum Schluss alles nach Gefühl mit Zucker und / oder Salz bestreuen. Fertig.

Grammar Stuff – Chapter 7

Verbs again – This time separable and inseparable verbs.

a) Prefixes are a funny thing because they change the meaning of the verbs.

sagen: Helmut **sagt** hallo.
=> *to say: Helmut says hello.*

absagen: Helmut **sagt** heute Abend seinen Kumpels **ab.**
=> *to cancel: Helmut cancels his evening date with his buddies.*

sich lossagen: Helmut **sagt** sich von seiner Familie **los.**
=> *to dissociate o. s. from: Helmut dissociates himself from his family.*

b) As you see there are separable and inseparable verbs. The most common inseparable prefixes are the following:

be-	***be**labern*	*to speak about sth.*
emp-	***emp**fangen*	*to receive / to conceive*
ent-	***ent**haupten*	*to behead*
er-	***er**schießen*	*to shoot*
ge-	***ge**fallen*	*to like*
ver-	***ver**suchen*	*to try*
zer-	***zer**matschen*	*to crush*

c) And then there are these funny things called separable prefixes. In case you want to get to know them: Here are the favourite ones.

ab-	***ab**schlachten*	*to slaughter*
an-	***an**zeigen*	*to report at the police*
auf-	***auf**spritzen*	*to pump up*
aus-	***aus**teilen*	*to deal out*
ein-	**ein**schlagen	*to smash in*
mit-	***mit**nehmen*	*to treat harshly*
vor-	***vor**kommen*	*to happen*
weg-	***weg**rennen*	*to run away*
zu-	***zu**treten*	*to kick*
zurück-	***zurück**schlagen*	*to strike back*
zusammen-	***zusammen**schlagen*	*to beat up*

And here is some final and important information about separable prefixes: The separable prefixes are always at the end of the sentence in statements and questions.

MC Feuermelder ***schlägt*** den Svengster ***zusammen.***
MC Feuermelder beats up the Svengster.

Zeigt Helmut viele Ausländer ***an?***
Does Helmut report many foreigners to the police?

In sentences with modal verbs the verb is in the last position of the sentence and the prefix is not separated from the verb.

Doreen möchte ihre Brüste ***aufspritzen.***
Doreen would like to pump up her breasts.

And then there are reflexive verbs. These verbs which will be presented in the next few lines can or must take a reflexive pronoun.

sich ärgern
Helmut ***ärgert sich*** über Ausländer.
Helmut gets angry at foreigners.

sich bewerben
Doreen ***bewirbt sich*** bei „Deutschland sucht den Superstar".
Doreen applies for "Germany's next Superstar".

sich waschen
Svengster ***wäscht sich*** dreimal am Tag.
Svengster washes himself three times a day.

And here are some more verbs like the ones mentioned above.

sich amüsieren
sich ärgern
sich hinstellen
sich bewerben
sich beschweren
sich freuen
sich kloppen
sich vorstellen
sich anschauen
sich selbstbefriedigen
sich setzen
sich duschen
sich bedanken

ich	beschwere	***mich***
du	beschwerst	***dich***
Sie	beschweren	***sich****
er / sie / es	beschwert	***sich****
wir	beschweren	***uns***
ihr	beschwert	***euch***
Sie	beschweren	***sich****
sie	beschweren	***sich****

The declination of the reflexive pronouns is the same as the declination of the personal pronouns in THE ACCUSATIVE! The only exception: *"sich"* s. a.*

Word formation is easy: Take the stem of a verb and put "-ung" at the end!

In case you have nothing better to do, just form yourself some German nouns. First take the stem of a verb and write the three letters *"-u"*, *"-n"* and *"-g"* in the right order *"-ung"* at the end of the stem. In case you wonder which gender the new words might have: It's easy because all German words with *"-ung"*-ending are feminine which means you have to use the article *"die"*. The only exception is the masculine word *"Dung"* (= cow shit): *"Der Dung"*

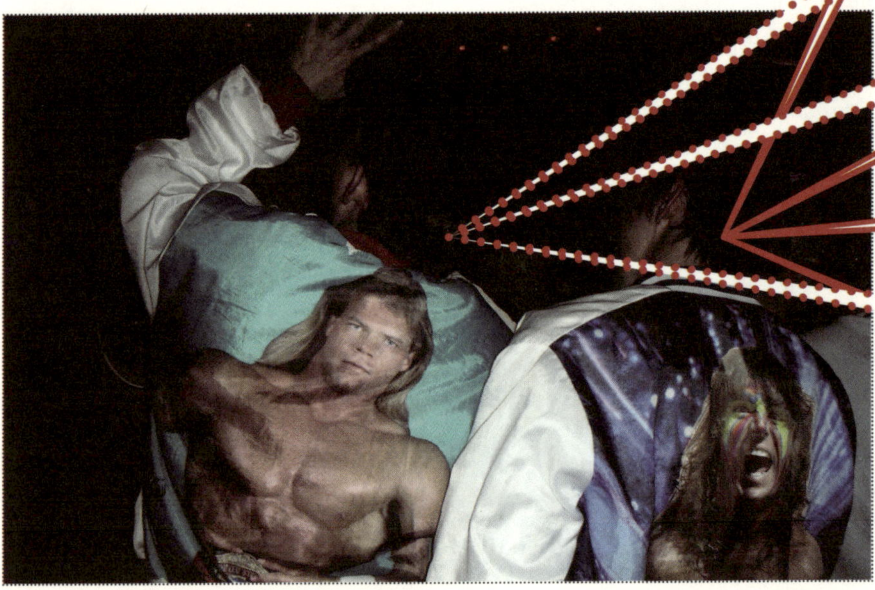

EY, DIE LEUTE HABEN EINFACH KEINEN STYLE.

ALSO ICH HAB DAMIT KEIN PROBLEM.

DAS SIEHT MAN DIR AN.

ACH? UND WORAN BITTE?

NA, DU HAST AUF DEINER JACKE EIN FOTO VON THOMAS GOTTSCHALK!

BESSER ALS HENRY MASKE MIT LANG-HAARPERÜCKE.

EGAL! JETZT SPIELEN SIE UNSER LIED! DAS IST DOCH „EYE OF THE TIGER“!

Exercises – Chapter 7

I guess you know what to do with the words given. Put them in the correct order and form.

der Taliban / Daniel Pearl / enthaupten / um 9 Uhr am Morgen

....

der / wegrennen / Dieb / möchten

....

müssen / den / wir / erschießen / Flüchtling

....

Doreen / gefallen / möchten / TV-Casting-Menschen / diesen

....

Achmadinedschad / zerstören / Israel / Präsident / möchten

....

einkaufen / Nordkorea / Atombombe / die / Pakistan / in

....

Papst Benedikt II / Lebenspartner / mitbringen / seinen / der / zum Abendessen

....

abholen / Eve / ihren / Svengster / Sohn

....

in Dallas / JFK / ermorden / Attentäter / der

....

And now fill in the correct reflexive pronoun. If you don't, the publishers of this book will hire some boys from da hood to break ya neck.

Helmut amüsiert .... mit sich selber.

Ich bedanke .... für die Schläge.

Eve: „*Helmut und ich, wir machen* ....*einen schönen Abend.*"

Svengster macht .... Sorgen, weil er schwul ist.

Wehe, Sie bedienen .... am Medikamentenschrank!

Become famous for inventing German nouns and look them up in your dictionary when you are done with inventing them!

a) vergewaltigen = ...

b) töten = ...

c) schlachten = ...

d) überraschen = ...

e) fisten = ...

f) zeichnen = ...

g) einschläfern = ...

h) heimsuchen = ...

Bonus-Track – Chapter 7

How-, what-, where- and why to eat in Germany

There are three things the Germans are really good at and therefore known for their excellence in these branches of society: humour, eating and world wars. This text is just a bonus track, so do not expect the authors of this book to write about all three of them. We will concentrate on the world wars … no, I remember the headline the publishers gave me, so I guess we should be nice and write about eating, food and everything that you can swallow in Germany to appease your hunger or for any other reasons.

The German Cuisine is known all over the blue planet and German cooks are the best in the world. They educated the French cooks and taught them everything – but the French weren't nice to the Germans and named fries that were fried in fat "French fries". That was the reason for World War I in which the German team was ahead for most of the time but lost in overtime.

The French took all deep-frying pans from the Ruhrgebiet and build up their own deep-frying-industry in the suburbs of Paris where to this day from time to time you can see groups of angry French teenagers without deep-frying pans who try to transform potatoes into French fries by setting cars on fire.

The most famous German dishes are *"Currywurst"*, *"Frikadelle"*, *"Frankfurter Würstchen"*, sausages in general and *"Leberkäs"*. All of them are made from each other or like the great Austrian philosopher Wolf Haas once put it in his own words: *"Weißt, woraus die Knackwiascht san? Aus die Abfäll' vom Leberkäs. Und weißt, woraus der Leberkäs ist? Aus die Abfäll' von die Knackwiascht."* ("Do you know what sausages are made of? They are made of the waste of liver loaf. And do you know of what liver loaf is made? The waste of the sausages.").

Essentially, you could get the impression that German food is all made of waste, but that is not completely true unless you say that milk is waste from the udder of the cow. Germany and its colony Switzerland are known for its chocolate culture. German chocolatiers invented the chocolate Santa Clause that you find in stores around March and the chocolate Easter Bunny, too. What you probably also didn't know: 87.5 % of the Cathedral of Cologne is made of chocolate. Precisely said, it is made of bitter chocolate. The other 12.5 % are made of concrete which is also a German invention, but nothing you should try to eat.

When you are hungry in Germany, don't be shy and ask other people in the streets if they have something to eat for you. If they say no or shake their heads, ask them *"Haste denn mal nen Euro für mich?"* ("Do you have a euro for me?"). Most Germans will be happy to meet someone as nice as you and help you out. If you want to sit in a restaurant, always remember that you agree to smoke at least every 5 minutes before your meal is served as soon as you sit at your table. In case you really enjoyed your food, express that by burping polysyllabic German words like *"Bauarbeiter"* (construction worker), *"Haftpflichtversicherung"* (liability insurance) or *"Polizeioberwachtmeister"* (special police sergeant) and the locals will love you and elect you as their chieftain. Do not forget to tip the waiter (in Germany the tip is called *"Trinkgeld"*) but not as you usually do in any other countries of the world! In Germany you do not express your gratitude with money but either with kisses or in cases of minor gratitude with painting a small picture or making a small sketch of the waiter or waitress. So don't forget your pens when travelling through Germany.

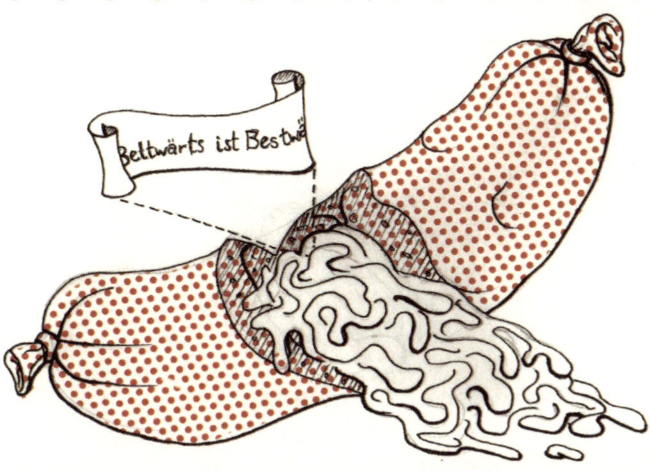

In Germany we do not have fortune cookies like in China. We do have fortune sausages (Glückswürste). You just have to bite in the sausage and there you will find a piece of paper with some wise advice on it or if you have bad luck with a curse. We Germans do also have "Glücksklöße" but no Kuglücksklöße!

Chapter 8

Svengster auf der Flucht

Svengster ist auf einem Hiphop-Event. Dort trifft er auf ein paar feindliche Rapper, mit denen er Rindfleisch hat. Die Lage eskaliert, als der böse Gangstarapper „Harter Sack" Svengster ein Bier über den Kopf kippt. Svengster ist stinkewütend und beschimpft „Harter Sack".

Svengster: *„Ey, Harter Sack! Fick deine Mutter!"*

Harter Sack: *„Fick DEINE Mutter!"*

Svengster: *„Ey, Alter! Was hast du gesagt?! Fick deine Mutter?!"*

Harter Sack: *„Ey, was hast DU gesagt?! Fick deine Mutter?!"*

Svengster: *„Fick dein' Vater! Fick deine Schwester! Fick deinen Hund, Hurensohn!"*

Harter Sack: *„Ich fick deinen Fernseher! Ich ficke deine Schwester und ich ficke deinen Fick!"*

Svensgter: *„Fick dich selber, Fickgesicht!"*

Da hat „Harter Sack" genug und holt sein Butterflymesser aus der Gürteltasche. Er möchte Svengster erstechen, doch der rennt weg. „Harter Sack" rennt hinterher und verliert seine Hiphophosen. Wütend zieht er seine Hose aus und verfolgt weiter den Svengster. Dieser läuft geradeaus nach draußen und versteckt sich mitten in einer Gruppe Rentner aus Hanau. Oben auf der Treppe steht „Harter Sack" und sucht Svengster: *„Wohin ist der?"* Die anderen Leute sagen, er ist hinaus gelaufen. *„Wenn ich den wieder sehe, dann gibt es Kasalla. Wie gerne ich den immer fertig mache!"*

Svengster krabbelt unter einen Bus. *„Vielleicht kann ich mich hier festhalten und entkommen? Ich möchte doch noch nicht*

sterben. Mist! Heute ist echt nicht mein Glückstag. Dieser verfickte Sohn einer Hundehurenmutter!"

Svengster hat sich wieder eingenässt. Der Busfahrer wundert sich über die Pfütze unter seinem Auto und entdeckt den verängstigten Svengster unter dem Bus.

Busfahrer: *„Was machen Sie denn dort? Kommen Sie sofort raus da unten!"*

Svengster: *„Entschuldigen Sie! Mein Name ist Sven Schmidt. Der Harter Sack will mich verkloppen, das blöde Fickgesicht!"*

Busfahrer: *„Na, junger Mann! Sagen Sie so etwas nicht! Das ist kein nettes Wort, verstehen Sie!"*

Svengster: *„Na, benutzen Sie nicht auch manchmal Schimpfwörter?"*

Busfahrer: *„Nein! Niemals! Kommen Sie mit. Ich fahre Sie mit meinem Bus nach Hause. Hier drin riecht es eh schon den ganzen Tag nach Urin."*

Der Busfahrer, die Rentner und der Svengster steigen in den Bus. „Harter Sack" findet den Svengster nicht mehr und geht wieder rein. Svengster sitzt vorne beim Busfahrer. Dieser spricht gerade in sein Mikrofon: *„Sehr verehrte Fahrgäste von Runter-Reisen. Wir machen jetzt einen kleinen Umweg und bringen diesen jungen Herren hier nach Hause. Bitte beachten Sie: Essen Sie keine Lebensmittel in diesem Bus!"* Der Bus fährt über eine rote Ampel und überrollt einen Kleinwagen mit 8 Leuten drin.

„Verdammter Dreck! Verfickte Scheiße! Jetzt muss ich wieder zum Idiotentest und darf beim Fahren keinen Alkohol mehr trinken!" Der Busfahrer weint. Svengster möchte ihn trösten. Die Rentner fragen sich, ob es später noch was zum Abendessen gibt.

Grammar Stuff – Chapter 8

Adverbs

What do they do?	**They modify verbs, adjectives, nouns and it is also possible that they modify whole sentences.**

Attention! Adverbs are NOT declined.

Groups of adverbs.	**There are three groups of adverbs** **- Adverbs of time** **- Adverbs of place** **- Modal adverbs**

Adverbs of time

heute = *today*
Heute ist Scheiße.
Today is shit.

morgen = *tomorrow*
Morgen ist auch noch ein Tag.
Tomorrow is another day.

gestern = *yesterday*
Gestern war blöd.
Yesterday was stupid.

wann? / jetzt = *when? / now*
Wann wollen Sie das Geld?
When do you want to have the money?

Jetzt geben Sie mir das Geld.
Now you will give me the money.

nachts / abends / nachmittags / mittags / vormittags = morgens
every night / every evening / every afternoon / every noon / every morning
Die Schmidts gehen **nachts** um 3 ins Bett.
The Schmidts go to bed at three o'clock at night.

dann = *then*
Dann kaufen wir Heroin.
Then we will go and buy Heroin.

danach = *after*
Danach schießen wir uns ab.
After that we we will get really fucked up.

einmal / zweimal / dreimal... = *once / twice / three times*
Sie drückt sich **zweimal** täglich was.
Twice a day she shoots herself up.

manchmal = *sometimes*
Manchmal geht Svengster in die Schule.
Sometimes Svengster goes to school.

wieder = *again*
Doreen hat **wieder** eine 5 geschrieben.
Doreen has written an "F" again.

Adverbs of place

wo? = *where*
Wo ist die Psychiatrie?
Where is the psychiatry?

da / dort / hier = *there / over there / here*
Da / Dort / Hier starb Elvis Presley.
There / Over there / Here Elvis Presley died.

links / rechts = *left / right*
Links / Rechts sind die Morphiumrezepte.
On the left / right there are the morphium prescricptions.

oben / unten = *up / down*
Der Leichnam liegt **oben** im 2. Stock / **unten** im Keller.
The corpse lies up on the second floor / down in the basement.

draußen = *outside*
Nachts ist es kälter als **draußen**.
At night it is colder than outside.

drinnen = *inside*
Drinnen gibt es nur Kännchen.
Inside you only get small cans of coffee.

mitten = *in the middle*
Mitten auf dem Marktplatz steht ein Exhibitionist.
In the middle of the market there is a flasher.

wohin? = *where to?*
Wohin floh Josef Mengele?
Where to did Josef Mengele escape?

hinauf / hinunter = *up / down*
Die Straße **hinauf / hinunter** ist der Puff.
Up / down the street there is the brothel.

hinein / heraus = *in / out*
Hinein geht er als Held, **heraus** kommt er als Depp.
He walks in as a hero and comes out as a fool.

geradeaus = *straight ahead*
Ihre Zelle liegt **geradeaus** den Gang runter.
Your arrest cell is straight ahead down the corridor.

Modal Adverbs

vielleicht = *maybe / perhaps*
Vielleicht ist Doreen schwanger.
Maybe Doreen is pregnant.

sehr = *very*
Svengster ist **sehr** hässlich.
Svengster is very ugly.

auch = *also*
Svengster nimmt Drogen, aber **auch** Helmut raucht Crack.
Svengster takes drugs, but Helmut also smokes crack.

noch = *for another*
Nach dem Drogenkonsum können Sie noch vier Tage wach sein.
After taking drugs you might be awake for another four days.

sogar = *even*
Sogar der Papst ist ein Mann, auch, wenn er keinen Sex hat.
Even the pope is a man, even though he doesn't have sex.

gerne = *please*
Ich möchte Dich heiraten. Ja, **gerne!**
I want to marry you. Yes, please!

Lern! Den! IMPERATIV! – The IMPERATIVE

You use the IMPERATIVE when you ask for favors and requests. It is always directed at a person or dog.

The second reason is because there are only two forms of the IMPERATIVE: the second person SINGULAR and the second person PLURAL.

DU-FORM: The DU-FORM is derived from the second person singular in the present. Just throw away the "*-st*"-ending and there it is: The DU-FORM-IMPERATIVE.

In case there is an irregular verb with an "*Umlaut*" in the second person singular form, just forget it in the imperative and use the vowel without the "*Umlaut*".

PRESENT:		IMPERATIVE:	
du gib**st**	=>	**Gib!**	*Give (it to...)!*
du geh**st**	=>	**Geh!**	*Go!*
du nimm**st**	=>	**Nimm!**	*Take (it)!*
du fähr**st**	=>	**Fahr!**	*Drive!*
du läuf**st**	=>	**Lauf!**	*Run!*

The IMPERATIVE PLURAL form is exactly the same as the second person PLURAL form of the PRESENT.

PRESENT:		IMPERATIVE:	
ihr gebt	=>	**Gebt!**	*Give (it to...)!*
ihr geht	=>	**Geht!**	*Go!*
ihr nehmt	=>	**Nehmt!**	*Take (it)!*

As all Germans are extremely polite there is also a polite form of the IMPERATIVE using the polite form of SINGULAR and PRESENT. Both of these forms, SINGULAR and PLURAL, have the same form. They look exactly like the THIRD PERSON PLURAL in the PRESENT.

PRESENT:		IMPERATIVE:	
sie geben	=>	**Geben Sie!**	*Give (it to...)!*
sie gehen	=>	**Gehen Sie!**	*Go!*
sie nehmen	=>	**Nehmen Sie!**	*Take (it)!*

As you have hopefully learned, there are different verbs in the German language. For example, there are separable verbs. Just keep one thing in your mind.

The only important thing is: The prefix comes at the end.

Example: umbringen *(to kill)*
SIE-FORM: **Bringen** Sie die Queen **um!**

Then you also have the reflexive verbs which might be a pain in the ass but do not care about that, just remember: In this case the reflexive pronoun comes at the end.

However, there is one last thing for you to remember. If you use the polite SIE-FORM, the relative pronoun comes between the verb and the reflexive pronoun.

Enough said. Here is an example!

sich einnässen	*(to wet oneself)*	
DU-FORM:	**Näss dich ein!**	Wet yourself!
IHR-FORM:	**Nässt euch ein!**	Wet yourselves!
SIE-FORM:	**Nässen Sie sich ein!**	Wet yourself / yourselves!

As you know meanwhile, the Svengster wets his bed and clothes from time to time. Your task now is to find out, what Svengster was dreaming of in the last few nights. Have a close look at the pictures and then guess! Talk with your teacher and discuss everything in class.

Wovon hat der Svengster heute Nacht geträumt?
Svengster hat heute Nacht .... geträumt.

a) von Micky Maus

b) vom Tod

c) von Captain Hook

d) vom Fliegen

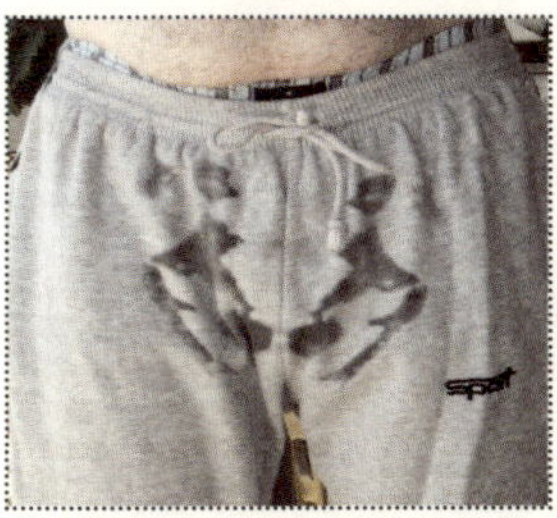

a) von kochenden Frauen mit Penis

b) von kochenden Frauen mit Penis

c) von kochenden Frauen mit Penis

d) vom Fliegen

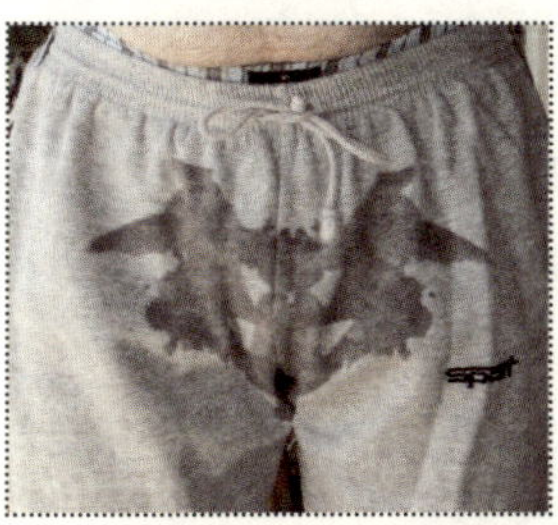

a) vom Coyote aus Roadrunner

b) von Batman

c) von zwei Vögeln

d) vom Fliegen

a) vom Sex mit einer Frau

b) von der Bundestagswahl

c) vom Fliegen

d) von nichts

Exercises – Chapter 8

Now that you have learned all these adverbs (modal adverbs, adverbs of time and adverbs of place) it is time to show that you have understood everything. So here is your chance to proof you are quite bright.

Adverbs:

***Fill in the right ones:* "auch", "zweimal", "gerne", "gestern", "hier", "danach", "wohin?", "rechts", "dort oben", "noch", "mitten", "links" *and* "heute"**

.... ist der Tag vor heute.

Du sollst nicht immer .... und ....verwechseln.

.... steht ein Selbstmörder auf dem Dach.

.... hast Du 200 Gramm Haschisch.

Helmut und Eve haben Sex. .... raucht Eve eine Zigarette.

Wird das .... noch was mit dem Geld?

Geben Sie mir .... eine zweite Line? Ja, ...

.... zwei macht vier.

.... ich will berühmt sein wie Osama Bin Laden.

.... ist der Dieb gelaufen?

MC Feuermelder schlägt dem Svengster .... ins Gesicht.

Adverbs of direction

***Fill in:* "in", "auf", "zu" *and* "nach"**

a) Dieter fliegt .... Paris

b) Herr Kramer geht .... Post.

c) Fred Baldus fährt .... Hause

d) Die Studenten gehen .... Bibliothek.

e) Heinz Herrmann braucht Geld. Er geht .... Bank.

... und nimmt Geiseln. *(takes hostages)*

... und hebt Geld ab. *(takes some money from his account)*

... und bettelt. *(asks for a dime)*

What do you do when you need money? Give me some examples or you have to pay lots of money, go back to the start and don't get 4.000 $ for not having given them to me.

Ich brauche Geld. Ich gehe ....

Ich ....

Ich ....

Ich ....

Ich ....

Ich ....

Ich ....

Give orders to everyone

No matter, how much sense they might have. And give them to everyone!

Example:
austrinken (du, ihr, Sie)

Trink aus! / Trinkt aus! / Trinken Sie aus!

exekutieren

.... / .... / ....

sich umbringen (du, ihr, Sie)

.... / .... / ....

sich befriedigen (du, ihr, Sie)

.... / .... / ....

scheißen gehen (du, ihr, Sie)

.... / .... / ....

Just tell the opposite of the word mentioned

draußen => ....

links => ....

unten => ....

der Tag => ....

der Winter => ....

schwarz => ....

der Vater => ....

Please write down more words and their opposite in the space provided below!

.... => ....

.... => ....

.... => ....

.... => ....

.... => ....

.... => ....

.... => ....

.... => ....

.... => ....

B Bonus-Track – Chapter 8

Driving a car in Germany

Driving a car in Germany is quite difficult if you compare it to driving a car at the North Pole or over the Atlantic Ocean. First thing you have to know: You are allowed to drive on a surface of your own choice, no matter if it is the pavement (*Bürgersteig* in German) or the trails or the autobahn. If you have chosen wisely, you drive on the autobahn or the pavement.

On the pavement there may be some stupid people running along called *Fußgänger* which means "pedestrian". Do not care about them and hit them hard with your car. They deserve it. On the autobahn everything is much easier. Drive as fast as you want to and use the headlamp flasher (German: *Lichthupe*) and your horn a lot. It is not allowed but highly recommended to bump other cars from the streets because you don't like the colour.

This behaviour comes from the 60s, when you could get your driving license by beating someone up in a dodgem-range (German: *Autoskooter*) of an entertainment park. The only other really important law on the streets is the Darwinian "Only the fittest survive!" In other words: Right for left and left for left or as the German aborigines say: "*Rechts vor links vor links vor links vor noch ein Tor!*"

If there is a really horrid crash in front of you, jump out of your car like the Germans, run to the car-wreck and try to take a nice picture before the others do it. You can become very rich with these pictures if you sell them to the media.

Last but not least two facts about the autobahn that have just recently been discovered. It was not Hitler who built them in the 30s – How could one man build thousands of kilometers of autobahn??? It was God who built the autobahn. Actually she wanted to build it in the middle of the Sahara desert, but then she could not find the right way, because she was too drunk and put the autobahn down on German ground.

Unfortunately, mankind isn't allowed to see God, so Hitler was cunning enough to claim the autobahn for himself when he awoke one morning in 1937. Actually God wanted to paint the Autobahn in bright pink because she thought that would look nicer from heaven but then decided on grey-black, because in the Do-it-yourself-store she thought that there was no reasonable explanation for why pink was twice as expensive as grey-black.

Hitler got it all back for his lies when he was forced to kill himself after God won the World War II against him. However, God had pity with Hitler and asked the Germans to name the main highway in Germany the Hitlerhighway, also known as A88 or Route 88.

Chapter 9

Frauengespräche

Eve und Doreen treffen sich in der Küche. Doreen findet sich in letzter Zeit hässlich und möchte von Eve wissen, ob das stimmt.

Doreen: *Mama, ich finde mich so hässlich. Findest du mich auch hässlich oder gefalle ich dir?*

Eve: *Aber Doreen! Ich antworte dir jetzt ganz ehrlich: Du bist nicht hässlich. Schau dir mal Vati an oder auch den Svengster. Neben den beiden Gesichtsbaracken siehst du aus wie ein schöner Schwan!*

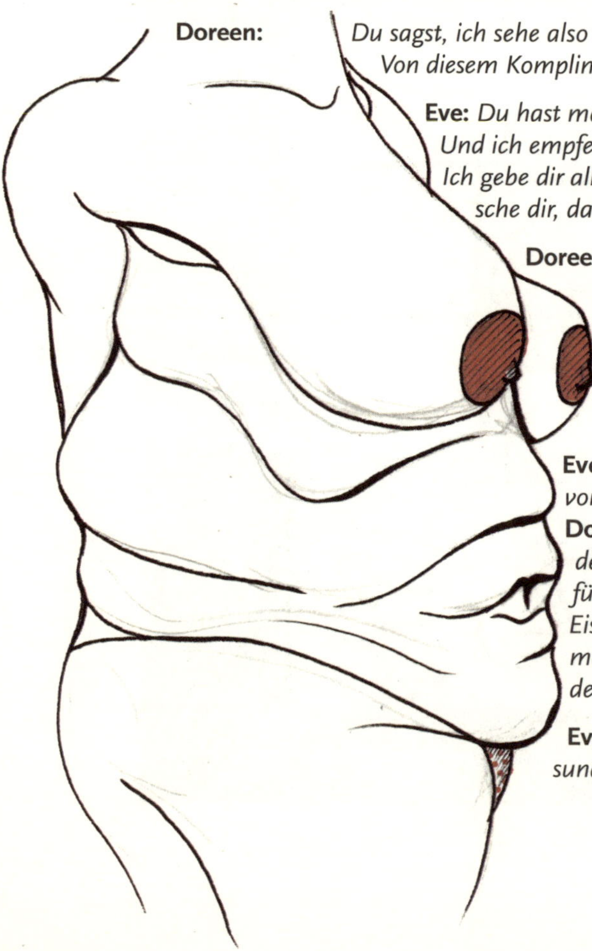

Doreen: *Du sagst, ich sehe also besser aus als zwei Gesichtsbaracken. Von diesem Kompliment wird es aber noch nicht besser.*

Eve: *Du hast mein Aussehen! Ich habe es dir geschenkt. Und ich empfehle dir, Doreen, glaube an deine Mutter. Ich gebe dir alle Tipps, die du wissen möchtest, wünsche dir, dass du genauso hübsch wirst wie ich…*

Doreen: *Du findest mich also nicht hübsch.*

Eve: *Doch! Natürlich! Wenn ich dich und Schacklihn sehe, dann denke ich immer wieder, da gehen zwei Grazien.*

Doreen: *Gratziegen?*

Eve: *Grazien! Zwei sehr schöne Frauen, von denen eine etwas zu dick ist, sicherlich.*

Doreen: *Die Schacklihn, nicht? Nach dem Essen bestellt die sich immer noch fünf Bällchen Eis mit Sahne bei der Eisdiele gegenüber von der Disko. Das macht die schon seit drei Jahren so mit dem Eisfressen.*

Eve: *Mach du das ja nicht! Eis ist ungesund! Merk dir das, Kind!*

Doreen: *Isst Vati auch ganz viel Eis?*

Eve: *Warum?*

Doreen: *Vati lief heute nach dem Duschen nackt durch die Wohnung und da habe ich unter seinem ersten Bauch, einen zweiten und einen dritten Bauch entdeckt.*

Eve: *An deinem Vati ist nun mal einiges dran. Wenn ich unter ihm im Bett liege und wir Sex haben, dann hoffe ich immer, niemand liegt unter uns in der Wohnung.*

Doreen: *Warum denn das?*

Eve: *Na, wenn der Vati mit seinen 100 Kilo da rummacht und die Decke einkracht.*

Doreen: *Dann kaufe ich euch irgendwann einmal die Wohnung ganz unten im Erdgeschoss.*

Eve: *Du bist süß, Doreen.*

Doreen: *Süß, aber nicht fett ... oder?*

Eve: *Neeee, nur süß.*

Doreen: *Mein Lehrer findet mich auch süß!*

Eve: *Dann sag dem Lehrer mal, dass das illegal ist und du auch eine süße Mami hast.*

Doreen: *In der Bibel steht aber doch: Du darfst nicht lügen!*

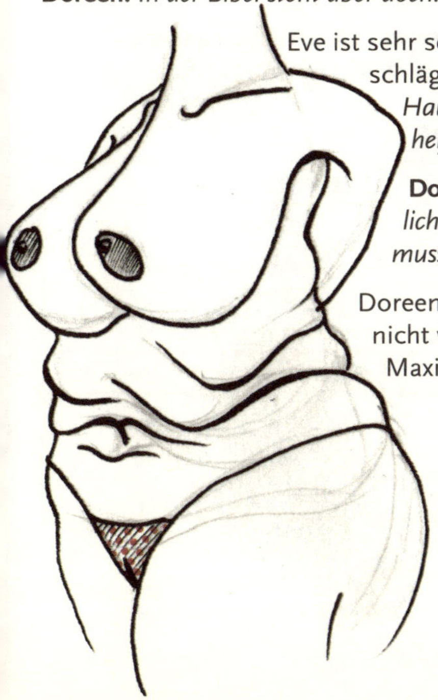

Eve ist sehr sehr sauer. Sie nimmt einen Holzlöffel und schlägt nach ihrer Tochter. Dann brüllt sie laut: *Hau ab, du fette Sau! Dir werde ich noch einmal helfen! Dir höre ich noch einmal zu!*

Doreen: *Ich danke dir! Endlich bist du mal ehrlich zu mir. Ich weiß, dass ich zu dick bin, aber musst du mir das so deutlich immer wieder sagen?*

Doreen weint sehr, weil ihre Mutter sie einfach nicht versteht. Aus Frust bestellt sie sich ein Maxi-Menu bei McDonalds.

Grammar Stuff – Chapter 9

The DATIVE case!

Before you get a lot of verbs that need a dative, you must know how the pronouns and the nouns look like when they are written in DATIVE. So here you get all you need to know about nouns and pronouns in THE DATIVE.

Definite and indefinite article in THE DATIVE

DATIVE	SINGULAR	PLURAL
Masculine	***dem*** / ein***em*** Zuhälter	***den*** / – Zuhälter***n***
Feminine	***der*** / ein***er*** Prostituierten	***den*** / – Prostituierten
Neuter	de***m*** / ein***em*** Sexmagazin	***den*** / – Sexmagazine***n***

Attention!

All nouns that do not end with an *"n"* do have an *"n"* in the PLURAL! The only exception: words that end with an *"s"* in the PLURAL, for example *"der / ein Porno"* which in the dative becomes ***"den / – Pornos".***

Not to confuse you, but just to remind you so you do not have to search around in your book, here are the cases you already know:

THE NOMINATIVE and THE ACCUSATIVE.

NOMINATIVE	SINGULAR	PLURAL
Masculine	der / ein Zuhälter	die / – Zuhälter
Feminine	die / eine Prostituierte	die / – Prostituierten
Neuter	das / ein Sexmagazin	die / – Sexmagazine

ACCUSATIVE	SINGULAR	PLURAL
Masculine	den / einen Zuhälter	die / – Zuhälter
Feminine	die / eine Prostituierte	die / – Prostituierten
Neuter	das / ein Sexmagazin	die / – Sexmagazine

Question words for persons – DATIVE

Der Tanga gehört ***Doreen.***	***Wem*** gehört der Tanga?
Die Drogen gehören ***Helmut und Svengster.***	***Wem*** gehören die Drogen?

"Wem?" can be translated as "to whom?"Do remember the other two question words you know. "Wer?" in the NOMINATIVE and "Wen?" in the ACCUSATIVE.

Verbs that are followed by the dative

Example:	**Deine Drogen**	**gefallen**	**dem Svengster.**
	Wer oder was?	Verb	Wem?
	NOMINATIVE		**DATIVE COMPLEMENT**

As you might have noticed the verb determines the case of the noun and the article. The following verbs are always followed by THE DATIVE. Learn them by heart and always connect them with THE DATIVE. If you forget them, it might be a sign that you get Alzheimer. In this case you should go and see a doctor.

antworten:	Svengster antwortet dem Untersuchungsrichter. *Svengster answers to the investigating judge.*
danken:	Der Drogendealer dankt Gott. *The drugdealer thanks god.*
gefallen:	Das Sexmagazin gefällt dem Pfarrer. *The sex magazine pleases the priest.*
gratulieren:	Der Papst gratuliert mir zum Geburtstag. *The pope congratulates me to my birthday.*
helfen:	Ivo hilft dem Zuhälter Branko. *Ivo helps pimp Branko.*
passen:	Der String passt Doreen. *The string tanga fits Doreen.*
widersprechen:	Der Teufel widerspricht dem Sohn Gottes. *The devil contradicts the son of god.*
zuhören:	Jesus hört den Menschen zu. *Jesus listens to the people.*
zusagen:	Helmut sagt dem Arbeitsangebot zu. *Helmut accepts the offer of the employment center.*
zuschauen:	Eve und Doreen schauen dem Boxkampf zu. *Eve and Doreen watch the boxfight.*

Verbs that are followed by THE DATIVE and THE ACCUSATIVE!

Isn't it great that every time you think "It is enough now!" some more things are coming? This time you get verbs that need a DATIVE and keep an ACCUSATIVE COMPLEMENT. The person is always in THE DATIVE and the objects are in THE ACCUSATIVE. Practically every verb we talk about is about "giving something to someone".

Eve	**wünscht**	**sich**	**eine andere Familie.**
Wer / was?		Wem?	Wen / was?
Subject	**verb**	**DATIVE C.**	**ACCUSATIVE C.**

And here are all the words with THE DATIVE and THE ACCUSATIVE.

anbieten:	Ivo	**bietet**	dem Lehrer	500 Euro **an.**
offer	*Ivo offers 500 euros to his teacher.*			
bringen:	Doreen	**bringt**	den Eltern	Kirschwasser.
bring	*Doreen brings her parents some cherry schnapps.*			
empfehlen:	Svengster	***empfiehlt***	Helmut	das neue Speed.
recommend	*Svengster recommends the new speed to Helmut.*			
erklären:	Eve	**erklärt**	den Kunden	die Preise.
explain	*Eve explains her prices to the customers.*			
erzählen:	Satan	**erzählt**	Gott	einen Witz.
tell	*Satan tells God a joke.*			
geben:	Die USA	**geben**	der Welt	Coca-Cola.
give	*The USA give Coca-Cola to the world.*			
sagen:	Boris Becker	**sagt**	Sandy	„Auf Wiedersehen".
say	*Boris Becker says "Good-bye" to his girlfriend Sandy.*			
schenken:	Svengster	**schenkt**	den Freunden	2 Gramm Marihuana.
g. a present	*Svengster gives his friends two grams of dope as a present.*			
schicken:	Das Gericht	**schickt**	Helmut	eine Vorladung.
send	*The court sends a citation to Helmut.*			

zeigen:	Doreen	**zeigt**	der Polizei	den Mittelfinger.
show	*Doreen shows her middle finger to the police.*			

Finally for this chapter there are also prepositions that are followed by THE DATIVE! THE DATIVE-only prepositions are* "aus" *(from)*, "bei" *(at)*, "gegenüber" *(opposite)*, "mit" *(with)*, "nach" *(after)*, "seit" *(since)*, "von" *(from) and* "zu" *(to).

Don't be too impressed by the words *"beim"* or *"vom"* or *"zum"*. They are just short forms of *"bei dem"*, *"von dem"* und *"zu dem"* which you usually use.

aus:	Der Pfarrer kommt ***aus*** dem Puff. *The priest comes from / out of the brothel.*
bei:	Svengster holt Drogen ***beim (bei dem)*** Dealer. *Svengster gets his drugs at the dealer.*
gegenüber:	Der Teufel wohnt ***gegenüber*** von Gott. *The devil lives opposite God.*
mit:	Der Mörder spielt ***mit*** dem Messer. *The murderer plays with the knife.*
nach:	***Nach*** dem Onanieren geht Helmut schlafen. *After masturbating Helmut goes sleeping.*
seit:	Helmut bezieht ***seit*** dem 2. Weltkrieg Arbeitslosengeld. *Helmut gets his unemployment paycheck since WW 2..*
von:	***Von*** der Schule kommt Doreen bestimmt nicht. *Doreen is definitely not coming from school.*
zu:	Es ist schön, ***zum (= zu dem)*** Schoren eingeladen zu werden. *It is a pleasure to be invited to shoot some drugs.*

„Immer wenn Du denkst, es geht nicht mehr, kommt von irgendwo ein Lichtlein her." *"Everytime you think, everything is totally fucked up, there comes a light from somewhere you wouldn't have expected." Here they are: Prepositions with both! Don't worry, be happy!*

THE ACCUSATIVE and THE DATIVE. Isn't that great?!

There are 6 prepositions which can be used with both, THE ACCUSATIVE and THE DATIVE. So be careful and look exactly at the sentences in which they are used.

All 6 of them in THE ACCUSATIVE – "an" (on), *"auf"* (on), *"in"* (into), *"neben"* (next to), *"unter"* (under) and *"vor"* (in front of) – are prepositions which take THE ACCUSATIVE when the question is where to? And the verb which is used expresses an activity.

If the question asked is WHERE and the verb which is used before expresses a state, then it shows that you need to take the dative for the following noun.

an, auf, in, neben, unter and vor with THE ACCUSATIVE

an:	Helmut klatscht den Svengster **an** die Wand. *Helmut smashes Svengster at the wall.*
auf:	Svengster haut Helmut den Hammer **auf** den Kopf. *Svengster beats the hammer on Helmut's head.*
in:	Helmut fährt Svengster **in** die Klinik. *Helmut drives Svengster to the hospital.*
neben:	Svengster setzt sich **neben** die Krankenschwestern. *Svengster sits down right next to the nurses.*
unter:	Helmut legt sich **unter** die Chefärztin. *Helmut lays down under the female head physician.*
vor:	Sven kniet sich **vor** die Lernschwester Elke. *Sven kneels down in front of student nurse Elke.*

an, auf, in, neben, unter and vor with THE DATIVE

an:	Helmut hängt **an** der Decke. *Helmut hangs from the ceiling.*
auf:	Svengster liegt **auf** dem OP-Tisch. *Svengster lies on the surgeon's table.*
in:	Helmut kennt einen Puff **in** der Stadt. *Helmut knows a brothel downtown.*
neben:	Die Mülltonnen brennen **neben** dem Haus. *The dustbins are burning right next to the house.*
unter:	Helmut liegt **unter** der Chefärztin. *Helmut lies under the female head physician.*
vor:	Sven steht nackt **vor** der Lernschwester. *Sven is standing naked in front of student nurse Elke.*

Dick und Doof stehen neben dem Cowboy. Die Störche stehen vor den Hunden mit Hut und die Frösche sitzen neben dem Afroamerikaner. *Come on! Play around and tell us who is where.*

Exercises – Chapter 9

Fill in! This time fill in either the correct definite / indefinite article in THE DATIVE. Be careful because if you fail, satan will haunt you tonight in your dreams and eat up your testicles – in case you have some.

Helmut und Svengster schauen .... Schlägerei (f.) zu.

Eve hört von .... Atombombenexplosion. (f.)

Doreen hilft .... Freundin (f.) Schacklihn in Mathematik.

Gott widerspricht .... Nietzsche. (m.)

Der Nachrichtensprecher gratuliert .... Wettermann. (m.)

Eves Brüste gefallen .... Mann. (m.)

Svengster dankt .... Academy. (f.)

Fill in, but this time the correct noun AND the correct articles of THE DATIVE and THE ACCUSATIVE.

Der Vater schenkt .... Pistole. (pl) (die Kinder)

Die Kanzlerin gibt .... Hitzefrei. (die Menschen)

Freddie schenkt .... zwei Flaschen Schnaps. (eine Oma)

Svengster bietet .... 300 Euro. (der Drogendealer)

Now fill in the correct DATIVE prepositons AND the correct article before the noun if it is neccesary.

Mc Feuermelder schläft .... (der Gangstarapper, pl.)

Helmut wohnt seit .... 1945 (das Jahr) mit Eve zusammen.

Ivo kommt .... (der Kosovo)

.... gehen alle Schmidts ins Wohnzimmer. (das Vollsaufen)

Mit .... ist nicht gut Kirschenessen. (der Teufel)

Now answer me some questions!

Wo kauft der Svengster seine Drogen? (der Dealer / bei)

Wo saufen sich die Schmitz voll? (das Wohnzimmer / in)

Woher kommt Ivo? (der Kosovo / aus)

Wo ist der Puff? (die Kirche / gegenüber)

Wo raucht Helmut immer? (das Bett / in)

Extra-work:

Read carefully and then answer the questions.

Eine Reise nach Deutschland

Die Familie Lodd aus New York reist im Sommer nach Deutschland. Herr und Frau Lodd haben 4 Flugtickets gekauft. Ihre Kinder Bob und Todd kommen mit nach Europa. Zuerst besichtigt die Familie Frankfurt, sieht sich den alten Bahnhof an und kauft in der Kaiserstraße ein. Danach fahren sie mit ihrem Mietwagen, einem Mercedes 500 SEL, nach Hamburg. Dort essen sie in einem Restaurant Heringssalat und treffen diesen Dr. Hannibal Lecker, der gerade einen Hamburger tötet und isst.

Sie fahren schnell  nach Berlin, damit er nicht auch sie tötet und isst. In Berlin besuchen sie das Brandenburger Tor und die Love-Parade. Bob und Todd tanzen die ganze Nacht lang und nehmen keine Drogen. Am nächsten Tag treffen sie wieder Dr. Lecker. Dieser Psychopath mit Dauerwelle hat zum Frühstück ihre Eltern, Herrn und Frau Lodd, gegessen. Traurig fliegen Todd und Bob mit Egypt Air wieder nach New York. Neben Ihnen sitzt Herr Fünfzigpfennig und strickt Merchandise-Artikel. Der Co-Pilot ist suizidal und das Flugzeug stürzt ins Meer.

Wann reisen die Lodds nach Deutschland?

[ ] Im Winter
[ ] Im Sommer
[ ] Im Herbst

Wie heißen die Kinder der Lodds?

[ ] Todd und Bob
[ ] Bill und Ted
[ ] Kirk und Dirk

Welche deutsche Stadt besichtigen die Lodds zuerst?

[ ] Berlin
[ ] Paris
[ ] Frankfurt

Was isst Hannibal Lecker in Hamburg?

[ ] Einen Berliner
[ ] Einen Kartoffelsalat
[ ] Einen Hamburger

Wie sterben Todds und Bobs Eltern?

[ ] Ihr Flugzeug stürzt ab.
[ ] Sie werden überfahren.
[ ] Hannibal Lecker tötet sie.

Mit welcher Fluggesellschaft fliegen Todd und Bob nach New York?

[ ] Mit Lufthansa
[ ] Mit Egypt Air
[ ] Mit Air France

50
CENT

B Bonus-Track – Chapter 9

Famous in Germany:
The Sandman, the Christ Child and the Nikolaus

It's there and then it's gone – a short story about German customs written by the famous German author Rolf Palmian.

Sirii is from Estonia and as someone mentions the Sandman, she asks "*Who's that?*" and I try to explain to her everything about the two German sandmen. There is a communist sandman and a capitalist one – by the way, the communist sandman won the battle and is still alive.

Their job is simply to spread sand in the eyes of children and other people's eyes at night to help them sleep. For sure, from the point of view of a doctor that probably wasn't the best sleeping-solution, Valium should be much better, but sand didn't need a prescription and no one ever heard of someone becoming addicted to sand.

Her question, how the Sandman is actually able to get into your room, is very difficult to answer. Maybe through the window ... anyhow, it really doesn't matter. One thing is sure: Be quiet and don't panic when it is late at night and someone you do not know is in your room. It's the sandman and he's there to throw sand into your eyes. Pure altruism! Just act as if you are already sleeping and it will move on and walk away in search of someone who is sleepless.

"And what about Christmas? Who brings the gifts?"

A controversy breaks out here. One colleague says, the Christmas gifts are being brought by angels, but that's a complete minority opinion. So I explain to Sirii that it is widely common that the Christ Child brings the gifts. No one has ever seen it doing so, but practically everyone has heard it because: *"When it's ready, it rings a bell. Then you rush into the room, but somehow it is just gone the second you enter. No one knows how it is able to disappear so fast. In a way, it's just like the 'Sandman', I mean the communist Sandman, you know. It's there and then it's gone. No traces left. Rififi on Christmas..."*

"Is it a boy or a girl?" "Well, I guess it's a boy ... but others may say, it's a girl... Maybe it's a hermaphrodite. That would explain why it's always disappearing faster than a 'streaker' at a soccer game. However, it's shy, very shy and maybe also a little bit ashamed that the others make fun of it. However, it has a good heart. Why else should it bring all those gifts?"

"So you got a hermaphroditic Christ Child and a communist Sandman in Germany."

"Well, actually I never thought about it that way, but... well. Yes, I guess you're right."

"And what about Santa Clause? I mean: Doesn't he come and bring gifts on December 24th?"

"No. He's there much earlier. He comes in the night from December 5th to December 6th. And he's not going under his artist's alias name. He uses his real one: Nikolaus. Just Nikolaus, no family name. When he's not travelling around he's living in a strange house that is made out of a square, an X and a triangle. And all these geometrical forms hang and depend on each other..."

"Hmm... and apart from his exquisite home... does he bring any gifts?!"

"Well, just small ones and he's also not coming alone, he's got a companion, but I think they are just friends..."

"?"

"Well ... if I think about it ... Knecht Rupprecht, that's his companion's name ... he is maybe into some kind of a fetish, you know. He's dressed all in black, wearing a

mask and some silver chains ... And on his hump he always carries a sack in which he'll stick children..."

"What?!"

"You know, Sirii, it's kind of a good cop – bad cop thing. Nikolaus is the nice guy and Rupprecht, well, you better take care of not coming too close to him."

"I see. And as with all other strange persons, Nikolaus and Rudolf..."

"No! Rupprecht!"

"Ok. Rupprecht and Nikolaus, they just materialize in your room or what?"

"No. Actually Nikolaus and Rupprecht always knocked on the door. Back in my childhood I even remember that I once saw them both coming with my godfathers BMW. Later they somehow managed to knock on the door, lay down their gifts and disappear just like the Christ child did. Maybe my godfather didn't want to rent his car to them anymore or the Christ Child gave them advice in high speed escaping – maybe at an advanced drivers training or a school for stuntmen led by a special police unit officer with autobahn-experience."

"Ah, well."

Sirii turns away. For now she seems to be satisfied, but maybe she just had enough. At least she has to tell something about Germany when she's back in Estonia. And I'm asking myself why everything in my childhood always seemed so normal.

Short biography of Rolf Palmian:

Rolf Palmian (*3. Juli 1921 in Prag, für † erklärt am 26. März 1969, am 24. Dezember 1979 nach mehrfachem Auftreten in der Öffentlichkeit und der Beantragung eines Nutzer-Ausweises bei Super-Video 2000 wieder offiziell für lebendig erklärt) gilt als größter Journalist, Schriftsteller und Werbetexter seiner Generation.

Zu seiner Bekanntheit trugen neben seiner Abhandlung *Schnick, Schnack, Schnuck* (1942, Suhrkamp Verlag) vor allem seine Reisetagebücher, seine Prominenteninterviews für die Gala und die Bunte, sowie seine großen Romane *Die Buddenbrooks, Die Pechtrommel, Ein weißes Pferd* sowie *Mit den Clowns kamen die Dänen.* Ein Großteil seines literarischen Schaffens ging verloren, als Palmians bester Freund Walt R. Schaft am 27. März 1969 sämtliche unveröffentlichten Romane, Kurzgeschichten und erfundenen Promi-Interviews in ein riesiges Fass voll Chlorix warf, um damit dem testamentarischen Wunsch des großen Palmian nachzukommen.

Palmian erhielt 1929 sowie 2001 den Nobelpreis für Literatur und war mehrfach für den Friedensnobelpreis vorgeschlagen, unterlag dabei aber immer wieder Mitbewerbern wie Helmut Kohl, Nelson Mandela oder Slobodan Milosevic. Verärgert gründete er eine eigene Akademie und verlieh sich von 2004 an alljährlich im Rahmen der Feierlichkeiten der Frankfurter Buchmesse den Friedenspreis des Deutschen Buchhandels.

Über seine persönlichen Lebensumstände ist wenig bekannt, da Palmian jede Interviewanfrage seit 50 Jahren ablehnt und auf sein Werk verweist, das „alles das ausdrückt, was ich bin." Mehrfach kam es zu Skandalen, da ihm Verstrickungen mit dem 3. Reich nachgewiesen wurden. So soll er Chief Managing Creative Director in Josef Goebbels Propagandaministerium gewesen sein und sich auch heute noch an Slogans wie „Wollt Ihr den totalen Krieg" und „Ein Volk, Ein Reich, Ein Führer" eine goldene Nase verdienen. Sein Kommentar auf die Vorwürfe lautet lapidar: „Ich weiß nicht, was Sie wollen. Der Grass war doch in der SS. Ich nicht."

Eine enge Freundschaft zu Barrack Obama, dem Dalai Lama und Peter Alexander ist belegt, ebenso zahlreiche Synonyme, unter denen er erfolgreich veröffentlichte. Hierzu zählen u. a. Günther Grass, Hermann Hesse und Martin Kleinwalsertal.

Chapter 10

Der Hobbykeller der Schmidts

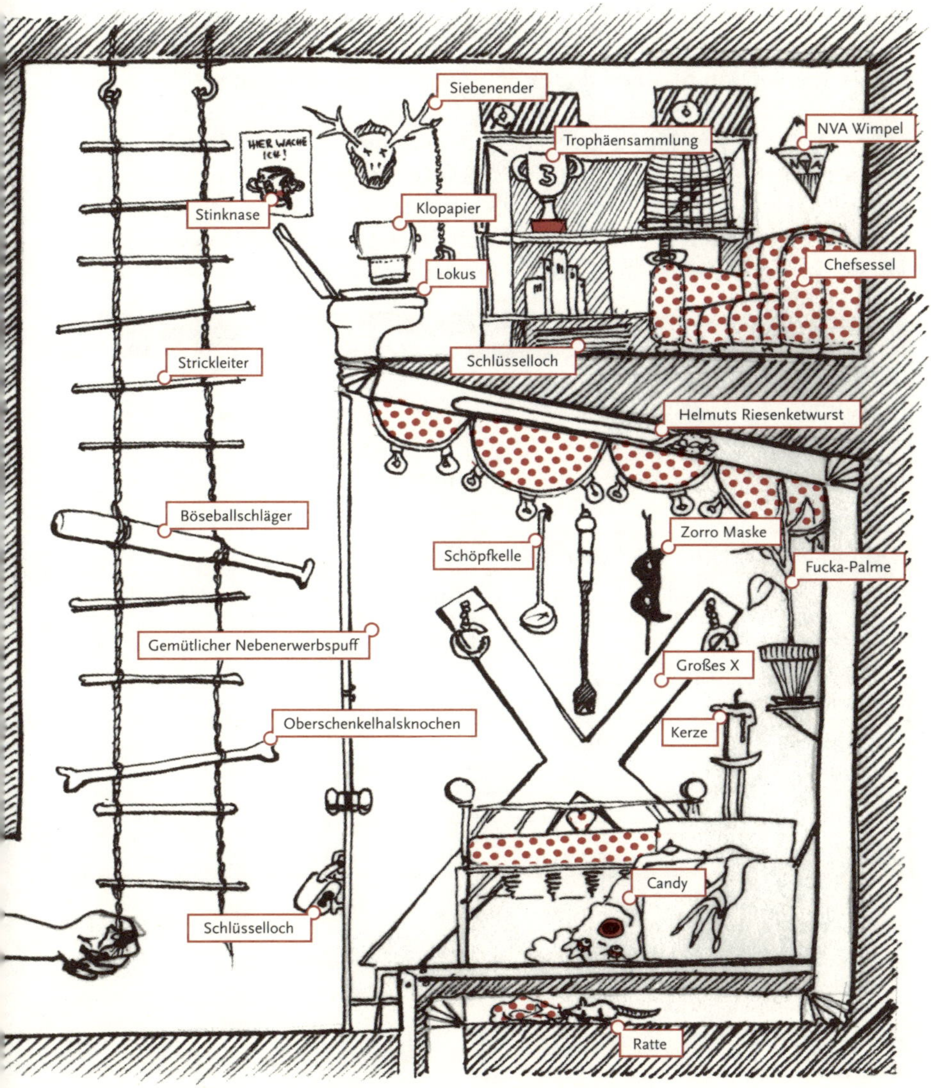
Siebenender
NVA Wimpel
Trophäensammlung
HIER WACHE ICH!
Stinknase
Klopapier
Lokus
Chefsessel
Schlüsselloch
Strickleiter
Helmuts Riesenketwurst
Böseballschläger
Zorro Maske
Schöpfkelle
Fucka-Palme
Gemütlicher Nebenerwerbspuff
Großes X
Oberschenkelhalsknochen
Kerze
Candy
Schlüsselloch
Ratte

Grammar Stuff – Chapter 10

Possessive pronouns and adjectives (NOMINATIVE, ACCUSATIVE, DATIVE)

For what reason do you need possessive pronouns and adjectives? Well, they show a connection between things and persons and also ownership. If you weren't able to express "This is MY girl. Do not touch her.", you would have to say "This is a girl. Don't touch her." And although it would make a lot of sense not to touch any girl that you see without asking her beforehand if it is allowed to touch her, it would still sound strange if you generalized the way I showed you in the example. People need to know what is theirs and what is yours. Here are the German possessive pronouns and adjectives.

Possessive pronouns and adjectives					
Singular personal pronoun	ich	du	Sie	er /es	sie
masculine / neuter	mein	dein	Ihr	sein	ihr
Feminine	mein***e***	dein***e***	Ihr***e***	sein***e***	ihr***e***
Plural	mein***e***	dein***e***	Ihr***e***	sein***e***	ihr***e***
Plural personal pronoun	wir	ihr	Sie	sie	sie
masculine / neuter	unser	euer	Ihr	ihr	ihr
Feminine	unser***e***	eu(e)***re***	Ihr***e***	ihr***e***	ihr***e***
Plural	unser***e***	eu(e)***re***	Ihr***e***	ihr***e***	ihr***e***

Personal pronouns
NOMINATIVE, ACCUSATIVE DATIVE

Hier ist Kokain. Woher kommt ***es?***
Here is some cocaine. Where is it from?

Spritzt du der Frau Drogen? Ja, ich spritze sie ***ihr.***
Do you shoot that girl some drugs? Yes, I will shoot her some.

Singular NOMINATIVE	**Singular ACCUSATIVE**	**Singular DATIVE**
ich	mich	mir
du	dich	dir
Sie	Sie	Ihnen
er	ihn	ihm
sie	sie	ihr
es	es	ihm
Plural NOMINATIVE	**Plural ACCUSATIVE**	**Plural DATIVE**
wir	uns	uns
ihr	euch	euch
Sie	Sie	Ihnen
sie	sie	ihnen
Question words	**Question words**	**Question words**
wer?	wen?	wem?
who?	*who?*	*who?*

Exercises – Chapter 10

The family of the authors of this book and some other people are very generous and go to buy some gifts and presents for other people they like. Unfortunately, they do not know how to use the dative. So now it is your turn to fill in the gaps with the pronoun that fits *("meiner", "seiner", "unserer", "einem", "einer", "dem", "der")*. And these are the persons which are available to use in any way: *"Oma Frieda", "Oma Hansie", "Mutter", "Vater", "Tante Mildred", "Onkel Wolf", "Kater Maxi", "der Nachbar" (Herr Masermann), "die Nachbarin" (Frau Masermann), "mein kleiner Bruder", "ich"*

Example:
Mein kleiner Bruder kauft ***meiner / seiner / unserer /*** Tante Mildred eine Badehose.

Tante Mildred kauft .... einen Kugelschreiber.

Mutter kauft .... ein Einwanderungsvisum. *(an immigrant visa)*

Onkel Wolf kauft .... nichts.

Oma Frieda kauft .... ein Sprachlabor.

Herr Masermann kauft .... eine Blume.

Frau Masermann kauft .... eine Flasche Bier.

Vater kauft .... einen Teppich.

Ich kaufe .... ein Klavier, einen Panzer *(a piano, a tank)* und drei ausgebildete *(professional)* Ninjas.

Now think about other persons buying strange things for other persons.

Beispiel:
Fritz kauft seiner Freundin ein Atom-U-Boot. *(Atomic Submarine)*

Give me 5 examples.

a) ....

b) ....

c) ....

d) ……………………………………………………………………………………

e) ……………………………………………………………………………………

Fill in the gaps or I'll search you and find you and punish you!

Der Mann und …………………… Frau.

Der Hund und …………………… Herrchen.

Die Schwester und …………………… Bruder.

Der Papst und …………………… Frau.

Die Großeltern und …………………… Enkelkinder.

Das Kind und …………………… Drogen.

Der Zuhälter und …………………… Puff.

Die Kanzlerin und …………………… perverses Hobby.

Der Showmaster und …………………… Tod.

So watcha, watcha, watcha want?! Or "Was Ihr wollt!"

Example: Was wollen Sie? (die Schwester) *Wir wollen die Schwester.*

Was sucht ihr? (das Geld und die Drogen) ……………………………………

Was wollt ihr? (die Macht) ……………………………………

Was sucht er? (das Kondom) ……………………………………

Und was suchst Du? (das ewige Leben) ……………………………………

Only possessive adjectives in the nominative, the accusative and the dative can save the world in this text. If you fail: Game over!

Helmut hat einen Opa.

……………………Opa wohnt mit …………………… Familie im brasilianischen Dschungel. Helmut bekommt ein Päckchen von …………………… Opa. In dem Päckchen ist ein Brief und ein Foto. Opa schreibt: Darf ich dir ……………………

jüngsten Sohn Adolf vorstellen? Eve schaut auf das Foto und fragt: *„Ist das ein Bild aus .... Kindheit, Helmut?* Helmut antwortet Eve: *„Nein! Das ist .... neuer Bruder aus Brasilien!“* .... *Vater Adolf hat ihn nach .... besten Freund benannt.“ „Aber er trägt doch .... Uniform, Helmut!“ „Nein! Das ist sicher nicht .... Uniform. Opa hat da doch .... eigene Fabrik.*

Do you have some personal pronoun in* THE DATIVE? *Or maybe also in* THE ACCUSATIVE? *Really? Why do you wait and do not start to fill in the gaps?

Wie geht es ....

Danke! .... geht es scheiße.

Möchtest du mit .... schlafen?

MC Utan, DJ Dooffresse und ich sind da. Kannst du

....ein paar Flaschen Schnaps mitbringen?

Könnt ihr .... auspeitschen?

Ja, gerne! Wir können .... gerne auspeitschen.

Komm doch mit zu den Schmidts! Komm doch mit zu

....

Keine Anzeige

Bonus-Track – Chapter 10

German Eaters

There are a lot of famous German eaters known and famous all over the world. For example there is the cannibal from Rotenburg who is somehow a plagiator of the famous Fritz Harmann but was not as successful in eating human beings like famous Fritz with his "Hackebeilchen"! Take care because it is "Hackebeilchen" and not "Hackebällchen". You get Hackebällchen at Ikea (there they call it "Kødbullar") and Hackebeilchen you get at Bauhaus or some other DIY-market. With a Hackebeilchen you chop wood or, in Haarmann's case, people. He caught and then later chopped several people, killed them by biting them in their throat and became one of the biggest mass murderers ever known. He seemed to be quite a DIY-man and sold meat to his neighbour who had a restaurant. So maybe involuntarily some other carnivore people in Hanover became cannibals by having lunch in the nearby restaurant.

Fritz Haarmann was executed in 1924 and became kind of a mass pop culture phenomenon. In the 60s there were even pop songs about him with lyrics like the following:

„Warte, warte nur ein Weilchen,	*"Wait, wait a while,*
Bald kommt Haarmann auch zu dir,	*Soon Haarmann will come and see you*
Mit dem kleinen Hackebeilchen,	*With his small little chopper*
Macht er Schabefleisch aus dir.	*He will make minced meat out of you*
Aus den Augen macht er Sülze,	*Of the eyes he will make aspic*
Aus dem Hintern macht er Speck,	*Of your ass he will make bacon*
Aus den Därmen macht er Würste	*Of your bowels sausages*
Und den Rest, den schmeißt er weg".	*And the rest, he will throw away."*

No one knows if Fritz Haarmann was the idol of the next famous cannibal coming from Germany. It's evident that Armin Meiwes from Rotenburg just ate one part of a man, while Haarmann is said to have eaten more parts of more men. Anyhow, Meiwes is German and showed that by looking for someone to eat on the internet. "Ordnung" must be, as we say in Germany. There he found someone who wanted to be killed but first wanted his penis to be cut off and eat it before dying. Meiwes agreed, they met, he cut the penis off, they tried to eat it but it was very difficult to get the penis done and they also didn't find any recipe for cooking a penis in any of the cook books that were available on the market or in the situation after the penis was cut off. So the victim died with a bad taste of burned penis in his mouth and Meiwes logged back into the internet to chat and find someone else who was willing to be killed and cooked. When the German police discovered his ad on the internet they were a little bit shocked and went to meet and greet Meiwes and later he was sentenced to 8 years in prison for manslaughter and not for murder, because he had slaughtered a man. However later, a higher court sentenced him for murder and the desecration of a corpse and he finally got a life sentence. He was not content with the judgement, but an appeal was not successful.

Hier das Rezept für Schwanz im Wein.
Here's the recipe for "Cock au vin"

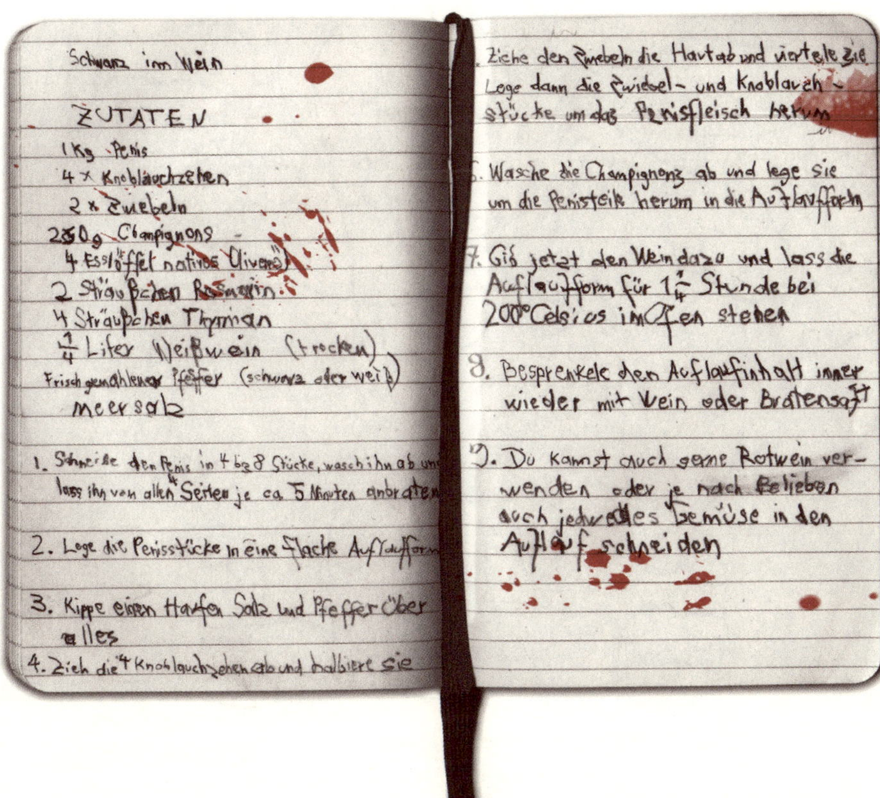

Chapter 11

Der Besuch von Opa

Eve, Doreen und der Svengster sind heute sehr aufgeregt. Opa Dolfi hat sich angekündigt. Eigentlich wohnt Opa Dolfi irgendwo in Brasilien. In seinen Briefen aus Brasilien schreibt er immer, dass dort ein kleines deutsches Dorf immer noch den feindlichen Übergriffen erbitterten Widerstand leiste. Was genau er damit meint, weiß niemand so genau und die, die es genau wissen, haben auch nicht so viel Lust, darüber zu sprechen. Nicht wahr, Eve, geborene Braun?

Helmut holt Opa Dolfi, den „alten Sack", am Flughafen ab. Er erkennt ihn schon von Weiten an seinem knallroten Koffer, auf dem ein interessanter Kofferaufkleber prangt: ein schwarzes, seltsames Kreuz auf weißem Grund. Erst denkt Helmut noch „Geschmackssache", dann aber sieht er zu, dass er den Alten schnell vom El-Al-Schalter wegbekommt, wo er gerade ein Streitgespräch anfangen möchte. Die Sicherheitsbeamten gucken schon seltsam, aber das stört Opa Dolfi nicht.

Im Auto ist der Opa sehr empört über seinen Schwiegersohn. *„Helmut! Du bist überhaupt kein Patriot! Dabei gehörst Du doch zur Elite des Deutschen Reichs, also ich meine, Deutschlands natürlich! Warum ziehst Du mich von diesem dummen El-Al-Schalter weg?"* Helmut stellt auf Durchzug und lässt den alten Mann Parolen dreschen und dummschwätzen. Zum Glück durfte der Opa per Sondergenehmigung in Tempelhof landen – keine Ahnung, ob er dafür mit dem Klaus Wowereit schlafen musste.

Helmut und Opa Dolfi kommen vorm Haus der Schmidts an. Eve hat sich und Doreen extra Zöpfe gebunden. Beide tragen lange Faltenröcke und der Svengster steckt in einer lustigen Lederhose. *„Hoffentlich sehen mich meine Rapperkumpels nicht so!"*, wünscht sich der Svengster, aber zu spät. MC Feuermelder kommt gerade um die Ecke und sieht wie der Svengster in Lederhosen einen alten Mann mit seltsamem Oberlippenbart auf den Mund küsst. *„Ein Glück"*, denkt sich MC Feuermelder! *„Ein Glück, dass ich mein Foto-Handy dabei habe! Das Bild schicke ich morgen an die Bildzeitung oder Youtube."*

Doreen macht noch einen Knicks vor Opa Dolfi und gemeinsam gehen alle ins Haus. Es gibt Schwarzwälder Kirschtorte und Spaghetti, weil das Opa laut Guido Knopp immer gerne gegessen hat. Alles ist eine Riesensauerei, weil

Opa Dolfis Parkinson in den letzten 60 Jahren auch nicht besser geworden ist. Zum Glück haben alle diese roten Spezialservietten an, die nur herausgeholt werden, wenn Opa Dolfi da ist, und die genauso aussehen wie sein Koffer mit dem Aufkleber drauf. Der Svengster würde so eine Serviette gerne als T-Shirt haben, aber die Eve sagt, das geht nicht.

Opa Dolfi erzählt von seinem Dorf. Dort gibt es eine Wolfsschanze, ein Führerhauptquartier und all das nach Plänen von Speer. Keiner der Schmidts versteht, was eine Wolfsschanze sein soll. Sprungschanze okay, aber Wolfsschanze? Im Regenwald? Und was ist ein Führerhauptquartier bitte? Und wer oder was sind Speerpläne? Lebt Opa Dolfi unter wilden Indianern? Die Schmidts schalten alle auf Durchzug, während Opa Dolfi von seinen Freunden, dem treuen Heinrich, dem Heydrich, dem Heini von der Post und vom schlimmen Badeunfall seines alten Kumpels Jupp erzählt: *„Rutscht aus, Peng, knallt auf seinen Kopf, eine Welle kommt und weg war er. Fast so, wie wir damals aus Berlin verschwunden sind!"*.

Svengster (wacht auf): *„Du bist aus Berlin, Opa?"*

Opa: *„Ja, äh, also nein, nicht genau. Eigentlich komme ich aus einem kleinen Ort am Inn."*

Svengster: *„Am Inn? Am Rhin? Also am Rhein?"*

Opa: *„Nein, mein Junge! Am Inn. Das ist ein Fluss in der Ostmark!"*

Svengster: *„Ostmark gibt's doch gar nicht mehr!"*

Opa: *„Ostmark, das ist Österreich..."*

Svengster: *„Nee. Die haben in Österreich auch schon Euro seit 2000."*

Opa: *„Ja, nein. Ostmark, das ist eine Bezeichnung, also ein Gebiet..."*

Svengster: *„Ist schon gut Opa ... Und in Berlin warst du dann auf Ferien?"*

Opa: *„Nun ja. Kann man so sagen. 1.000-jährige Ferien ... waren geplant, aber dann lief das nicht so. Das Leben, mein Junge, ist kein Wunschkonzert!"*

Svengster: *„Ich will auch 1.000 Jahre Ferien!"*

Opa: *„Keine Bange. Das kommt schon wieder. Ganz bestimmt."*

Svengster: *„Und wann? Und warum bist du jetzt in Brasilien?"*

Opa: *„Ich sage nur die Flugscheibe von Neuschwabenland. Im ewigen Eis des Pols!"*

Svengster: *„Welche Polen? Opa? Alles in Ordnung? Willst Du noch etwas Wasser?"*

Opa: *„In Brasilien bin ich quasi zur beruflichen Neuorientierung. Mein Job war hart und ich war sehr ausgepowert. Burn-Out-Syndrom sozusagen. Letzte, wenn nicht gar Endstufe. Brennendes Benzin und nicht mal das will brennen…"*

Der Svengster schaltet wieder auf Durchzug und Opa Dolfi redet die ganze Nacht durch mit seiner krächzenden, schnarrenden rrrrrollenden Stimme. Aber dem wollen wir überhaupt nicht zuhören, denn jetzt gibt es hier ja wieder grammatische Aufgaben zu erfüllen und Fragen zu beantworten.

Questions! Answer them in correct sentences!

Womit bezahlt man in Österreich?

....

Seit wann ist Opa Dolfi in Brasilien?

....

Wer ist beim Baden gestorben?

....

Wie heißt der Fluß, an dem Opa Dolfi geboren ist?

....

Mit wem möchte Opa Dolfi streiten?

....

Was trägt der Svengster?

....

Wen küsst der Svengster auf den Mund?

....

Grammar Stuff – Chapter 11

Time preposition and time question word

"seit"

"seit" is another DATIVE preposition. You use it before dates and times. You use it in the present tense, but it always refers to the past.

Seit 60 Jahren lebt Opa Dolfi in Brasilien.
For 60 years Opa Dolfi has been living in Brasil.

Helmut läuft seit 5 Stunden auf Standby.
Helmut has been on standby for 5 hours.

"wann"

"wann" is a simple question word.

Wann kommt die Flut?
When does the flood come?

You can also combine "seit" and "wann" just like you can do it in English.

Seit wann macht Sven in sein Bett?
Since when does Sven wet his bed?

Exercises – Chapter 11

Seit wann?

Seit wann gibt es in Österreich Euros?

.... (100 / Jahre)

Seit wann kannst du Deutsch?

.... (1 / Tag)

Seit wann stinkt es hier so?

.... (17 / Furz)

Seit wann trinken Sie Alkohol?

.... (47,5 / Monat)

Seit wann ist Mord illegal?

.... (2 / Stunde)

Fill in the gaps with the correct endings of the adjectives

Einer der Autoren erzählt Geschichten aus seinem Leben.
One of the authors tells tales from his life.

Gestern aß ich grün........ Krokodil (n) mit gelb........ Bohnen (pl). Ich hatte die gut........ Lebensmittel (pl) im nah........ Supermarkt (m) gekauft. Danach fuhr ich mit meinem schwarz........ Ferrari (m) zu meinem groß........ Haus (n) in den schön........ Hollywood Hills (pl). Dort traf ich meine häßlich........ Freunde (pl) mit ihren dumm........ Frauen (pl). Die dümmst........ Frau hatte den dickst........ Mann (m). Zusammen hatten beide 13,5 rothaarig........ Kinder (pl). Die Kinder liebten kalt........ Erdbeereis (n) mit groß........ behaart........ Spinnen (pl).

Nach dem Essen sprangen wir in den warm.......... Swimmingpool (m) und fingen die weiß.......... Haie (pl), die darin schwammen. Ein Hai fraß die sieben allerdümmsten Kinder. Die extrem dumm.......... Mutter (f) war deswegen sehr sehr traurig. Ich sollte meinen Lieblingshai, den ich mit meinen eigen.......... Händen (pl) vor Australien gefangen hatte, töten. Aber ich machte das nicht. Ich warf lieber die dumm.......... Frau, ihren dick.......... Mann (m) und die ander.......... Kinder (n) der groß.......... Familie (f) in den blau.......... Pool (m).

Dann wurde ich von der schlau.......... Polizei aus Hollywood verhaftet. Der Richter sagte mir im Prozess, daß ich wegen 15,5fach.......... Mord (m) ins Gefängnis müsse. Im Gefängnis schrieb ich ein lang.......... Buch (n) und viel.......... gut.......... Freunde (pl) aus der Drogenszene besuchten mich in meiner klein.......... schön.......... Zelle (f). Heute wird mein gut.......... Buch (n) in Hollywood verfilmt. Die Hauptrolle in dem best.......... Film aller Zeiten spielt:

[ ] Sylvester Stallone

[ ] Sean Connery

[ ] Puff Daddy

[ ] John Malkovich

Bonus-Track – Chapter 11

Humour and Comedy in Germany

Harald Schmidt: Rich like Hitler but not as funny.
Funny because: Gets paid for not working.

Roland Koch: Always laughs in the end.
Funny because: Signed a poster on which he was painted as a child molester.

Mario Barth: Successful like Hitler (70.000 watched his show in the Olympia stadium).
Funny because: Has a girlfriend, he says.

Otto Waalkes: Successful like Uwe Boll (lots of great movies).
Funny because: Yodohüti! No prescription of Ritalin.

Karl Dall: just watch that face.
Funny because: see above.

Heinz Schenk: Prehistoric Hessian comedy relict.
Funny because: drinks from Bämbels and was an asshole to the "Bunny of Fortune".

Josef Goebbels: Successful comedy partner of Hitler.
Funny because: funny foot and funny accent.

Der Maddin: Hessian comedian with preprehistoric comedy sense.
Funny because: Laughs about his own jokes and fat mouth.

Otto Schily: Really good at watching what people do.
Funny because: Look at his haircut! If that's not funny!

Cindy aus Marzahn: Former jobless giant 30ft woman.
Funny because: She's fat! That's funny enough for any German.

Oliver Pocher: Former Jehova's witness who thinks he's funny...
Funny because: ...but is not. In no way.

Joschka Fischer: The funniest foreign secretary of state (E. g.: Kosovo and stuff).
Funny because: –

Kai Diekmann: Makes the funniest German newspaper.
Funny because: His haircut, his face, his dentist wife Katja K.

Chapter 12

Helmut und die Polizei

Helmut ist ein begeisterter Autofahrer. Leider ist die Polizei nicht so von Helmut begeistert, weil er wie ein Idiot heizt und sich an keine Verkehrsregeln hält. In den letzten drei Wochen hat Helmut schon 27 Punkte in der Verkehrssünderkartei gesammelt. Er ist in einer Spielstraße statt Schrittgeschwindigkeit 120 km / h gefahren, er hat mindestens fünf rote Ampeln missachtet, er hat diverse Beamten beleidigt, am Steuer seines Fahrzeugs bei Tempo 200 mit seinem Handy telefoniert, auf der Autobahn gedrängelt und seinen Auspuff abgebaut. Heute fährt Helmut unangeschnallt mit seinem tiefer gelegten knallgelben Ford Capri über einen Fahrradweg und stupst ganz leicht einen Mann an, der ihm mit seinem Krankenfahrstuhl den Weg versperrt.

Dabei wird Helmut von einem Streifenwagen beobachtet. Als Helmut nicht anhält, wird eine Straßensperre errichtet und Nägel werden auf der Straße verstreut, damit die Reifen von Helmuts Auto platzen. Fünfzehn Polizeiwagen kreisen Helmut in seinem Auto ein und Er ist böse und sehr angefressen, weil seine Reifen jetzt kaputt sind und bestimmt auch die Alufelgen, die er zu seinem letzten Geburtstag

von Eve geschenkt bekommen hat. Er springt aus seinem Wagen und brüllt die Polizisten an. Diese zücken ihre Pistolen, aber das stört Helmut nicht.

Helmut: *„Ihr blöden Idiotenwichser! Was habt ihr mit meinem schönen Auto gemacht? Habt ihr sie noch alle? Ich kann euch eure Autos auch kaputtmachen, ihr Bullenschweine!“*

Helmut rennt mit Schwung und mit gestrecktem Bein zu einem Polizeiwagen und tritt die Frontscheibe ein. Dann schlägt er mit bloßen Händen die Scheinwerfer kaputt und wirft eine brennende Packung Streichhölzer in den Tank des Wagens. Plötzlich trifft ihn der Schlag und Helmut fällt in Ohnmacht.

Als er wieder aufwacht, liegt er mit ganz vielen blauen Flecken, einer gebrochenen Nase und zwei gebrochenen Armen in einem Straßengraben. Sein Ford Capri kokelt noch ein bisschen. In seiner Jackentasche findet er einen Brief von der Polizei.

Sehr geehrter Herr Schmidt,

es reicht. Auf Grund Ihrer nicht angemessenen Fahrweise, sind wir gezwungen, Ihr Auto zu zerstören. Es hat uns sehr viel Spaß gemacht, auch Ihre Arme zu brechen, damit Sie in nächster Zeit erst recht nicht mehr Auto fahren können. Ihren Führerschein haben wir konfisziert und aus der klaffenden Wunde auf Ihrer linken Wange haben wir eine Blutprobe entnommen. Die Analyse hat ergeben, dass Sie betrunken gefahren sind. Ihr Alkoholspiegel lag bei 2,3 ‰, was genau 1,5 ‰ zuviel sind. Bitte haben Sie Verständnis für unser Handeln, aber wir können Ihre Fahrweise einfach nicht mehr tolerieren. Ihr Führerschein ist fürs erste weg u. wenn Sie uns fragen, dann bleibt er das auch noch lange.

Mit freundlichen Grüßen!
Ihre Polizei bzw. wie Sie uns nennen, Ihre „Bullenschweine“

Helmut ist jetzt noch wütender als vorher. Sein schönes Auto ist abgefackelt und hinüber, sein Führerschein weg und seine Arme gebrochen. Vergeblich versucht er, zu Hause anzurufen, aber er trifft die Tastatur seines Handys nicht. Er muss zu Fuß nach Hause gehen. Helmut weint, denn er geht nicht gerne zu Fuß.

Als Helmut zu Hause angekommen ist, schlafen Eve und die Kinder schon. Helmut ist traurig, aber zum Glück ist noch etwas zu trinken da. Nach vier Stunden mit Korn und Schnaps ist Helmut wieder etwas glücklicher. Zufrieden zündet er sich eine Zigarette an und schläft auf der Couch ein.

Questions! Answer them in correct sentences!

Wie nennt Helmut die Polizisten?

....

Was für ein Auto fährt Helmut?

....

Was hat Helmut gebrochen?

....

Wie viele Promille hat Helmut?

....

Seit wann hat Helmut 27 Punkte in der Verkehrssünderkartei gesammelt?

....

Wer ist schon eingeschlafen, als Helmut zu Hause ankommt?

....

B ED 1953H

Grammar Stuff – Chapter 12

If you want to talk about the past, there are two times you can use: THE PERFECT TENSE and the preterite tense. THE PERFECT TENSE is mainly used in spoken language, while the preterite is more often used in written language. In this chapter we will concentrate on the perfect tense which is formed by using the auxiliary of *"haben"* or *"sein"* + PAST PARTICIPLE.

Here are two sentences in THE PERFECT TENSE, just to give you an impression:

Opa Schmidt hat in Berlin gewohnt.
Grandpa Schmidt has lived in Berlin.

Opa Schmidt ist nach Berlin geflogen.
Grandpa Schmidt has flown to Berlin.

PERFECT TENSE with *"haben"*

Most of the normal verbs and the reflexive verbs form the PERFECT TENSE with *"haben"*.

Example: Svengster hat Haschisch geraucht.
(rauchen: PAST PARTICIPLE: geraucht)
Svengster has smoked dope.

haben

	PRESENT		PAST PARTICIPLE
ich	habe	Crack	geraucht
du	hast	Crack	geraucht
Sie	haben	Crack	geraucht
er / sie / es	hat	Crack	geraucht
wir	haben	Crack	geraucht
ihr	habt	Crack	geraucht
Sie	haben	Crack	geraucht
sie	haben	Crack	geraucht

PERFECT TENSE with *"sein"*

However, as it is always with the German language: There are exceptions. And these exceptions do NOT have *"haben"* in THE PERFECT TENSE, but instead from THE PERFECT TENSE with *"sein"*. These verbs are verbs concerning movement or the change of a state and also the two verbs *"sein"* and *"bleiben"*.

Examples:

Svengster ist um 5 Uhr morgens eingeschlafen.
Svengster fell asleep at 5 am.

Helmut und Eve sind aus der Kurve geflogen.
Helmut and Eve flew out of the curve.

Ich bin am Mittwoch im Puff gewesen.
On Wednesday I was in the brothel.

Sie sind 5 Jahre im Knast geblieben.
You have stayed in prison for 5 years.

sein

	PRESENT		PAST PARTICIPLE
ich	bin	gestern	gerannt
du	bist	gestern	gerannt
Sie	sind	gestern	gerannt
er / sie / es	ist	gestern	gerannt
wir	sind	gestern	gerannt
ihr	seid	gestern	gerannt
Sie	sind	gestern	gerannt
sie	sind	gestern	gerannt

The regular verb's PAST PARTICIPLE

Forming the PAST PARTICIPLE with the regular verbs is really simple. Just put the prefix *"ge-"* at the beginning of the verb and a *"-t"* at the end of the verb and everything is fine. If you have a regular separable verb, the *"ge"*-part has to be placed in the middle of the verb.

INFINITIVE		PAST PARTICIPLE
sagen	*to say*	**ge**sag**t**
kaufen	*to buy*	**ge**kauf**t**
morden	*to murder*	**ge**morde**t**
zahlen	*to pay*	**ge**zahl**t**
machen	*to make*	**ge**mach**t**
foltern	*to torture*	**ge**folter**t**
fragen	*to ask*	**ge**frag**t**
abkaufen	*to believe*	ab**ge**kauf**t**
abfragen	*to query sth.*	ab**ge**frag**t**
zulabern	*to bend so's ear*	zu**ge**laber**t**

There are also regular inseparable verbs as you might know. These have prefixes like *"be-"*, *"emp-"*, *"er-"*, *"ge-"*, *"miss-"*, *"ver-"* and *"zer-"*. And all these verbs form the PAST PARTICIPLE without *"ge-"* but have the same ending *"-t"*.

INFINITIVE		PAST PARTICIPLE
beerdigen	*to bury*	beerdig**t**
zerstören	*to destroy*	zerstör**t**
morden	*to murder*	gemorde**t**

Irregular verbs and their PAST PARTCIPLE

The irregular verbs do have a different PERFECT TENSE PAST PARTICIPLE. However, it is only the ending which is different. The prefix *"ge-"* is the same but the ending is *"-en"*. Concerning the separable verbs, there is also nothing new for you, because just as the regular verbs they have *"ge-"* in the middle.

a) Normal irregular verbs:

INFINITIVE		PAST PARTICIPLE
geben	*to give*	**ge**geb***en***
fliegen	*to fly*	**ge**flog***en***
hauen	*to beat*	**ge**hau***en***
schlagen	*to beat*	**ge**schlag***en***
essen	*to eat*	**ge**gess***en***
finden	*to find*	**ge**fund***en***
kommen	*to come*	**ge**komm***en***
treffen	*to meet*	**ge**troff***en***
nehmen	*to take*	**ge**nomm***en***
bleiben	*to stay*	**ge**blieb***en***
ankommen	*to arrive*	an**ge**komm***en***
wegfahren	*to drive away*	weg**ge**fahr***en***
zurück kommen	*to come back*	zurück**ge**komm***en***
abrufen	*to access*	ab**ge**ruf***en***

b) Attention! There are three exceptions!!! These three are the verbs:

INFINITIVE		PAST PARTICIPLE
bringen	*to bring*	**ge**brach***t***
denken	*to think*	**ge**dach***t***
wissen	*to know*	**ge**wuss***t***

c) More exceptions

There are inseparable irregular verbs which do NOT have a *"ge-"* at all. These verbs are all of those with the prefixes *"be-"*, *"emp-"*, *"ent-"*, *"er-"*, *"ge-"*, *"miss-"*, *"ver-"*, and *"zer-"* plus also practically all verbs ending with *"-ieren"*. The last group of verbs, the verbs with *"-ieren"* in the INFINITIVE always end on *"-t"* in the PERFECT TENSE.

INFINITIVE		PAST PARTICIPLE
beginnen	*to begin*	***be***gonnen
belügen	*to tell so. a lie*	***be***logen
betrügen	*to betray*	***be***trogen
empfehlen	*to recommend*	***emp***fohlen
entscheiden	*to decide*	***ent***schieden
erfinden	*to invent*	***er***funden
erschießen	*to shoot so. dead*	***er***schossen
gewinnen	*to win*	***ge***wonnen
genießen	*to enjoy*	***ge***nossen
missverstehen	*to misunderstand*	***miss***verstanden
verkloppen	*to spank so.*	***ver***kloppt
versuchen	*to try*	***ver***sucht
vergessen	*to forget*	***ver***gessen
verzeihen	*to pardon so.*	***ver***ziehen
zerlegen	*to deconstruct*	***zer***legt
masturb***ieren***	*to masturbate*	masturbier***t***
urin***ieren***	*to urinate*	urinier***t***
stud***ieren***	*to study*	studier***t***

The position of the auxiliary and the participle in a PERFECT TENSE sentence

Svengster **hat** auf die Fresse **bekommen.**
Svengster has had his face beaten up.

Du **bist** zu dumm **gewesen.**
You have been too stupid.

Wir **sind** in der Hölle **angekommen.**
We have arrived in hell.

Seid ihr blöde **geworden?**
Have you become retarded?

Hat Helmut mir den Mittelfinger **gezeigt?**
Has Helmut shown me his finger?

Haben wir die Cholera **bekommen?**
Have we been infected with Cholera?

Adverbs: Word order exchange

Hier spricht Helmut gerade.
Helmut is just talking.

Deswegen möchte ich dich schlagen.
That is why I want to beat you.

As you see:
If the adverb is at the beginning of a sentence, the word order changes.

Example: Eve ist **bestimmt** am Ketwurststand.
Bestimmt ist Eve am Ketwurststand.

Exercises – Chapter 12

To be or not to be or in this case: sein oder haben – that is the question! Complete the sentences!

Wo.......................................Helmut sein Bier getrunken?
Wann.................................Svengster ins Bett gemacht?
Was...................................Opa Dolfi im Dschungel gemacht?
Was...................................am 11. September 2001 passiert?
Ihr.......................................vor Jahren nach Peking geflogen.
Wir......................................uns einen Ferrari geleast.
Eve......................................Ärger mit dem Gesundheitsamt gehabt.
Helmut...........................beim Arbeitsamt gewesen.
Doreen...........................schon mit 12 ein Piercing getragen.

Talk about what you did last weekend with the expression of time at the beginning of each sentence.

Um 12.00 Uhr aufwachen

....

Um 12.07 Uhr auf der Toilette sitzen

....

Um 13.15 Uhr in der Dusche urinieren

....

Um 13.23 Uhr die Haare kämmen

....

Um 16.67 Uhr Kondome einkaufen

....

Um 20.15 Uhr „Wetten Dass“ gucken

....

Um 23.10 Uhr in die Disco gehen

....

Von 23.15 Uhr bis 1.30 Uhr ein Mädchen abfüllen

....

Anschließend das Mädchen abschleppen

....

Im Bett dann die Kondome vergessen

....

Am Montag um 8.00 Uhr beim Urologen Termin haben

....

***Be kind, talk to strangers and ask them curious questions in the* "SIE"-FORM.**

ihre Kinder schlagen	=>	Haben **Sie** ihre Kinder **ge**schlagen?
Drogen verkaufen	=>	....
Exhibitionist sein	=>	....
Steuern hinterziehen	=>	....
Mutter ficken	=>	....
Schwarz fahren	=>	....

Now be so kind and answer these questions honestly and always remember: Everything has already happened but the people who ask you these stupid questions are simply retarded and work for the publishing house which published this book.

Example:
Wann kommt Jesus auf die Erde? (vor gut 2000 Jahren)
Jesus ist vor gut 2000 Jahren auf die Erde gekommen.

Wann fliegen Terroristen ins World Trade Center? (am 11.09.2001)

....

Wann heiratet der Papst einen schwulen Moslem? (vor 2 Tagen)

....

Wann trinkst du dein erstes Bier? (um 12 Uhr mittags)

....

Wann stürzt die Concorde ab. (am Vormittag)

....

If I asked you to marry me, would you agree? If I asked you to jump out of the window, would you? And if I asked you to put the adverbs at the beginning of the sentence, would you be so kind and do it?

Die Drogendealer haben mittwochs Ruhetag.

....

Opa Dolfi hat vorgestern die Flagge gehisst.

....

Helmut hat leider seinen Führerschein verloren.

....

Doreen geht heute mit Schacklihn shoppen.

....

Ich hätte gerne zwei Bällchen Erdbeereis mit Sahne.

....

Bonus-Track – Chapter 12

Famous German Inventions: The wheel, bread and communism

Germany is well known in the world for its inventions that changed Germany and the world and made it a better place. There are smaller inventions like the atomic bomb, the H-bomb or the Red Cross, but there are also inventions that have become extremely huge and useful, for example the wheel.

The wheel was invented in 1517 bei a man named Martin Luther whose famous great-great-great-great-great-great children Luther Vandross and Martin Luther-King later also became famous for their music with the Luther Five. The most famous Luther, or as we call him in Germany Luther 1st didn't like that he couldn't drive around on his bicycle because there was nothing like wheels in his time. He became so angry that he wrote a protest note to the Vatican but didn't get an answer and that is why he forced himself to invent the wheel. The first wheels were not really as round as wheels nowadays. In fact, they looked more like triangles and it was not that easy to ride on your bike with triangle wheels. However, it was easier than before when you didn't even have wheels at all. Throughout his life, Martin Luther became wiser and in his final year he decided that the best thing to do would probably be to make wheels round. Beforehand though he had experimented with pentagon wheels, octagon wheels, trapezoid wheels and even completely indescribable wheel forms. Then he died and was buried and the wheel became more successful than any invention before apart from the fire that was – as everyone knows – invented by Gustav Benz in 1889.

Another famous story of success was the story of communism. Karl Marx, quite an unsuccessful hair stylist and three times world championship winner of the Mustache-Olympics, awoke one morning in 1848 and thought it would be a great and also funny idea if anything belonged to anyone and there wouldn't be any criminal bank houses or managers or stock exchange assholes. If anything belonged to anyone, then everyone would be rich. He was completely astonished that no one before had had this idea and wrote it down in a manifest. Then he put many of these manifests in envelopes and sent them to lots of governments around the world but only the Eastern governments approved of his idea and built up their societies just like Marx wanted them to be built plus some smaller amendments – but they didn't inform Marx about these amendments. Marx was happy, except for the itchy rash he always had and then died. In the communist countries everyone was happy but they would have been happier if these amendments hadn't been written down in Marx's manifest. Later, a few years after Marx, communism died too, but everyone wasn't too sad about it because capitalism, another German invention, was also sick to its bones. The stock market crashed and there were millions of dislikeable and now jobless bankers on the streets which on the other hand made a lot of other jobless people happy because now, they were no more alone.

The last famous invention that was invented in Germany is bread. Before bread was invented the poor people had to eat their sausages (invented by Herr Peter Wurst in 1632 during the Thirty Years War in Munich) and their cheese (invented by Fritz Werner Keese in 1943 in Stalingrad which was German at that time) without any support. In fact, they often put the sausages on a piece of meat which nowadays seems a little bit odd. In those days butter was not that popular to most of the people because there was no bread to smear it on. Rich people often ate butter by biting off little pieces and then chewing it which is still very delicious but just doesn't look right. Today this can only be seen in the Secret Butter Societies of the most northern southern parts of Germany. However, it is difficult to get access to one of the secret gatherings of these societies on which it is said real butter orgies take place. Over there, but only over there, bread is still forbidden, but in all other places in Germany and the rest of the free world you are allowed to have bread in your pockets and to eat it in public. It is still not known who actually invented bread and when exactly it was invented. No one knows who might have been so intelligent to mix up all that stuff like rye, flour and some other chemicals and put it into an oven for some time but as this idea is so magnificent and pure and fantastic there is no other possibility than the fact that bread must have been invented by a German – maybe even a woman.

Chapter 13

Helmut und die Politik

Helmut liebt seine Lieblingskneipe, den Bierhimmel. Hier ist er so oft, wie es nur irgendwie möglich ist, und trifft sich mit seinen Freunden. Dann trinken alle viele Liter Bier und Schnaps und sind glücklich. Heute aber hat Helmut keine gute Laune, denn früher ist alles viel besser gewesen, meint er.

Helmut: *Früher hat das Bier hier viel besser geschmeckt. Es war viel gelber und der Schaum war viel schaumiger. Überhaupt war der Bierhimmel früher auch schöner. Die Leute sahen besser aus als die Leute heute, die Bardame war bestimmt 20 Jahre jünger und auch viel unterhaltsamer. Auch ihr, meine Kumpels, auch ihr wart lustiger und hattet auch viel mehr Haare auf dem Kopf.*

Erich: *(ein Kumpel Helmuts): Und erst die Politiker!*

Helmut: *Und erst die Politiker! Früher hatten wir den Willy Brandt, den Franz-Josef Strauß und den Herbert Wehner! Heute haben wir die Merkel und diesen Geheimdienstler Steinmeier! Der hat meinen Führerschein geklaut! Die Politiker sind die schlimmsten, die wir je hatten. Überhaupt das ganze politische System. Die Demokratie ist ja schön, aber ich finde eine Diktatur viel effektiver. Und ich als Diktator!*

Erich: *Prost, Helmut! Auf dich als den besten Diktator aller Zeiten, den größten Diktator aller Zeiten, den GröDaZ!*

Helmut: *Danke, Erich. Aber schau dir doch das politische System an! Der Russe, der Putin hat das Gas. Der Exkanzler Schröder gehört dem Putin und der Gasmafia. Die Gasmafia erpresst den Westen. Die Merkel gehört der Industrie genau wie die CDU, die FDP und die SPD. Die Industrie erpresst die Merkel. Die Merkel arbeitet für die Industrie und die Banken. Den Banken gehören die Häuser und die Autos. Noch wohnen die Leute in den Häusern, aber die Merkel und die Banken und die Industrie sorgen dafür, dass die Deutschen erpresst werden und dann bald in den Autos schlafen müssen. Und wenn sie kein Auto haben, dann eben auf der Straße. Die Grünen sind die FDP geworden, die Linke macht Opposition. Die Autoindustrie geht kaputt, aber deutsche Autos sind auch nicht besser als amerikanische oder indische.*

Erich: *Trink doch noch etwas, Helmut. Du musst deine Stimme schonen! Prost!*

Helmut:
Ist doch so. Alles geht den Bach runter. Gerade wir und der kleine Mann von der Straße.

Erich: *Welcher kleine Mann von der Straße?*

Helmut: *Na Leute wie du und wie ich. Alle erpressen den kleinen Mann von der Straße. Und die kleine Frau auch. Ich sag nur Eve. Was die an Abgaben und Steuern und Kram zahlen muss! Von dem Gewinn kann ich bestenfalls eine Woche trinken!*

Erich: *Sag, Helmut! Kannst du mir mal aufmalen, wie das politische System in Deutschland aussieht und funktioniert? Dann kann ich das morgen auch mal meinen Kindern erklären. Die nehmen das gerade in der Schule durch.*

Helmut: *Rosi! Bedienung! Ich brauch mal dringend einen Kuli, Buntstifte und ein bisschen Papier.*

Rosi: *Hier das Papier!*

Helmut: *Nein! Kein Zewawischundweg! Hier hat niemand andersrum gegessen! Nen Block bitte.*

Rosi: *Ach so. Moment.*

DAS POLITISCHE SYSTEM NACH HELMUT SCHMIDT

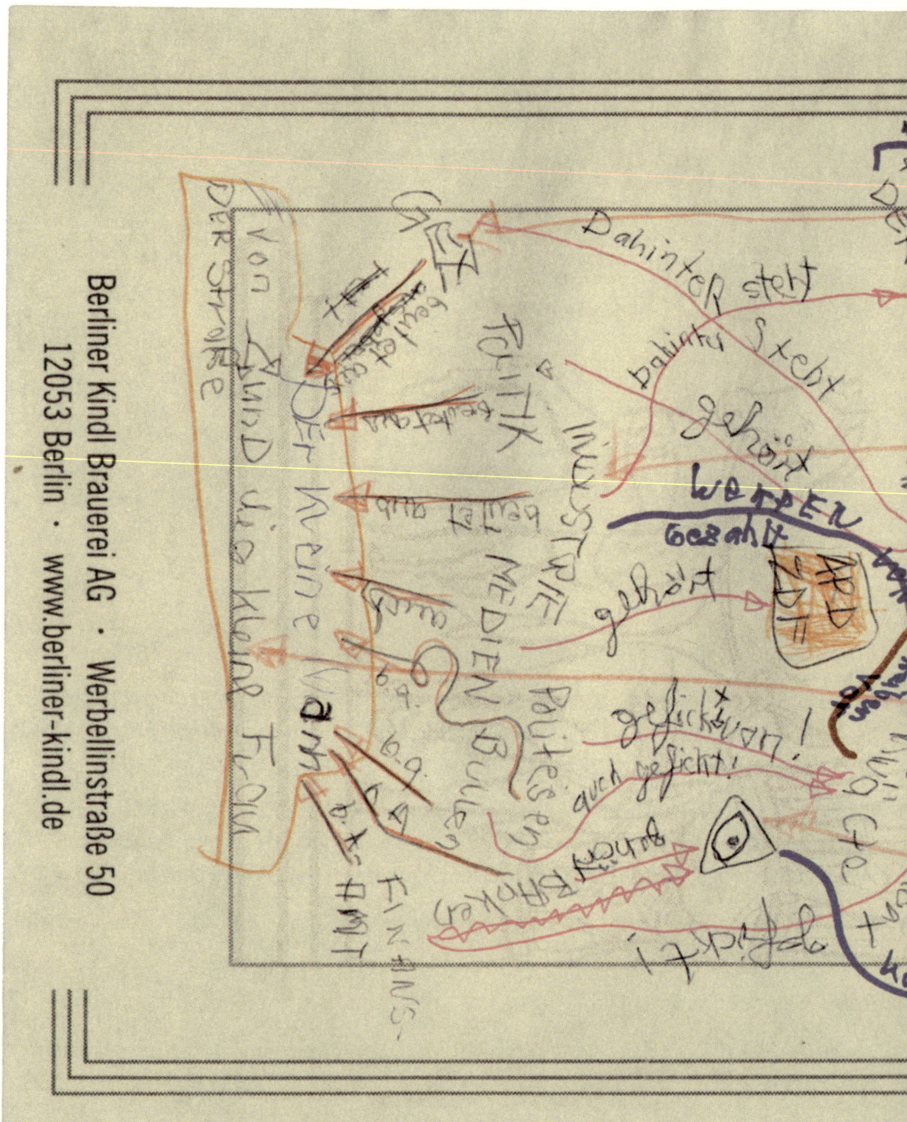

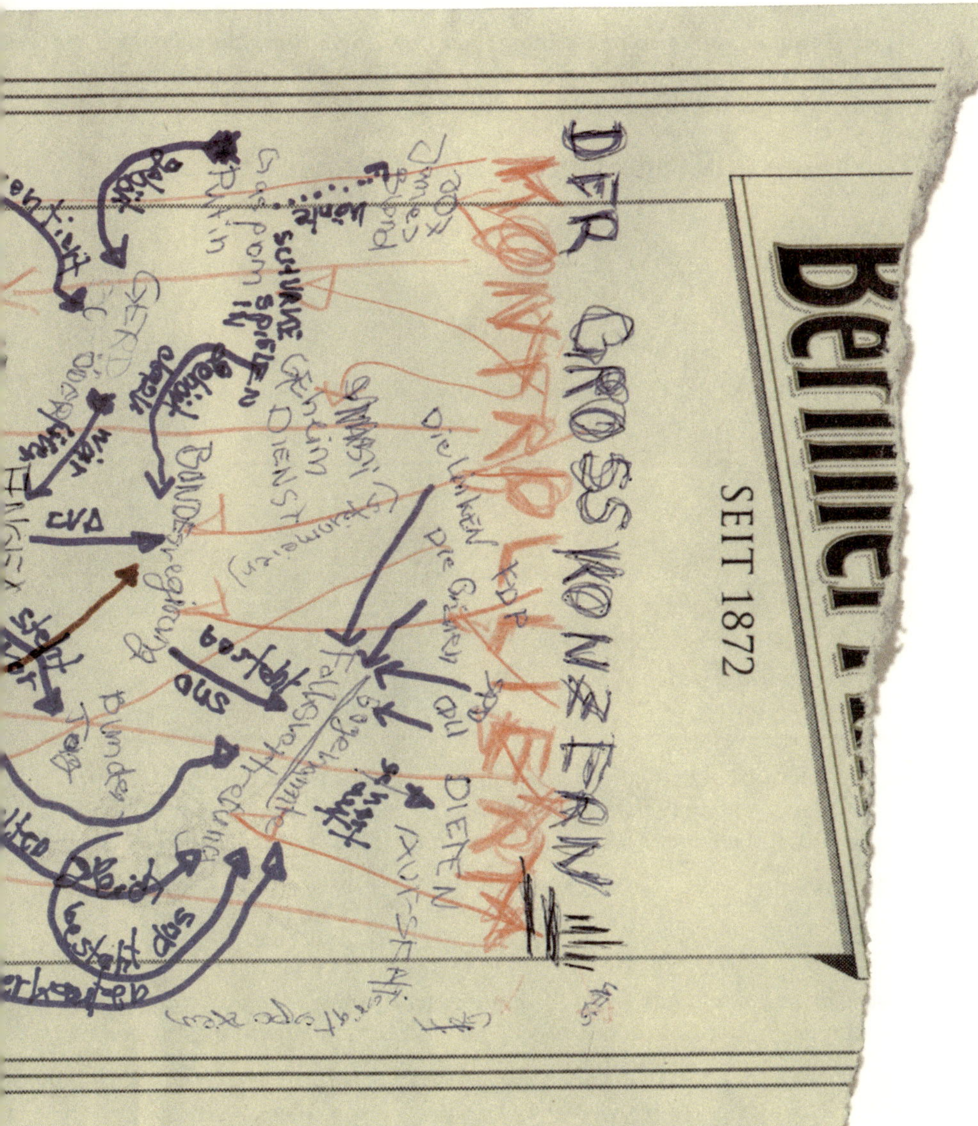
SEIT 1872

Grammar Stuff – Chapter 13

As we Germans like to compare things you have to do that, too, when you are in Germany and want to infiltrate our system. So in this part of the book you will learn about the comparison of adjectives.

The three different degrees of comparison

POSITIVE	COMPARATIVE	SUPERLATIVE
dumm	dümm**er**	am dümm**sten**
dumb	*dumber*	*dumbest*

Example

Diese Frau ist dick.	Doreen ist dick**er.**	Eve ist am dick**sten.**
This woman is fat.	*Doreen is fatter.*	*Eve is the fattest.*

As you might be able to guess, the comparative has the ending *"-er"*. The superlative's ending is *"-sten"* but before you form that adjective with *"-sten"* at the end of the word you have to place *"am"* in front of the adjective!

POSITIVE	COMPARATIVE	SUPERLATIVE
dünn	dünn***er***	am dünn***sten***

***However, as you already know there are special forms in any Germany case of the language. And here they are:* "a", "o" *and* "u" *change to* "ä", "ö" *and* "ü"**

arm	***ä***rm***er***	am ***ä***rm***sten***
poor	*poorer*	*the poorest*

groß *large*	grö**ßer** *larger*	am grö**ßten** *the largest*
krank *sick*	kränk**er** *sicker*	am kränk**sten** *the sickest*

after* "-t-", "-ß-" *and* "-sch-" *there is the ending* "-est" *in THE SUPERLATIVE

gescheit *clever*	geschei**t**er *more clever*	am gescheit**est**en *the cleverest*
weiß *white*	wei**ß**er *whiter*	am weiß**est**en *the whitest*
hübsch *pretty*	hüb**sch**er *prettier*	am hübsch**est**en *the prettiest*

And then there are the irregular forms, because everything in the German language and in Germany in general is irregular. We are the kings of irregularity. Learn the following irregular foms by heart!

gut *good*	besser *better*	am besten *the best*
viel *much*	mehr *more*	am meisten *the most*
gern *many*	lieber *more*	am liebsten *the most*
hoch *high*	höher *higher*	am höchsten *the highest*
nah *near*	näher *nearer*	am nächsten *the nearest*
teuer *expensive*	teurer *more expensive*	am teuersten *the most expensive*
dunkel *dark*	dunkler *darker*	am dunkelsten *the darkest*

Attributive Adjectives

Svengster raucht den ***größeren*** Crackbrocken vor dem ***kleinsten*** Crackkrümel.
Svengster smokes the larger lump of crack before smoking the smallest piece.

There are two things you have to keep in your memory:

1. The ending of the comparative attribute adjective is always ***"-er"*** plus the adjective ending.
2. The ending of the superlative attributive adjective always has the ending ***"-st"*** plus the adjective ending.

Comparison with *"als"*

***If you want to make a difference – and who doesn't want to make that?! – you have to use the comparative plus* "als".**

Helmut wiegt 103 kg. *Helmut weighs 103 kg.*	Doreen wiegt 72 kg. *Doreen weighs 72 kg.*
Helmut ist ***schwerer als*** Doreen. *Helmut is heavier than Doreen.*	Doreen ist ***leichter als*** Helmut. *Doreen is lighter than Helmut.*
Svengster ist 21 Jahre alt. *Svengster is 21 years old.*	MC Feuermelder ist 16 Jahre alt. *MC Feuermelder is 16 years old.*
Svengster ist ***älter als*** MC Feuermelder	MC Feuermelder ist ***jünger als*** Svengster.
Svengster is older than MC Feuermelder	*MC Feuermelder is younger than Svengster.*

"dass" – subordinate clauses with that funny SS word

Example:
Doreen sagt zu Helmut: Ich ärgere mich, ***dass*** du getrunken hast.
Doreen says to Helmut: I'm angry that you have been drinking.

The word "dass" is a conjunction between the main clause ***"Ich ärgere mich"*** and the subordinate clause ***"dass du getrunken hast"***. ***"Dass"*** is the link between these clauses. It is very often used after verbs like *"sagen"* (say), *"glauben"* (believe), *"meinen"* (think), *"hoffen"* (hope), *"wissen"* (know), *"wünschen"* (wish), *"vorschlagen"* (suggest), *"mögen"* (like), *"sich freuen"* (to be happy / glad). To cut it short, these are words which express some kind of wish, feeling or opinion. Note that main and subordinate clauses are separated by a comma and that the verb is always at the end of the subordinate clause.

Subject	verb	conjunction	subject	verb
Helmut	sagt,	***dass***	er	Hunger hat.
Helmut says that he is hungry.				
Eve	glaubt,	***dass***	Svengster	Drogen nimmt.
Eve believes that Svengster is taking drugs.				
Wir	meinen,	***dass***	wir	Deutsch können.
We think that we know how to speak German.				
Ihr	wisst,	***dass***	ihr	nichts wisst.
You know that you do not know a thing.				
Ich	wünsche,	***dass***	die Welt	untergeht.
I wish the world would go down.				
Der Papst	freut sich,	***dass***	es	Rotwein gibt.
The pope is happy that there is red wine.				
Wir	möchten,	***dass***	das Attentat	funktioniert.
We want the assassination to work fine.				
Sie	hoffen,	***dass***	die Bombe	explodiert.
They hope that the bomb explodes.				

Exercises – Chapter 13

1. Use just superlatives for the best in the world.

Example: Jamaika = (schön) => Jamaika ist die schönste Insel der Welt.

a) Der Ferrari F 40 = (teuer, Auto) ....

b) Der Nil = (lange, Fluß) ....

c) Die Autobahn = (gut, Autobahn) ....

d) Der Smart = (hässlich, Auto) ....

e) Svengster = (groß, Rapper) ....

f) Doreen = (geil, Tussi) ....

g) Eve = (lecker, Wurst) ....

2. Compare with *"als"*. What is superior or inferior?

a) Helmut Kohl ist .... ein Elefant. (groß)

b) Bernd ist .... ein guter Staubsauger. (intelligent)

c) David Beckham spielt .... Fussball .... ich. (schlecht)

d) Mein Auto ist .... ein Mini Cooper. (teuer)

e) Mein großer Bruder ist .... mein kleiner Bruder. (klein)

f) Dracula trinkt .... Blut .... Wein. (gern)

And now I want you to write down 5 own examples in which you compare two things or persons or countries and express what you like more than the other.

a) ....

b) ....

c) ....

d) ....

e) ....

3. Who of these persons is POSITIVE, who is SUPERIOR and who is SUPERLATIVE. Use the adjectives:

"drogensüchtig", "fertig", "idiotisch", "schön", "kriminell", "blöde", "abgefuckt"

a) Bushido, Sido, Smudo

....

b) Svengster, MC Feuermelder, Saddam Hussein

....

c) George W. Bush, Angela Merkel, Nicolas Sarkozy

....

d) Pete Doherty, Amy Winehouse, Michael Jackson

....

e) Die Queen, der Papst, der Teufel

....

f) Heidi Klum, Claudia Schiffer, Nadja Auermann

....

g) U2, die Rolling Stones, Coldplay

....

Tell us (in German!) the history...

...of the car industry starting with Daimler and Benz and always think of the pollution produced by exhaust fumes... No! Just joking. Form sentences using the word "dass" and the other words given.

Ihr erzählt mir / ihr liebt den Fremdsprachenlehrer

....

Wir hoffen / Vater Helmut bekommt den Nobelpreis

....

Manche Leute glauben / Hitler ist der aktuelle Kanzler in Deutschland

....

Ich schlage vor / wir ziehen uns alle nackt aus und haben Spaß

....

Die Scientologen glauben / sie sind immun gegen Atombombenstrahlung

....

Read and answer the questions!

Opa Dolfi erzählt vom Flug nach Deutschland

Als ich noch in Brasilien gewesen bin, haben sich mein jüngerer Bruder und meine Frau beide das rechte Bein gebrochen. Kurz darauf hat mein Hund Blondie schlimme Zahnschmerzen bekommen. Er ist zum Zahnarzt gegangen. Mein Bruder und meine Oma haben im Krankenhaus gelegen. Heute können sie wieder gehen. Im Flugzeug nach Deutschland habe ich mich dann erkältet. Neben mir hat eine Frau gesessen. Sie hat Schnupfen gehabt und mir von ihren Krankheiten erzählt. „Ich habe Magenschmerzen, Halsschmerzen und eine Lungenentzündung. Mein Mann ist an BSE, der „Mad-Cow-Disease", gestorben und meine Tochter fällt immer mittwochs in Ohnmacht!"

Die Frau hat mich schrecklich aufgeregt. Außerdem hat sie aus dem Mund gestunken. Sie hat erzählt, dass sie sich nicht gerne die Zähne putzt. Acht Stunden habe ich neben ihr gesessen und konnte nicht atmen. Ich bin sehr froh gewesen, als ich aus dem Flugzeug steigen konnte.

Wer brach sich ein Bein?
Mein jüngerer Bruder und meine Frau. [ ]
Mein Vater. [ ]
Mein Vater und meine Oma. [ ]

Was ist mir im Flugzeug passiert?
Ich habe mir ein Bein gebrochen. [ ]
Ich habe mich erkältet. [ ]
Ich habe mich verbrannt. [ ]

Welche Krankheiten und Schmerzen hatte die Frau?
Halsschmerzen, Magenschmerzen und eine Lungenentzündung. [ ]
Kopfschmerzen, Schnupfen und Liebeskummer. [ ]
Husten, Grippe und eine Nierenentzündung. [ ]

Wann fällt ihre Tochter immer in Ohnmacht?
Immer, wenn sie Liebeskummer hat. [ ]
Immer mittwochs. [ ]
Immer, wenn sie sich die Haare föhnt. [ ]

Warum hat die Frau aus dem Mund gestunken?
Sie putzt sich nicht gerne die Zähne. [ ]
Sie hat sich nicht ihren Bart rasiert. [ ]
Sie hat Hustenbonbons gelutscht. [ ]

Wie lange hat Opa Dolfi neben ihr gesessen?
2 Minuten. [ ]
7 Stunden. [ ]
8 Stunden. [ ]

Bonus-Track – Chapter 13

The internet

The internet was brought to Germany by Pope Benedict in 2006 when there was this huge clerical commitment in Cologne. Since then the internet has grown to a huge and massive hot spot in the media. Every newspaper who knows what to do, every journalist who knows how to move his hand on a keyboard or a typewriter to produce sentences and relative clauses and stuff like that writes about the internet. Nowadays, it is even possible to meet other people than the pope on the internet, to see them in reality, to fall in love immediately and plan a future with them with a bunch of kids, lots of money and even more fun, because isn't fun the most important thing in life and on the internet?

The internet lives in Cologne where there is this famous cathedral called the "Kölner Dom". There are other domes in Germany, for example the "Hamburger Dom" which is no cathedral and in fact not even a house but more of a northern beer festival like the Oktoberfest in Munich. Another "Dome" is "The Dome" which is a music festival for kids under the age of 14. This festival starts at 2 pm and ends at 7 pm because the kids have to be in bed early in Germany – and the artists who play on stage have the same desire. Sleeping is one fine hobby of most Germans, except for a small group of sleepless people. However, for these people who cannot sleep the pope provided the internet. So they can get together online, chat a bit – while all other non-sleepless people sleep – about their problems with sleeplessness and then maybe sometimes see each other, fall in love and later then fall asleep happily ever after.

Nevertheless, there are critics of the internet who say that it has committed several crimes like bank robbery, exhibitionism, snuff films and animal pornos and stuff like that. And these reproaches are tough and severe! But no one has any evidence that it is all the internet's fault. Several other suspects have been asked questions, several suspects have somehow disappeared like oppositional politicians in China or some dark Southern American countries or maybe even in Guantanamo. No one knows and this is exactly why no one knows what to know. The German police and the German secretary of interior really want to know what other people know and this is why they started to suck out every piece of information from the internet and the sleepless people surfing around in the widths of the internet.

Imagine the secretary of interior surfing! Surfing in his wheelchair. I would really like to see this picture and I am very happy that the graphic guy and co-editor and co-publisher of this book is such a great artist who was able to paint a picture.

Hopefully you are as happy as we both are with the painting. And if you want, we allow you to take a piece of very thin paper and lay it over the painting to copy it that way, put it in a frame and then hang it above your bed or above your toilet or under your bed or under your toilet – just do as you wish and feel as if you are at home when you are at home.

You see: There are not only bad things the pope with his evil eyes is responsible for. There is more than being anti-preservatives, anti-abortion or anti-homosexuals. There is the internet, there is the Red Cross, there is Jesus, god, the Holy Ghost and the eternal life for all of us. Hopefully.

Chapter 14

Die Schmidts kaufen Mielke

Doreen ist auf dem Heimweg vom Shopping und hat noch 25 Euro in der Handtasche. Plötzlich sieht sie einen Hundehändler an der Straße stehen. Dieser hat einen kleinen süßen Hund im Angebot und Doreen schmilzt das Herz.

Doreen: *„Hallo Hundehändler! Wie viel kostet dieser Hund da?"*

Hundehändler: *„40 Euro."*

Doreen: *„Ich gebe dir 10 Euro!"*

Hundehändler: *„Nein, niemals nicht zu diesem Preis. Spinnst du? 30 Euro!"*

Doreen: *„22 Euro, aber das ist mein letztes Wort."*

Hundehändler: *„24,50 Euro ist mein letztes Wort. Das ist ein echter Pitbull! Scheckheftgepflegt, eine Beißmaschine, Vollwaise. Hat seine Eltern aufgefressen."*

Doreen: *„Abgemacht. Gekauft! Was hat der denn da vorm Mund?"*

Hundehändler: *„Das ist ein Körbchen zum Pilze sammeln! Nein! Quatsch! Ein Maulkorb natürlich. Den musst du unbedingt dran lassen, damit nichts passiert."*

Doreen nimmt den Pitbull, den sie liebevoll Cocky nennt und geht mit ihm nach Hause zu ihren Eltern. Eve und Helmut sind nicht begeistert. Niemals haben sie ihren Kindern erlaubt, Haustiere zu haben. Schon, als sie die Läuse hatten, waren Helmut und Eve entsetzt. Jetzt steht ein 80 Kilogramm schwerer Pitbull in ihrem Wohnzimmer und blinzelt sie böse aus seinen Schweinsäuglein an. Doreen bittet und bettelt und weint, aber Eve bleibt hart.

Eve: *„Niemals kommt die Bestie in mein Haus! Wenn wir Glück haben, frisst er uns nur die Haare vom Kopf! Wenn wir Pech haben, dann beißt er uns die Hälse durch!"*

Doreen: *„Aber er hat doch einen Maulkorb! Wir füttern ihn einfach durch einen Strohhalm mit Sondennahrung! Schacklihns Oma lebt auch schon seit Jahren so."*

Eve: *„Helmut! Sag du doch auch einmal was! Das geht doch nicht mit dem Hund!"*

Helmut: *„Naja. So ein Hund macht schon was her. Und hier in der Nachbarschaft ist erst letztens eingebrochen worden."*

Eve: *„Aber das war doch der Svennie mit seinen Kumpels."*

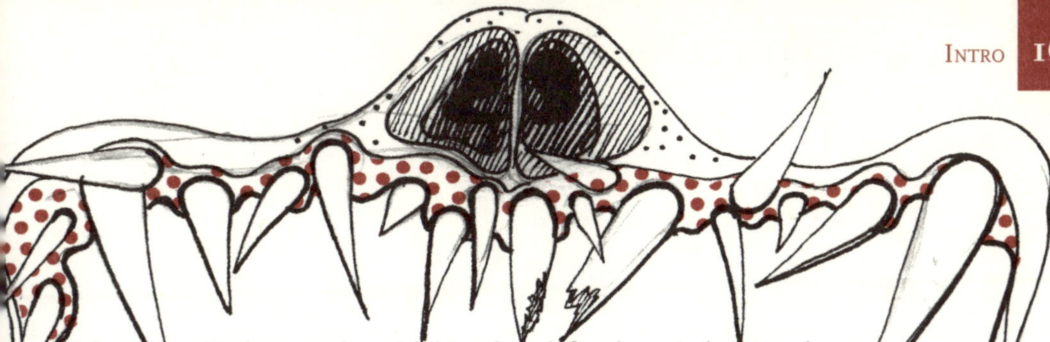

Helmut: *„Und wenn schon. Ich bin schon dafür, dass wir den Hund zum Schutz behalten. Ich kümmere mich darum.“*

Eve: *„Du kümmerst dich um nichts! Du tust nichts! Ich habe dich noch nie arbeiten sehen! Du bist ein totaler Nichtsnutz!“*

Helmut: *„Jetzt braucht der Hund nur noch einen Namen.“*

Doreen: *„Ja! Cocky! Er heißt Cocky!“*

Helmut: *„Bitte?! Nein! Dann können wir ihn ja gleich ‚Penis‘ rufen! Er muss einen deutschen Namen tragen, einen Namen, der Respekt einflößt, böse klingt und gleichzeitig unberechenbar. ‚Führer‘? ‚Hasso‘? Ich hab es! ‚Mielke‘! Ich taufe dich auf den Namen ‚Mielke‘, ‚Cocky‘!“*

Helmut nimmt Mielke und geht mit ihm in den Park um zu trainieren. Auf dem vergitterten Street-Soccer-Feld spielen gerade auch ein paar Jungs Fußball und Mielke will mitspielen, aber Helmut will das nicht. Er schlägt und tritt Mielke, der immer wieder dem Fußball oder einem Spieler hinterher hetzt und dabei jault und wimmert. Schließlich will Helmut wissen, ob Mielke bissig ist.

Er holt einen dicken Stock und stellt sich vor das Gitter des Spielfelds. Von dort entfernt er durch das Gitter Mielkes Maulkorb und reizt ihn mit dem Stock. Mielke schnappt zu und zieht Helmut beinahe durch das Gitter nach innen. Dann verliert er das Interesse und sucht neue Stöcke. Am schönsten findet Mielke die beweglichen Stöcke, die unten an den Fußballspielern dran sind. Mielke weiß nicht, dass das Beine sind. Hauptsache ist doch, dass sie ihm schmecken.

Helmut weiß jetzt, dass Mielke bissig ist. Er weiß jetzt auch, dass Mielke eine Mörderbestie ist, obwohl er das gar nicht herausfinden wollte. Er ruft die Polizei an und erzählt, dass ein Pitbull auf einem Fußballfeld im Park zwei komplette Fußball-Mannschaften aufgegessen hat. Doreen und Eve erzählt er: *„Auf einmal ist Mielke verschwunden. Keine Ahnung, wohin er ist. Manchmal sind Tiere eben seltsam.“*

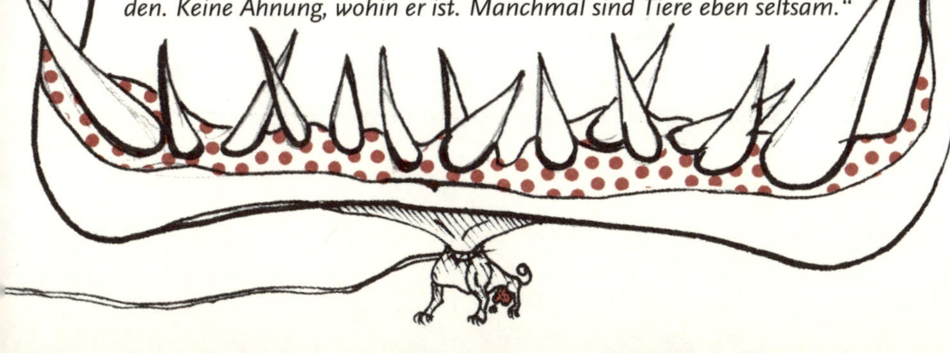

Grammar Stuff – Chapter 14

This chapter is all about negativity. Up to now you couldn't say "no" in German and always had to say *"Ja und amen."* to anything. Be it that someone asked you to kiss him / her frenchstyle, be it that someone told you to go and fuck yourself or be it that someone asked you if it was okay if he peed over your feet. All you could say was *"Ja!"* Well, at least you didn't say *"Jawohl!"* like all the Nazis in the Hollywood movies do.

Anyway, here is everything about negation in one chapter.

"*Nicht*" and "*kein*"

There are two things to remember:

a) If the noun has a definite article, the negative particle *"nicht"* is used.
b) If the noun has an indefinite article or no article at all, then the negative particle *"kein"* is used.

Examples:	Hast du das Geld für die Drogen? *Do you have the drug money?*	Nein. Ich habe es ***nicht.*** *No. I do not have it.*
	Haben Sie etwas Geld für mich? *Do you have any money for me?*	Ich habe ***kein*** Geld für Sie. *I don't have any money for you.*

"*Nicht*" and "*nichts*"

***The only thing* "nicht" *does: It makes a sentence negative.* "Nichts" *on the other hand stands for a* NOMINATIVE *or* ACCUSATIVE COMPLEMENT.**

Svengster hat den braunen Afghanen geraucht.
Svengster has smoked some brown Afghan.

Negative: Svengster hat den braunen Afghanen ***nicht*** geraucht.
Svengster hasn't smoked any brown Afghan.

Svengster möchte etwas trinken.
Svengster would like to have something to drink.

Svengster möchte braunen Afghanen rauchen.
Svengster would like to smoke some brown Afghan.

Negative: Svengster möchte ***nichts*** rauchen.
Svengster doesn't want to smoke anything.

More negativity! Say no to anything!

nie
Der Hund bellt nie. — *The dog never barks.*

niemals
Helmut ist niemals nüchtern. — *Helmut is never ever sober.*

niemand
Niemand kennt Kurt Beck. — *No one knows Kurt Beck.*

nirgends
Nirgends gibt es Arbeit. — *There are no jobs anywhere.*

nirgendwo
Nirgendwo ist es toll. — *It is not great anywhere at all.*

nie und nimmer
Nie und nimmer hat Deutschland einen Weltkrieg gewonnen.
Never ever Germany has won a world war.

niemals nicht
Angela Merkel hat mal gut ausgesehen? Niemals nicht!
Has Angela Merkel ever looked nice? Never ever! You're kidding!

"nicht nur... sondern auch"

The word construction *"nicht nur... sondern auch"* shows that there is something more to say, something more to add to something that has already been said. *"Nicht nur... sondern auch"* joins other words or groups of words as coordinating conjunctions.

Examples: Helmut ist nicht nur Alkoholiker, sondern auch ein Psychopath.
Helmut is not only an alcoholic but also a psychopath.

Eve spricht nicht nur Deutsch, sondern auch Sächsisch.
Eve doesn't only speak German but also Saxonian.

Exercises – Chapter 14

Is it *"nicht"* or is it *"kein"*. Don't guess! Know it!

Haben Sie einen Pitbull, Herr Schmidt?

Nein! Ich habe .... Pitbull, Herr Wachtmeister!

Wo ist Doreen?

..................Ahnung! Ich weiß es ....

Was ist denn mit dir los, Svengster?

Ich habe das Klo .... schnell genug gefunden!

Opa Dolfi hat einen komischen Bart, aber er hat .... Holzbein.

Eve hat ein Nagelstudio gehört. Eve besitzt heute .... Bestattungsinstitut.

Equivalents:

What is the same but completely different? What's the negative? Draw lines!

Irgendwo	jemand	einmal	einer	etwas
Nichts	keiner	nirgendwo	niemand	nie

There is more than just one thing!

***Joint he sentences with* "nicht nur ... sondern auch"**

MC Feuermelder kaufen Drogen – Maschinengewehr

....

Der Terrorist lieben Blumen – Songs von James Blunt

....

c) Der Heilige Geist mögen skifahren – surfen

....

d) George W. Bush keinen Krieg führen können – essen keine Brezel

....

e) Du Mord begehen – sein unschuldig

....

Complete the following text

Use:* "nicht" *(5x)*, "nichts" *(1x)* "nie" *(1x)*, "niemand" *(1x)*, "keiner" *(1x)*, "kein" *(1x)*, "keine" *(1x)* "nie und nimmer" *(1x)*, "niemals nicht" *(1x)*, "nicht nur ... sondern auch" *(2x)

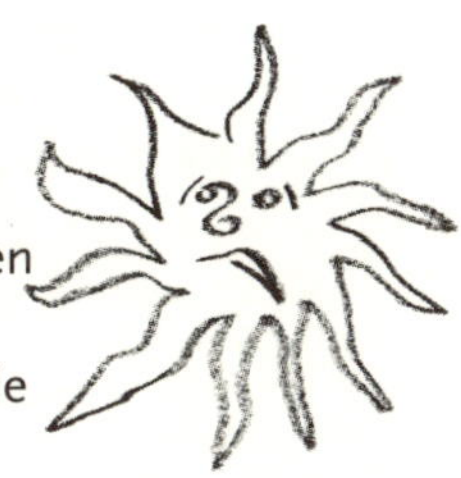

Der Tag der Sonne wendet sich zum Guten

Die Sonne hat .... so tolle Laune, als sie draußen in der Stadt rumspaziert. Überall sind so viele Menschen und dann hat sie ja auch noch diesen hässlichen eingewachsenen Zehnagel. Noch .... hatte sie solche Schmerzen.

Sie ärgert sich sehr, dass sie überhaupt auf die Idee gekommen ist, mit einem eingewachsenen Zehnagel in der Stadt spazieren zu gehen. Da kommt eine alte Frau und spricht sie blöd von der Seite an: *„Hallo Sonne! Wie geht's?"*

..................spricht die Sonne ungestraft von der Seite an. Die Sonne zieht sich wortlos den Stiefel vom Fuß, den Socken auch und klatscht der alten Frau den eitrigen Zeh ins Gesicht: *„Da! Bitteschön!"* Die alte Frau allerdings mag es, wenn ihr jemand eitrige Zehnägel ins Gesicht haut, doch das kann die Sonne und .... nur die, das kann ja wirklich .... hier wissen. Wer rechnet schon damit, dass es alte Frauen gibt, die gerne eitrige Zehnägel ins Gesicht gehauen bekommen?! Also ich jedenfalls .... So etwas passiert doch ....
Bei Jüngeren Leuten, ok! Wenn die das gern haben, dann ist das ja noch verständlich, die mögen ja auch Tokio Hotel, aber alte Menschen!? ....

Die alte Frau hat sich in genau dem Moment in die Sonne verliebt, als diese mit ihrem wehen Fuß dazu anhob, ihr den eitrigen Zeh ins Gesicht zu pfeffern. *„Vorfreude war und ist doch einfach die schönste Freude,* .... *wahr?“*, dachte sie jetzt, als die Sonne *„Da! Bitteschön!“* sagt und legt ihr den Arm um die Schulter. *„Autsch, tat das weh!“* Die Sonne ist schließlich .... die Sonne, ... noch wütend wegen ihres Zehs. ....Wunder, dass sich die alte Frau den Arm verbrennt.

Aber das stört sie .... Wer verliebt ist, spürt ....Verbrennungen dritten Grades. Sie lädt die Sonne auf einen Café Latte Macchiato beim Italiener um die Ecke ein und die Sonne verliebt sich in die alte Frau. Noch am selben Tag ziehen sie .... zusammen, ... heiraten auch. Seit diesem Tag wohnen die alte Frau und die Sonne in einer Parterre-Wohnung in Weißensee, und wenn die alte Frau ganz lieb zur Sonne ist, dann erbarmt sich diese und schlägt ihr den immer noch eitrigen Zeh ins Gesicht. Und ....kann die beiden trennen!

CUSTOMERS WHO ENJOYED THIS STORY MIGHT ALSO LOVE

100%
PURE
MEAT!
Keine Anzeige
Oh boy!
SCHLACHT-
SCHÜSSEL-
FÜHRER
Bayern

B Bonus Track – Chapter 14

German TV

TV was introduced to Germany in 1987. Before this time there were travelling theater companies whose actors played behind a big frame and reenacted things, events and processes that the Germans had read of in their newspapers like the first man on the moon, the extinction of Hiroshima or Godzilla destroying some Japanese islands. The spectators were all sitting in a big room and had their binoculars or telescopes turned in the wrong way. With the introduction of TVs everything became different. The foremost reason for allowing TVs in Germany was that many Germans had complained about being bored of having to talk to other people or watching on their wall without the walls watching back at them or telling them stories or showing them anything else than the wallpaper. The political leaders of Germany had a lot of arguments about whether it is right or whether it is wrong but in the end they came to the conclusion that TV wouldn't be as bad as anyone knew it would be.

Every German got an "Abwrackprämie" (a 2.500 euro wrecking bonus from the government if you gave away your old wallpapers and instead bought yourself a flat screen TV set) and famous shows like "Wetten dass ..?!" ("What the fuck?!"), "Wer wird Millionär" ("Who wants to be a millionaire") and "Vier gegen Willy" ("Four against Willy") showed the world what the world still doesn't want to believe: The Germans are not only unable to win a war, but they are also not able to create a good TV program. Lots of actors that were stars of the theatre times when there still was no TV now turned into TV actors which made things even worse. Remember famous German actors and entertainers like Til Schweiger, Josef Goebbels and Hildegard Knef? I guess you know what I mean.

In the last few years from 1987 until today which might be 2009 but can also be any point later in time as we, the authors, do not know when you will read and hopefully will have bought this book. Anyway, today there has been found some proof that there are effects of watching TV which are in fact quite useful. For instance, the ability to see has increased by 23% (see "And then there was orange. Increases in seeing colours." Rolf Palmian Ph. D., Berlin University Press 1992). In his work Palmian tells us about the first time when a German person living in Germany was able to see the colour orange. First everyone declared the patient of Dr. Palmian insane, but Palmian believed in his people, made several tests and could finally prove to other scientists that his patient was no liar and that the colour of orange even existed in Germany. Palmian was nominated for the Nobel Prize in Physics but wasn't able to attend at the ceremony because he was run over by a passing car whose driver didn't see the red lights. Palmian died immediately but in his hometown there are still several statues showing his face, body and buttocks.

Today's TV program has quite a big variety – if you ignore the fact that there is only one channel which is controlled by the government which is controlled by the biggest leader and commander the world has ever seen who goes by the name of Kim Yong Il. That leader is praised throughout the whole program, even in late night pornos and the reports about World War VI.

Chapter 15

Helmut in der Arbeitsagentur

Immer wenn Helmut Geld braucht, geht er in die Agentur für Arbeit, um dort Ärger zu machen. Heute trifft Helmut um 13 Uhr in der Agentur ein. Er hat sich nicht extra schick gemacht und die Haare sind auch seit 5 Tagen nicht gewaschen. Die Frau am Tresen schnauzt ihn grundlos an, um ihn einzuschüchtern, aber Helmut zeigt ihr nur seinen Mittelfinger. Den kennt die Frau noch nicht, denn sie arbeitet erst seit ein paar Tagen in der Agentur. Geschockt ruft sie beim Sicherheitsdienst an, aber die kennen Helmut schon und tun ihm nichts.

Wenn Helmut im Arbeitsamt ist, dann brauchen die Sicherheitsfuzzis gar nicht erst zu kommen. Helmut ist mittlerweile auf dem Weg zu seinem Sachbearbeiter Herrn Koleps. Der Sachbearbeiter weiß meistens noch weniger als der Gummibaum, der in seinem Zimmer steht. Das Einzige, was Helmut tun muss: Er muss ihn einschüchtern. Er muss ihm drohen und er muss notfalls etwas laut werden. Der Sachbearbeiter hat Angst vor Helmut und hat heute frei. Helmut bemüht sich, die Tür zum Sachbearbeiter-Zimmer zu öffnen. Schließlich tritt er die Tür ein, um nachzuschauen, ob sich Herr Koleps dort auch wirklich nicht versteckt hat.

Herr Koleps ist wirklich nicht da, aber Helmut gefällt die Schreibtischlampe sehr gut. *„Die nehme ich mir mal mit"*, denkt er sich und steckt sie unter seine Trainingsjacke. *„Wenn die mir schon kein Geld geben, dann darf ich mir Naturalien mitnehmen, oder etwa nicht?"* Helmut verlässt gerade den Raum, als er einem anderen Sachbearbeiter, Herrn Dschango, über den Weg läuft. *„Na, mein lieber Kunde! Was machen Sie denn hier?"*

Helmut: *„Ich brauche Geld und krieg keines von euch!"*

Herr Dschango: *„Kommen Sie mal mit und wir sammeln was in der Kantine für Sie."*

Helmut: *„Wirklich?"*

Herr Dschango: *„Bin ich die Wohlfahrt oder was? Wenn Sie hier Türen eintreten, dann kriegen sie doch nichts von uns. Um Kohle zu kriegen, musst du freundlich sein!"*

Herr Dschango nimmt Helmut mit in sein Büro und zeigt ihm dort ein Foto in einem goldenen Rahmen.

Herr Dschango: *„Hier! Das ist unser Lieblingskunde, Herr Tobstarr! Im großen Jahresendvoting zum freundlichsten Arbeitslosen des Jahres 2008 hat er mit weitem Abstand den ersten Platz gewonnen. Herr Tobstarr ist nicht nur freundlich, sondern auch gut aussehend, musikalisch, intelligent und humorvoll. Naja. Am Thema „humorvoll" kann er noch etwas arbeiten, aber wir haben ja auch nicht den witzigsten Arbeitslosen gesucht, sondern den freundlichsten."*

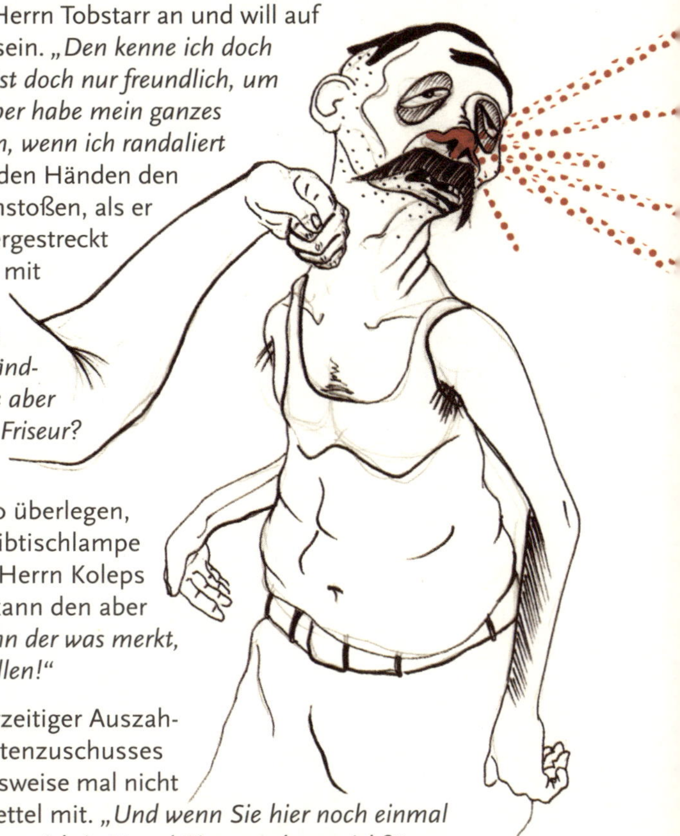

Helmut schaut sich das Bild von Herrn Tobstarr an und will auf einmal gar nicht mehr freundlich sein. *„Den kenne ich doch irgendwoher"*, denkt er sich. *„Der ist doch nur freundlich, um zu seinem Geld zu kommen! Ich aber habe mein ganzes Geld bisher auch immer bekommen, wenn ich randaliert habe."* Helmut will gerade mit beiden Händen den Schreibtisch Herrn Dschangos umstoßen, als er von Herrn Dschangos Faust niedergestreckt wird. Durch den Nebel hört er ihn mit einem anderen Mann sprechen. *„Das war eindeutig Notwehr! Nicht wahr, Herr Tobstarr?" „Selbstverständlich, Herr Dschango! Das haben sie aber gut gemacht. Ach, waren Sie beim Friseur? Hübsch geworden..."*

Herr Tobstarr und Herr Dschango überlegen, ob sie Helmut die geklaute Schreibtischlampe wieder abnehmen sollen, um sie Herrn Koleps zurückzugeben. Herr Dschango kann den aber sowieso nicht abhaben. *„Und wenn der was merkt, dann soll er sich mal nicht so anstellen!"*

Helmut bittet freundlich nach vorzeitiger Auszahlung seines monatlichen Heizkostenzuschusses und Herr Dschango will ausnahmsweise mal nicht so sein und gibt ihm einen Zahlzettel mit. *„Und wenn Sie hier noch einmal Ärger machen, Schmidt, dann setzt es richtig Haue! Sie verstehen mich?"*

Helmut nickt, lässt sich das Geld in einem anderen Raum auszahlen und verlässt die Arbeitsagentur. Zu der geht er in nächster Zeit bestimmt nicht mehr. Vor allem nicht zu Herrn Dschango.

Grammar Stuff – Chapter 15

Conditional clauses

Not everything can be done without any thinking or without any condition that must be given beforehand. That is why we have to talk about conditional clauses.

a) Conditional clauses with "wenn" give a condition that has to be fulfilled before the things said in the main clause can be true, possible or done.

b) The verb is always found at the end of the sentence in a subordinate clause.

Example:

Wenn du Polizist bist,	darfst du Drogen nehmen.
If you are a policeman,	*you are allowed to take drugs.*
Subordinate clause	***Main clause***

It is also possible to change the clauses and start with the main clause followed by a subordinate clause. However that does not change the meaning of the sentence.

Example:

Du darfst Drogen nehmen,	***wenn*** du Polizist bist.
You are allowed to take drugs	*if you are a policeman.*
Main clause	***Subordinate clause***

"um ... zu" + INFINITIVE – another form of subordinate clauses

There are two points you have to be careful with if you use an* "um ... zu" *+ infinitive construction.

a) Always remember that the conjunction *"um ... zu"* + INFINITIVE refers to a destination or an intention.

b) The persons in the main clause and in the subordinate clause have to be the same.

Example:

Um Geld vom Arbeitsamt ***zu bekommen,*** müssen Sie freundlich sein.
To get money from the labour exchange *you have to be nice.*
Subordinate clause ***Main clause***

Sie müssen freundlich sein, ***um*** Geld vom Arbeitsamt ***zu bekommen.***
You have to be nice *to get money from the labour exchange.*
Main clause ***Subordinate clause***

"Der", *"die"* and *"das"* as demonstrative pronouns

Bushido! Unglaublich! ***Den*** haben Sie schon in Grönland gesehen?
Bushido! Unbelievable! You've alredy seen this guy in Greenland?

Und die Rapper da hinten? ***Denen*** hab ich gesagt, sie sollen sich ficken gehen.
And these rappers over there? Well, I've told them to go and fuck themselves.

SINGULAR	MASCULINE	FEMININE	NEUTER
NOMINATIVE	der	die	das
ACCUSATIVE	den	die	das
DATIVE	dem	der	dem
PLURAL	**MASCULINE**	**FEMININE**	**NEUTER**
NOMINATIVE	die	die	die
ACCUSATIVE	die	die	die
DATIVE	denen	denen	denen

In spoken German or some other people may say "in bad German" it is quite common to use *"der"*, *"die"* and *"das"* as demonstrative pronouns which then stand instead of personal pronouns. The demonstrative pronoun then refers to a person or thing mentioned in the sentence before. The form of the demonstrative pronouns is the same as in the definite articles with just one exception, the dative plural form of *"denen"*.

Exercises – Chapter 15

Tell us what you have to do if something you've planned goes wrong.

Example:
alles geht schief – von der Brücke springen
=> Wenn alles schief geht, springe ich von der Brücke.

meine Freundin betrügt mich – sie auch betrügen

....

ich habe kein Koks mehr – Klebstoff schnüffeln

....

Michael Jackson nochmal tourt – die Apokalypse nah sein

....

Keine Gänse abzuschießen sind – eben eine Mieze schießen

....

Mir ist übel – kotzen gehen

....

Mein Onkel hat keinen Penis – meine Tante sein

....

Der Esel wird mutig – aufs Eis gehen

....

Es ist Nacht – dunkel sein

....

Helmut hat Durst	–	3 Liter Bier in 5 Minuten trinken
Svengster liegt im Bett	–	sich einnässen
Doreen hat Zeit	–	shoppen gehen
Eve steht am Ketwurststand	–	immer wieder Ketwürste essen

Link sentences to form *"um ... zu"*-clauses

Example:
Helmut geht zur Agentur für Arbeit. Er möchte Geld bekommen.
=> Helmut geht zur Agentur für Arbeit, um Geld zu bekommen.

Doreen möchte dünner sein. Sie will bei Germany's Next Top Model gewinnen.

....

Der Papst kauft Kondome. Er will kein Vater werden.

....

Mielke zerfleischt die Fußballer. Er möchte wissen, wie Menschen schmecken.

....

Eve verkauft Ketwurst. Irgendwie Geld verdienen wollen.

....

Svengster trägt Hiphophosen. Er will cooler aussehen, als er in Wirklichkeit ist.

....

Match the sentences

Kennst du The Notorious B.I.G.?	Die kostet 100.000 Euro.
Wohin fliegt dieses Flugzeug?	Den haben wir schon nackt im Internet gesehen.
Kann ich mal einen Euro haben?	Den habe ich selbst erschossen.
Was kostet die Goldkette da im Schaufenster?	Das fliegt in die Twin Towers.
Möchtet ihr euren Deutschlehrer nackt sehen?	Den gebe ich dir doch gerne.
Wie finden Sie meine neue Frisur?	Nein, der ist mir völlig unbekannt.
Du hast noch nie von Thomas Mann gehört?	Die ist eher so halbgut.
Was machen eigentlich Guns N' Roses?	Deren Platte kauft kein Mensch.

WARTE-
MARKEN
NIETE

B Bonus-Track – Chapter 15

Hitler, D! und Schäfer-Gümbel – German Celebrities

In Germany you can be famous for everything – as you can see above when you read the headline carefully. Two of the persons mentioned in it are politicians, both of them famous for losing. The first one for losing the Hessian parliamentary elections in 2009 and the third one for starting World War II and then losing it. Both of them have strange names that normally do not exist any more in the world and for which there is no explanation at all. It is said that Hitler is physically dead and Schäfer-Gümbel is politically dead, but you never know when a "Flugscheibe" from "Neuschwabenland" will land at Frankfurt City airport to save Opel.

D! is some kind of a mixture of Hitler and Schäfer-Gümbel, but instead of the other two guys, he has an African born father. That doesn't make any of them superior to the others but D! is convinced he is a great dancer – something like the German version of Fred Astaire or Michael Jackson. He is the head of a TV show named "Popstars" in which he pushes around stupid girls with bulimia who try to sound like Anastacia who doesn't sound very well either. In this show he is kind of a dictator (see also: Schäfer-Gümbel) but one who shows his emotions. That means that he cries together with the girls who he made crying by telling them they were complete crap and should jump out of a window in a skyscraper just a few seconds before. As you can see – becoming a celebrity in Germany is not so easy and it is always important to be an asshole if you want to be a celebrity.

However, there are also other German people you should know when you want to understand Germany and the German culture. You have already seen the most famous comedians of Germany, now it is time for you to get to know some more celebrities including the most important facts about them so you can easily take part in a party conversation at the Berlinale 2013.

Thomas Gottschalk: former teacher now show master, famous movies like "The Super Noses", "2 Noses fuel with Super" or "The Return of the Super Noses". His hair is said to be fake.

Jesus: Son of GOD, born when Bethlehem was still German, lots of miracles, saved mankind with his death. Dead for a long time but resurrected.

Barbara Salesch: First German TV Judge with red hair, drives English car (probably in red), likes her red dyed hair.

Goethe: famous for his great poems, stories, novels, genius and phallus collection. To name one of his most famous book titles: Fist (in German Faust).

Marlene Dietrich: THE German actress everyone knows for her genius. Berlin born, leading actress in "Der Blaue Engel", against Hitler and pro allied troups, later retired and lived in Paris in an apartment which she would never leave for 20 years. Then she died.

Günther Jauch: Host of the German edition of "Who wants to be a millionaire". Saved mankind and the jungle by drinking lots of Krombacher beer. Or was it Bitburger?

Heidi Klum: German top model who doesn't seem to be bright. Married with Seal, not with a seal, works for McDonalds and is the domina in "Germany's Next Top Model".

Karl Lagerfeld: famous couture designer for Chanel, a few years ago lost 100 kg to fit into skinny jeans, then started wearing lots of silver jewelry (especially skulls), hates Heidi Klum.

Jürgen Klinsmann: Best actor ever born in Germany, did not act but instead was the person he had to play. Always happy and laughing. Played in hundredths of films, just was "in it for the money". Died in California by a heart attack in early 90s.

Klaus Kinski: Greatest football coach Germany has ever seen. Lived in California, then nearly became Champion of the world in 2006 but then lost against Italy in the semi finals. Later moved from Germany to Bavaria where he unsuccessfully tried to become "Deutscher Meister".

Angela Merkel: First chancelorette in Germany if Hitler was not female. Has a strange haircut and lived in the GDR (German Democratic Republic). Former chancellor Helmut Kohl had kind of a crush on his "little girl" and helped her to rise. She likes to watch what others do and then not to do anything. Showed her breasts in Norway.

DJ Bobo: Swiss Eurodance musician known for his dance moves that always look like he is unsuccessfully trying to "fan out" a burning forest. Greatest hits are "Somebody dance with me", "Keep on dancing", "Chihuahua" and "There's a party". Has a very big nose and lesser and lesser hair.

Arnold Schwarzenegger: Austrian born, nowadays US-American actor and governor of California. As bodybuilder he liked anabolic steroids, later was the Terminator, married a Kennedy and then turned into a politician. Has a funny Austrian accent (See: "I'll be back!" or "Hasta la vista, baby!").

Franz Beckenbauer: Best football player of the world, in Germany known as "Der Kaiser" which means "The Emperor". Doesn't know what he talks but just does it – although he is a representative for Adidas and not for Nike.

Bud Spencerterrencehill: Siamese dizygotic twins that became famous by beating up rugby teams, GIs, evil people, other boxers, and sometimes themselves. Later one of them joined Silvio Berlusconi's questionable party while the other one only acted as a priest.

Sissy: Austrian queen, played by Romy Schneider. Both were often depressed. The reason for Sissy's depression might have been the country she lived in.

HP Baxxter: Famous shouter of German Powerpopband Scooter ("Hyper Hyper", "How much is the fish", "Dop, Döp, Dop, Dödel öp öp öp") and voice behind the first techno ballad called "Break it up". Nowadays also panel show grimace judging over tits and asses of teenagers.

Leni Riefenstahl: One of the great faces of German film and moviemaking (others: Veronika Ferres, Veronika Ferres and Veronika Ferres). Had some Nazi friends and made some questionable but highly artificial films in the Nazi era. Later filmed black Africans and fishes.

Tobstarr: First and only German Hiphop producer – Germany's equivalent to Dr. Dre. Bonus features: Extremely good-looking, wise and with an exclusive sense of taste.

Pope Benedict: The artist formerly known as Josef Ratzinger. Wears funny clothing, says strange things that infuriate others like Muslims, Jews and Protestants and has – as one would say in Austria – "schiache" (evil) eyes. First German pope since Jesus Christ.

Chapter 16

Eve geht fremd

Eve arbeitet heute schon seit 7 Stunden in ihrem Ketwurst-Imbiss. Sie hat geschuftet und konnte sich nicht einmal 5 Minuten hinsetzen, hinlegen oder einfach nur rumhängen. Ständig hat sich jemand vor den Imbiss gestellt und eine Ketwurst oder Grilletta bestellt. Eve ist sehr müde und erschöpft. Sie hat schon 12 Ketwürste gegessen – nicht, weil sie hungrig gewesen ist, sondern aus Frust.

„Zu Hause hängt Helmut bestimmt wieder besoffen auf der Couch rum. Die Kinder liegen mir auch auf der Tasche und stehen jeden Tag vor mir und wollen Geld. Wie gerne würde ich alles stehen und liegen lassen!“, murmelt sie in ihren Damenbart, als plötzlich ein junger Mann ihr Interesse erregt. Er steigt gerade aus seinem 30-Tonner-LKW aus und geht in Richtung Eves Ketwurst-Imbiss.

Mann: *„Hallo! Ich bin Mobutu und ich hätte gerne eine Ketwurst.“*

Eve *(schaut in den Schritt Mobutus und errötet): „...warum ... warum das denn?!“*

Mann: *„Ich habe Hunger. Ich sitze seit 8 Stunden auf dem Bock und höre die ganze Zeit Truckstop und Tom Astor.“*

Eve: *„Ach! Ach so. Also eine Ketwurst für Sie, Herr Mobutu?“*

Mann: *„Mobutu ist mein Vorname. Wenn Sie „Herr Mobutu“ sagen, dann nenne ich sie „Frau Eve“ ... oder vielleicht „Fräulein“?“*

Eve: (errötet noch mehr): *„Nein, Frau, also Fräulein, also ist ja auch egal. Nennen Sie mich einfach Eve.“*

Mobutu errötet ebenfalls und grinst: *„Gerne, Eve!“*

Eve schießt eine ordentliche Ladung Ketchup in die Ketwurst-Stulle. Dann stopft sie eine Ketwurst von Trioland in die Ketwurst-Stullenöffnung und verreibt so den Ketchup gleichmäßig an den Innenrändern der Stulle. Mobutu schaut interessiert zu. Er sieht, wie zärtlich und wie liebevoll Eve das Essen für ihn zubereitet. Jede Bewegung sitzt, jeder Handgriff passt und der ganze Körper Eves scheint bei jedem Zucken mitzuschwingen. Mobutu verliebt sich sofort. Sicher, er hat schon viele Frauen gesehen, aber bestimmt noch keine wie Eve. Es gab welche, die hübsch waren und welche, die hässlich waren, aber keine wie Eve. Eve ist eine wie keine.

Eve: *„Herr Mob ... Mobutu, was ist denn los mit Ihnen? Alles in Ordnung? Ihre Ketwurst ist fertig."*

Mobutu (er erwacht wie aus einem schönen Traum): *„Was? Wie? Wo bin ich? Eve ... ich weiß nicht, wie ich es sagen soll. Ich liebe Sie. Ich habe Sie vom allerersten Moment an geliebt. Ihr Lächeln, Ihren Körper, Ihre Anmut, Ihre Ketwurst ... Verzeihen Sie mir, aber ich kann nicht anders."*

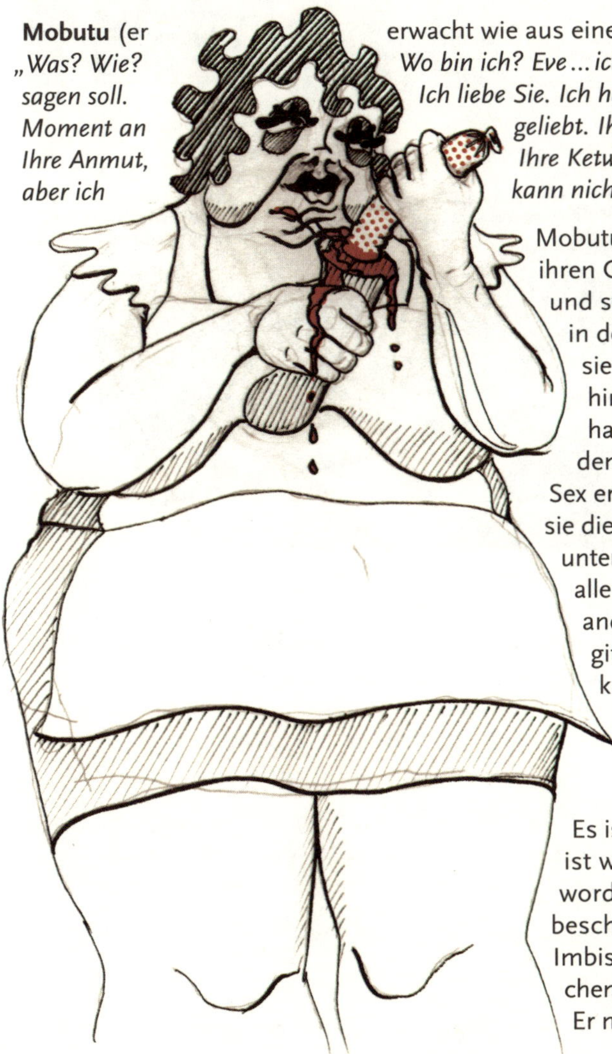

Mobutu und Eve klatschen mit ihren Gesichtern aufeinander und stecken sich ihre Zunge in den Mund. Dann ziehen sie sich aus und legen sich hinter die Ladentheke. Eve hat Angst, dass andere Kunden Mobutu und sie beim Sex erwischen. Deshalb zieht sie die große Tür zum Staufach unter der Theke auf und stellt alle Tiefkühlpommes sowie andere Vorräte und Rattengift in den Fußraum. Dann krabbeln Mobutu und sie in das Staufach des Imbiss und schlafen miteinander.

Es ist 6 Uhr abends. Helmut ist wieder einmal wach geworden und hat Hunger. Er beschließt, zu Eve und ihrem Imbiss zu gehen und die restlichen Ketwürste wegzuessen. Er macht sich auf den Weg.

Um 5 Minuten nach 6 Uhr sind Eve und Mobutu fertig mit dem Sex. Sowohl Eve als auch Mobutu überlegen, noch einen schlechten Witz von wegen Ketwurst und Penis zu machen, verkneifen sich das aber. Sie küssen sich kurz und Mobutu geht zurück zu seinem LKW. Er dreht sich noch einmal um und ruft Eve zu: „Ich vergesse Dich nicht, Schatz! Und wenn Du in den nächsten Nächten im Bett liegst und auf einmal sehr erregt bist… dann haben wir Fernverkehr, hahahaha!"

Eve lacht, aber sie lacht nicht lange, denn gerade biegt Helmut um die Ecke. Hat er etwas mitbekommen? Helmut sieht verärgert aus. Verärgert und hungrig. Er reißt die Tür auf, setzt sich auf einen Hocker und fängt an zu hetzen:

Helmut: *„Hast du den Neger gesehen? Der nimmt mir den Arbeitsplatz weg!"*

Eve: *„Aber du hast doch gar keinen Arbeitsplatz!"*

Helmut: *„Das ist es ja gerade! Wenn der nicht den LKW da fahren würde, kann ich den fahren!"*

Eve: *„Aber du hast doch gar keinen Führerschein mehr."*

Helmut: *„Ich könnte aber einen haben! Und nicht mal Deutsch kann der!"*

Eve: *„Warum das denn?"*

Helmut: *„Hast Du nicht gehört, was der gerufen hat?"*

Eve wird ganz schlecht, sie muss sich setzen. Aber Helmut redet weiter.

Helmut: *„Der wollte sich über mich lustig machen! ‚Haben wir Fernseher!' Was soll das? Sehe ich etwa so aus? Ich habe zwar keinen Job, aber einen Fernseher hab ich schon!"*

Grammar stuff – Chapter 16

"legen", "stellen", "hängen" *vs.* "liegen", "stehen", "hängen"

You have to differentiate between the verbs* "legen", "stellen", "sich setzen", "hängen" *and the verbs* "liegen", "stehen", "sitzen", "hängen". *They sound nearly the same in your ears, they nearly look like each other and* "hängen" *even is exactly the same verb as* "hängen". *However, you always have to see the difference in the use of these verbs.

1.) The first group of verbs *("legen", "stellen", "sich setzen", "hängen")* are regular verbs which express an activity. You can always ask the question *"Wohin?"* which indicates that these verbs often stand with prepositions of place and by that need to be followed by the accusative.

2.) The second group of verbs *("liegen", "stehen", "sitzen", "hängen")* are irregular verbs that are focussed on the result of the activity which happened before. In that case the prepositions of place are followed by the dative. In these verbs nothing happens, something stays where it is. So you can always ask the question *"Wo?"*.

You may have seen several examples in the text about Eve and Mobutu but over here you will also get a number of examples so you better understand.

legen = *to put*	liegen = *to lie*
Eve legt die Ketwürste auf den Grill.	Helmut liegt auf dem Sofa.
Eve puts the sausages on the grill.	*Helmut is lying on his sofa.*
INFINITIVE = **legen**	INFINITIVE = **liegen**
PRESENT PERFECT = **hat gelegt**	PRESENT PERFECT = **hat gelegen**
stellen = *to put*	**stehen = *to stand, to be***
Sven stellt eine Stange Wasser ins Klo.	Doreen steht in Hundescheiße.
Sven puts a rod of water in the toilet.	*Doreen is standing in dog shit.*
INFINITIVE = **stellen**	INFINITIVE = **stehen**
PRESENT PERFECT = **hat gestellt**	PRESENT PERFECT = **hat gestanden**
hängen = *to hang*	**hängen = *to hang***
Die Iraker hängen Saddam Hussein.	Saddam Hussein hängt am Galgen.
The Iraqis hang Saddam Hussein.	*Saddam Hussein hangs on the gallows.*

INFINITIVE = **hängen**	INFINITIVE = **hängen**
PRESENT PERFECT = **hat gehängt**	PRESENT PERFECT = **hat gehangen**
sich setzen = *to sit down*	sitzen = *to sit*
Israelis und Araber setzen sich zusammen zu Gesprächen.	Israelis und Araber sitzen in einem Bus.
Israelis and Arabs are sitting down to have a talk.	*Israelis and Arabs are sitting in a bus.*
INFINITIVE = **sich setzen**	INFINITIVE = **sitzen**
PRESENT PERFECT = **hat sich gesetzt**	PRESENT PERFECT = **hat gesessen**

The indefinite pronouns "*ein-*" and "*kein-*"

The pronouns *"einer"*, *"eine"*, *"ein(e)s"* stand for one person or object from a number of persons or objects (see also the English equivalent "a" or "no"). The plural in the nominative and the accusative is always welche and in the dative it is *"welchen"*. The negative form is *"kein"* which is declined like *"ein"*.

Too much theory? You want any examples? Here you get them.

Ich habe sieben Verkehrsunfälle gehabt.
Einen hatte ich erst gestern.

I have had seven car crashes.
One of them was just yesterday.

3 Taschendiebe sind geschnappt worden.
Keiner hatte eine Atombombe gestohlen.

Three pickpockets have been caught.
None of them had stolen an a-bomb.

Haben Sie Kinder entführt?
Ja. Ich habe ***welche*** entführt.

Have you kidnapped any children?
Yes. I have kidnapped some.

To make it easier for you here is another table we made.

SINGULAR	MASCULINE	FEMININE	NEUTER
NOMINATIVE	ein***er*** / kein***er***	ein***e*** / kein***e***	ein***(e)s*** / kein***(e)s***
ACCUSATIVE	ein***en*** / kein***en***	ein***e*** / kein***e***	ein***(e)s*** / kein***(e)s***
DATIVE	ein***em*** / kein***em***	ein***er*** / kein***er***	ein***em*** / kein***em***
PLURAL	**MASCULINE**	**FEMININE**	**NEUTER**
NOMINATIVE	welch***e*** / kein***e***	welch***e*** / kein***e***	welch***e*** / kein***e***
ACCUSATIVE	welch***e*** / kein***e***	welch***e*** / kein***e***	welch***e*** / kein***e***
DATIVE	welch***en*** / kein***en***	welch***en*** / kein***en***	welch***en*** / kein***en***

Exercises – Chapter 16

"Legen" ***or*** **"liegen?" "Stellen"** ***or*** **"stehen?" "Sitzen"** ***or*** **"sich setzen?" "Hängen"** ***or*** **"hängen"** ***or*** **"hängen?"** ***Too many words, too little sense? Then why don't you take the above mentioned words and put them correctly in the gaps we left in the text below because we are nice people.***

.... die Hände über den Kopf!

Helmut .... eine Flasche Bier in den Kühlschrank.

Eve .... auf Mobutu, wenn sie Sex hat.

Doreen .... im Nagelstudio und nicht in der Schule.

Opa Dolfi .... im Garten eine Deutschlandfahne auf.

Schacklihn .... sich auf ihren dicken Hintern.

Opa Dolfi .... seltsamerweise nicht im Kriegsverbrecherverzeichnis.

Svengsters Hosen .... fast auf dem Boden.

We desperately need to complete the sentences with indefinite pronouns. If we do not do so, our ship will sink and we all will drown or freeze to death in this wide blue and icy ocean.

Ich hole mir gleich auf dem Strich einen Tripper. Möchtest Du auch ....

Nein! Ich hatte schon .... Ich will echt .... mehr haben.

Haben Sie auch ein BigMac-McTasty-Menu in ihrem Imbiss?

Nein, aber da vorne ist ein McDonalds. Da gibt es bestimmt ....

Ein paar Kondome liegen im Wohnzimmer herum. In der Küche, dem Bad, Doreens Zimmer und auf der Fensterbank hin zum Hof liegen auch noch ....

Haben Sie Kontakt zu diesem Mann mit einem Bein gehabt, Frau Schmidt?

Nein. Ich kenne Männer mit zwei Beinen und Männer mit drei Beinen, aber .... mit nur einem Bein, kenne ich nicht.

Sprechen Sie auch Kishuaheli?

Nein. Und ich kenne auch .... aus Kishuahelistan.

B Bonus-Track – Chapter 16

Public holidays in Germany

All in all there are 73 public holidays in Germany. You might guess that the Germans are very lazy but that is wrong. They are only quite inventive when it comes to holidays. For example every single German has the right to proclaim 4 to 6 personal public holidays per annum. Let's just give you an example.

Let's have a look at Bernd Müller. Bernd Müller is *"Sachverwaltungsbeamter"* at a revenue office. On Monday on his way back from work he sees a bright purple car in which a white dog is barking at him. Bernd Müller is shocked and angry and starts getting nausea. On the next day he calls the office and instead of calling in sick he says that today is his personal public holiday, the "First annual Day against bright purple cars with white barking dogs inside". Instead of firing him immediately his bosses will congratulate him on the next day he comes back to his office. This is because he proved to be inventive. And isn't that what every economy needs nowadays: Ideas, ideas, ideas and innovations, innovations and innovations.

Germany is one of the leading nations concerning new ideas and inventions and patents as has already been mentioned some chapters before. Throughout the year there are tournaments and competitions of who had the greatest public holiday idea and at the end of every year there are the finals where every company and every public office sends their best contenders to. Since the beginning of these "Public Holidays Idea Championships" there have only been two contestants that didn't work in an office. To give you a better impression of what the winners in the last five years were, here is the list of champions.

2005 – Friedrich Müllerslust:	1. Ich-hab-heute-einfach-keine-Lust-Gedenktag *1st Today-I-just-don't-wanna-do-a-thing-Memorial Day*
2006 – Paul-Hans Franz:	1. Durchfall-durch-unabgekochtes-Kranenwassertrinken-Feiertag *1st Diarrhea-because-of-drinking-uncooked-water- from-out-of-a-water-tap public holiday*

2007 – Herbert Siebenhoden:	1. Erster-Amselschiss-auf-meinem-neuen-strahlend-gelben-Auto-Gedenktag *1st First-feces-of-blackbird-on-my-shiny-yellow-new-car-Memorial Day*
2008 – Kevin Bindegeweber:	1. Erster-Alles-Gedenktag *1st First-of-all-Memorial Day*
2009 – Zebbedäus Adolph:	1. Abwrackprämiengedenktag *1st Wreckage-Bonus Memorial Day*

It is evident that the list of honour is completely conquered by men. You may wonder why, but isn't it evident? You really do not get it? Why should women be forced to invent something when they are not allowed to work? German women usually sit at home gardening their gardens and children, cooking meals like potato mash or Wiener Schnitzel for their husbands. Sure, there are some women who really want to work, but they are fooled by the men who hire them as gardeners, kindergarten teachers or cooks or – much more cunning – as personal assistant who then has to cook, garden or teach the children of the male employer. As you see, we German men are extremely cunning – some might even say that we are assholes but who cares about these stupid, short-dicked imbeciles who only talk shit when they open their stinking mouths?

Chapter 17

Der Svengster wird schwul

Svengster und Doreen schauen gemeinsam Fernsehen, als auf einmal Bruce Darnell (der ehemalige Supermodel-Coach) zu sehen ist. Dem Svengster wird auf einmal ganz mulmig und Doreen merkt das natürlich.

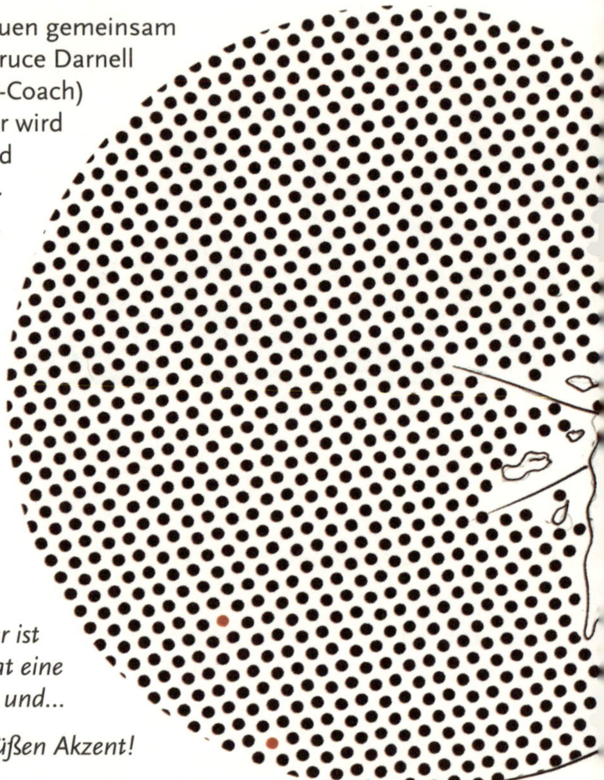

Doreen: *Was ist denn mit dir los, Sven?*

Sven: *Ich weiß auch nicht. Irgendwie ist mir nicht so gut.*

Doreen: *Seltsam. Das ist so, seit Bruce zu sehen war.*

Sven: *Bruce, Bruce, Bruce! Was soll denn an dem schon dran sein!*

Doreen: *Na, er ist schwarz, er ist dünn, er ist austrainiert, er hat eine Glatze, er kann sich bewegen und...*

Sven: *...und er hat voll den süßen Akzent!*

Doreen glaubt, sie hat gerade eben nicht richtig gehört. Ist Ihr Bruder auf einmal schwul geworden? Ihr Bruder, ein schwuler Gangsterrapper und Bettnässer! Mit großen Augen dreht sie sich zu Svengster um, schaut ihm zuerst in den Schritt (ist da nicht eine Beule zu sehen?) und dann ins Gesicht.

Doreen: *Svengster!*

Sven: *Ja? Was ... was ist?*

Doreen: *Du hast gerade gesagt, du würdest Bruce süß finden ... Bist du jetzt auch noch schwul?*

Sven: *Das würde ich ja wohl wissen! Nur, weil ich Bruce süß finde, seine Geschmeidigkeit anbete und seinen Körper verehre wie einen nubischen Tempel, bin ich doch nicht schwul!*

Doreen beobachtet ihren Bruder. Dem Svengster steht Schweiß auf der Stirn, sein Gesicht ist knallrot, seine Zunge streicht immer wieder über seine Lippen; verzweifelt versucht er, eine Erektion zu verbergen. Doreen hat genug und schaltet um auf die RTL 2 Action News.

Zwei Wochen später.

Es ist 22 Uhr. Vor dem Haus der Schmidts steht ein dunkelhäutiger Mann mit tief ins Gesicht gezogenem Kapuzenpulli. Er drückt eine Klingel und nach kurzem Warten wird ihm die Tür geöffnet. Der Mann verschwindet im Hauseingang.

Helmut kommt heute ausnahmsweise früher aus seiner Stammkneipe nach Hause. Die Frau seines Wirtes ist am morgen zerstückelt aufgefunden worden und der muss sich jetzt um die Beerdigung kümmern. Helmut ist nicht gut gelaunt, weil er noch nicht genug getrunken hat. Übel gelaunt pinkelt er ans Auto der Nachbarn, ehe er das Haus betritt. Er wankt zu seiner Wohnung, schließt auf, öffnet den Kühlschrank und ist entsetzt. Da sind doch gestern noch drei Bierflaschen gewesen!

Wütend macht sich Helmut auf die Suche nach dem verschwundenen Bier. Er sucht im Elternschlafzimmer, im Hobbykeller, in Doreens Zimmer, ja sogar im Bad und im Spülkasten der Toilette sucht Helmut. „Natürlich sind alle weg, wenn man mal was sucht! Wenn Eve wenigstens da wäre! Die würde mir neues Bier holen gehen!"

Aber Helmut gibt nicht auf und sucht weiter. Auf dem Balkon hat er noch nicht nachgeschaut. Als er dort steht, hört er seltsame Geräusche. Es schabt, es quietscht und zwischendrin meint er, er würde den Svengster jammern hören. Helmut ist verwirrt. Da! Dieser Schrei! Das war doch der Svengster! Bestimmt hat der wieder Ärger mit irgendwelchen anderen Rappern.

Aufgeregt stürzt Helmut in Svengsters Zimmer und erstarrt. Sein Bier! Zwei Bierflaschen stehen ausgetrunken auf dem Boden. Svengster liegt auf dem Bauch im Bett, im Hintern Svengsters steckt ein schwarzer Mann und im Hintern des Schwarzen steckt eine volle Bierflasche. Helmut handelt sofort. Mit Schwung zieht er die zum Glück noch volle Flasche aus dem Hintern des Schwarzen.

Erst jetzt bemerken Svengster und der Schwarze Helmut. Helmut wischt den Flaschenhals kurz mit etwas Spucke und seinem Unterhemd ab und verlässt den Raum. Kurze Zeit später kommt auch Eve nach Hause. Als sie gerade ihren lila Lackmantel an der Garderobe aufhängt, kommt ein schwarzer junger Mann aus Svengsters Zimmer. Eve und der junge Mann erschrecken sehr, denn sie kennen sich gut. Es ist Mobutu! Aus dem Wohnzimmer ruft Helmut: *„Hey, Eve! Unser Sohn ist jetzt schwul! Erst Gangstarapper, jetzt schwul! Ich hab es ja immer schon kommen sehen!"*

Mobutu wird leicht rot und ist sehr verlegen. Ehe Helmut aus dem Wohnzimmer gewankt kommt, gibt er Eve noch schnell einen Zungenkuss. Dann verlässt er die Wohnung. Eve weint im Flur, Svengster weint in seinem Zimmer, Helmut hat Freudentränen in den Augen, weil er doch noch ein Bier gefunden hat.

GROSS
KONZERN

Grammar Stuff – Chapter 17

In this chapter you will learn a lot about word formation in the German language. There are several possibilities to form words and the good thing about them is that it is not really that difficult.

From a verb to a noun

The easiest thing to form a noun from a verb is by putting the article before the verb and writing the former verb with a capital letter.

Examples:	rauchen	***das R***auchen
	ficken	***das F***icken
	saufen	***das S***aufen

From adjectives to nouns

It is also quite easy to form a noun from an adjective. To do that you also have to capitalize the adjective and in some cases you also have to add the ending "-e".

Examples:
Das ***Kriminelle*** am Amoklaufen ist, dass ***Unschuldige*** getötet werden.
What's criminal about runnig amuck is the killing of innocent people.

Dr. Tod von der CDU: Das ***Langhaarige,*** das ist der Herr Lamp.
Dr. Death from the CDU: That long haired thing over there is Mr. Lamp.

Das ***Grün*** steht Dir kein bisschen.
That green doesn't fit you at all.

Das ***Große*** an dieser Sache ist, dass niemand weiß, worum es geht.
The big thing about it is that no one knows what it's all about.

Verb + noun = new noun

Another possibility to form a new noun is taking a verb, dropping the ending "-en" and then adding a noun.

Examples:	schwitzen	der Kasten	**der Schwitzkasten**
	to sweat	*the box*	*headlock*

Examples:	essen *to dine*	das Zimmer *the room*	**das Esszimmer** *dining room*

adjective + noun = new noun

However you can also form a new noun by combining a noun with an adjective.

Examples:

voll *absolute*	der Wichser *the wanker*	**der Vollwichser** *absolute wanker*
dumm *dumb*	die Fresse *the face*	**die Dummfresse** *dumb face*

Subjunctive with *"würde"* and INFINITIVE

You use the subjunctive with **"würde"** ***+ INFINITIVE when you express wishes or ask for favors in a polite way.***

Examples:

Ich würde dir gerne die Fresse einschlagen.
I would like to trash your face.

Würdest Du mich mal am Arsch lecken?
Would you please go and fuck yourself?

Just to help you a little bit: Here is the conjugation of the subjunctive of **"sein".**

SINGULAR	
ich	würd***e***
du	würd***est***
Sie	würd***en***
er / sie / es	würd***e***
PLURAL	
wir	würd***en***
ihr	würd***et***
Sie	würd***en***
sie	würd***en***

Exercises – Chapter 17

There you have several words, nouns and adjectives and verbs. Now make the best of it and combine them in the right way.

brechen	hacken	billig	grün	lecker	hundert
Schmecker	Nutte	Fresse	Schimmel	***Durchfall***	Füßer

Example: Der Brechdurchfall

....

....

....

....

....

Complete the following sentences with the appopriate nouns which are constructed out of the following verbs: **"wichsen", "Nase bohren", "springen", "singen"**

Das .... aus dem 40. Stock ist ungesund.

Beim.. kannst du verbluten.

Das .... macht dich irgendwann blind.

Das .... in der Fußgängerzone bringt nichts.

What do you really want to do? We know it. So build sentences from what we gave you using the subjunctive and tell us what you would wish to do.

in die Bank gehen, alles Geld abheben und es an den Grosskonzern schicken

....

die beiden Herausgeber dieses Buches heiraten

....

Herrn Heldrich und Herrn Lamp viele viele Kinder schenken

....

oben genannten Männern immer gut kochen und auch das Geschirr abspülen

....

More "würde" + INFINITIVE

Many people daydream and would like to be another person or to do something extraordinary...

Sie sind Dr. Evil:
(gerne die Welt beherrschen)

....

Sie war Saddam Hussein
(gerne wie Mr. T sein)

....

Sie sind Herr und Frau Blutwurst.
(gerne Rindfleisch verkaufen)

....

Das sind die Herausgeber von „Deutsch für den Ausländer".
(gerne drei Millionen Exemplare dieses Buches verkaufen)

....

Bonus-Track – Chapter 17

Germany on a smaller scale – The German Vereinswesen

Italy has the Mafia, Russia, too and the Americans have their evangelical Christians and the Germans, they have their *"Vereine"* – or as one says in English "clubs". Sure, every country has clubs like football clubs, baseball clubs or any other sport club, but Germany's clubs are much more than that. The German *"Vereinswesen"* (club culture) is something completely different, especially in more rural countrysides.

Over there, the clubs are more powerful than anywhere else. The main clubs that lead smaller communities are mostly the *"Freiwillige Feuerwehr"* or the *"Musikvereine"*. Approximately 80 % of the people living in villages are members of these clubs and because of this fact these clubs elect the mayor, who is very grateful and gives money from the village to the clubs who in return re-elect him. Of course the mayor is also a member of these clubs. If you do not join at least one of the clubs, you become some kind of an outsider and it would be better if you leave the village sooner or later. The clubs will ask you for protection money and if you do not pay, they'll burn down your house, car or your house and the garage in which your car seemed protected.

The police will not help you because they belong to the clubs, the church will not help you because the *"Musikverein"* plays on Good Friday processions or on Christmas Eve and so it is best to join one of the clubs. However, how do you join one of them? First of all, you have to swear an oath that there is only one thing which is important to you: The *"Verein"*. You have to show you do not care about your family or your loved ones by sacrificing one of them or at least one or two limbs of yourself, preferably toes because if you sacrificed a finger it would be difficult for you to play an instrument like the trumpet, the flute or the tuba. People who sacrifice a finger have to play the kettledrum, the tymbal or become conductor of the *"Musikverein"*.

The thing is that the senior members of the club want to see that you are ready to bleed for the community. Secondly, you have to eat at least seven Schnitzels in a row and drink two bottles of schnapps called *"Himbeergeist"*. Some of the readers might be reminded of Spring Break in the US, but Spring Break is nothing compared to the German *"Vereinswesen"*. Having eaten and drunk as much as any human is possibly able to do, you have to sing German *"Schlager"* and *"Volksmusik"* (which has nothing to do with "folk music") for two and a half hours without puking. If you are not already dead after that, the final task may finish you off. The last thing you have to do is to get in your car and drive drunk at least 50 kilometres through an area in which there is no civilization at all, just forest.

There are however other possibilities to join a club which, on the other hand, are not much better. You can try and bribe the chairman of the club (always remember: Bribing is very big in Germany. Just look at wikipedia or google *"Bestechung"* and *"Volkswagen"* or *"Siemens"* or *"Politiker"*) or you can marry the ugly children of high-ranking club members. If you chose the second possibility always remember that a divorce is impossible in this case and marriage ends with the death of one of the partners.

At this point you are probably a little bit frightened and intimidated by the German *"Vereinswesen"* but everything sounds harder than it actually is. Why don't you found your own *"Verein"* and intimidate other existing clubs? All you need is strong and healthy followers, psychotic behaviour, a few weapons and some unlucky coincidences that dispatch your enemies. It is a little bit more difficult than in the US to get weapons in Germany but it is still not impossible. The easiest way to get them is to join a *"Schützenverein"* (shooting club) or to buy them at Frankfurt main station or on other black markets. If you need information just go to an *"Internet-Verein"* and look it up, but be sure that Wolfgang Schäuble or Ursula von der Leyen (another strange-looking German secretary of state) isn't sitting right next to your computer.

B Bonus-Track – Chapter 17

Die Autoren

FLORIAN LAMP

(* 20.01.1977 in Siershahn / Westerwald) machte sich einen Namen als „Mann mit Ideologie", den „man hier nicht gebrauchen könne" (vgl. H. Sendlmeier), Rebellenführer der „Generation P bis Z", und Gründer der Roto-Bewegung, deren Rotor I er auch ist. Schon in frühester Kindheit war er zu außergewöhnlichen Leistungen fähig, wie sein erster Platz bei den DLRG-Meisterschaften der Ortsgruppe Wirges 1986 beweist.

Nach einem Studium der Meedchenwissenschaften und Sozial- und Wirtschaftsgeschichte in Marburg, der Teilnahme am „Schreiblabor Pornographie" beim bekannten Autoren Thomas Hettche, diversen Praktika und einem sagenumwobenen Irak-Aufenthalt, in dessen Rahmen er als Supervisor der US-Army tätig war und doppelt ausgezeichnet wurde, entschied er sich fürs Exil im Luftkurort Schlüchtern.

Dort absolvierte er ein Volontariat im Verlagswesen beim damals noch feinen Rockbuch Verlag und sammelte Kräfte für die Verlagsgründung von „DER GROSSKONZERN" in Berlin.

Diverse Fernsehauftritte (u.a. bei arte, RTL, SAT 1, dem RBB und Phoenix) im Rahmen seiner Rebellentätigkeit bleiben hier nur kurz am Rande erwähnt. Zudem erwarb sich Lamp einen Ruf als „Millionär der Herzen", als er zweimal erfolglos versuchte, bei „Wer wird Millionär?" in die Mitte zu kommen und dort die Frage mit „Ich!" zu beantworten.

Lamp lebt, liebt und arbeitet in Berlin und wenn man Glück hat, kann man ihn in Vollmondnächten durch den Tiergarten heulen hören.

HELDRICH JOHANNES

(* 13.02.1979 in Alzenau / i. Ufr.) entstammt, nach eingehender Ahnenforschung von Sebastian Th. Lollschied, dem Herrschergeschlecht der Merowinger und soll nach Ls. Angaben direkter Nachfahre von Theuderich I. sein. Dies ist allerdings nicht durch Quellenzeugnisse gesichert. Parallelen sind jedoch besonders in der frühen Affinität zur Infantrie zu erkennen. H. erziehlte dort als Junker besondere Erfolge bei ihm übertragenen Lehraufgaben im Bereich Führernachwuchs. Allerdings erlangte er innerhalb seiner Militärzeit lediglich den Rang des Generalisten. Dies veranlasste Ihn, dem Ruf des Redundanten zu folgen, um sich künftig als Propagandist zu verdingen.

In dieser Zeit hatte H. die erste jungfräuliche Begegnung mit der großen Weltliteratur als er als 19-jähriger Adoleszent E. Henscheid eine Wurfsendung in den Briefkasten steckte. Von diesem nachhaltig prägenden Ereignis beflügelt schuf er dann noch kurz mit Herrn Lamp eine Kanzlerin und entschwand in die leichte Zunft, um fortan die Welt als Kunstmaler zu beglücken.

Zusätzlich zu Farbe und Form widmet sich H. insbesondere seiner floralen Leidenschaft: der Züchtung und Veredelung von Acer Heldreichii, dem, seiner botanischen Erfolge zu Ehren, nach ihm benannten Griechischen Ahorn.

Neben leicht tyrannischen Tendenzen sagt man ihm nach, ganz gut kochen zu können, was sicherlich nicht auf die – wie man munkelt – Verbindungen zu den Musikergrößen Reimer Reiner, Karl Kühl und Heinz Heiz zurückzuführen ist.

H. arbeitet nach Wagners „Die Kunst und die Revolution“ und überlegt z. Z., im Sinne des Gesamtkunstwerks, neben dem Master of the Universe, parallel noch einen Master of Arts im Fach „Holocaust und Toleranz” zu machen oder die Malerei ganz an den Nagel zu hängen, um nach Lederhose zu ziehen und dort Falkner zu werden.

Thanksgiving

Wir danken Gott, unseren Lisas (spezielles Danke für die Englisch-Korrektur des gesamten Buchs sowie hervorragende Suppen) und Lenas (besonderes Danke für die Druck-Ratschläge, Homepagedesign-Ratschläge und Druck-Beratung) und natürlich unseren Familien für Liebe, Unterstützung und so.

Außerdem sind wir sehr froh, dass wir mit Paul Nissler einen echten Englisch-Muttersprachler kennen. Paul hat alle Übersetzungen der deutschen Kapitel ins Englische besorgt und außerdem noch alle Bonus-Tracks in korrektes Englisch gebracht.

Nicht vergessen wollen wir außerdem alle Korrekturleser und –Leserinnen. Wenn man sein eigenes Buch mehrmals durchgelesen hat, wird man einfach betriebsblind. Danke, der Frau Doktor und der Lamp-Mama.

Außerdem danken wir Herrn Hübner von der Existenzgründerhilfe für die tolle Beratung bei der Gründung des GROSSKONZERNS. Merci, liebe Esther von den Zeugen Jehovas für diverse Besuche, die uns Kraft durch Ablenkung gaben. Noch zwei Sachen: Du sahst immer viel besser aus als deine Begleiterinnen und deine Stimme ist einfach unglaublich. Übrigens: Johannes mag frische Blumen, aber wir sind nicht schwul.

Womit wir bei unserem Kapellmeister Fist Pückler angekommen sind. Er hat uns allein durch seine Abwesenheit immer wieder zu Höchstleistungen getrieben und für Svengsters erste Singelauskopplung extra ein heißblütigen Araberhengst erschossen: Hey, Ho! We love yo!

Ebenfalls liebsten Dank schulden wir unserem Handmodel Tina Köhler, unserem Kniemodel, dem Rorschach-Einnässer und den Fotomodels auf den diversen Schwarzweißaufnahmen. Auch unseren echten Schmidts möchten wir ein dickes Danke hinterherbrüllen. Ihr wart noch besser als die Zeichnungen von Euch, und wir hoffen sehr, dass ihr uns jetzt, nachdem das Buch fertig ist, nicht übermäßig hasst. Aber mal abgesehen davon: Wer außer Hape Kerkeling kann von sich schon sagen, er sei eine wichtige Figur aus einem Bestseller? Die Buddenbrooks vielleicht, aber die waren Fake.

Wir danken dem Goethe-Institut, das ungefragt von einer Förderung des Projekts abgesehen hat und sich jetzt bei dem Riesenerfolg, den „Deutsch für den Ausländer" hat, bestimmt in den Arsch beißt, fast allen Massenmedien für hervorragende Propagandadienste, den diversen Feuilletonisten und Feuilletonistinnen, die unser Buch zerrissen, gelobt oder nicht mal reingeguckt haben, den Rand- und Nichtrandgruppen, die sich durch dieses Buch beleidigt fühlen. Wir entschuldigen uns bei all denen, die wir zu empören vergessen haben. Bitte schreiben Sie uns, damit wir im zweiten Teil auch Sie beleidigen können.

Wir freuen uns, wenn Sie sich an diesem Buch freuen, wenn Sie sich aber nicht freuen, dann freuen wir uns trotzdem, weil Sie das Buch ja bereits gekauft haben. Schreiben Sie uns, beleidigen Sie uns, loben Sie uns, beweihräuchern Sie uns.

ACHTUNG: Wenn Sie jemand anderes beleidigen, loben oder beweihräuchern wollen, wenden Sie sich bitte nicht an uns.

Folgende Kontaktmöglichkeiten stehen Ihnen offen:

Elektrisch: lob@der-grosskonzern.de
motzen@der-grosskonzern.de
buchkaufen@der-grosskonzern.de

Mental: Der kosmische Bestellservice

Translations

Preamble

Textbooks are usually boring. Language textbooks are usually somehow okay because they can be pictorially glamorized – for example you can draw revolvers and machine guns in the hands of all the people in the drawings and photos. In the 1990s this was still possible without any danger for you to be directly dragged to the school psychologist when these improved pictures were discovered.

But we don't want to be stuck reminiscing of the good old days. The present book is a language textbook. Really horrifying were – and they definitely still are – math books. Due to the fact that none of us editors is really good at maths, we've principally concentrated on the German language because this is what we understand. We've mixed ze whole zing wizz English because we also know zis quiet very good well, please, mein Führer!

The foreigner, who inherits this book, in order to learn the wonderful German language, should get an unprettified and above all non-falsified picture of Germany, its inhabitants, its customs and traditions. One should discern that we Germans can really be very ugly, without any sense of humour and that we're not even the perfectionists that other people abroad always think we are.

Despite this, the foreigner should be conscious of how important Germany and the Germans are, when this planet wants to overcome the financial crisis, and later other crises like global warming, birth crises or an impact from a one kilometre-long meteorite not far from the French Atlantic coast.

The German genius is largely unbroken. Not too long ago the first auto-scrap bonus premium was invented, a good 100 years ago the car, and shortly before that the wheel – all original German inventions just like the world-war, National Socialism and a week of tenant-responsible cleaning of staircase and pavement. We, the inventors of this book, want to contribute to this, that the world may enjoy the German essence but don't have any plans to invade Poland and can only reiterate and point out that there is definitely no Heldrich-Putin-pact.

We are peaceful pacifists, who wouldn't touch a fly, as long as it's beyond our reach and we don't have any fly swatters. Until now, there's only been one universal language: the language of love. With help from this book, German should equally become a language of love. Then it shouldn't matter that world-wide and until now other languages like English, Russian, Portuguese or French are spoken by more people than German.

We plan to be more successful with this book than Charlotte Roche with her "Wet areas" or God with the bible. If this isn't the case, then the publisher will continue to print this book until it comes to what would happen if that stupid math lesson in which a chess board and rice grains play a big role became true. You know the lesson, in which you have a chess board and then put 1 grain on the first square, then 2 grains on the next, then 4 on the next, then 16, then 256, then... In the end you would have so many rice grains on the chess board that the whole world would be covered in rice.

If you now change the words "rice grain" to "German for the Foreigner", the whole surface of the earth (including the oceans) would be covered 2.3 centimetres high with copies of "German for Foreigners". Buy this book, learn with this book and give this book to the male and female foreigner. They'll be thankful.

Chapter 1 – The Schmidts

This is the Schmidt family. The Schmidts are a typical German family.

"Hello Schmidt family!"

Father: *"Ah, keep your mouth shut!"*

Reporter: *"Mr. Schmidt, are you from Germany?"*

Father: *"Where else do you think I'm from? The moon?"*

Helmut Schmidt is unemployed. He was educated to be a parachute jumper and worked as an unofficial employee of the Stasi which was the secret intelligence service of the German Democratic Republic. Apart from that he likes to drink a lot of alcohol.

Reporter: *"Cheers, Mr. Schmidt!"*

Daughter: *"Hello! I am Doreen Schmidt. I'm 14 years old and I don't go to school. School sucks!"*

Mother: *"You don't go to school, Doreen? Well, it doesn't matter. My name is Eve and I work at a snack bar. I love Ket sausage, my husband and life. Where is our son, Sven?"*

Son: *"Here I am. I am Svengster, an original big gangster and when it's not hot, then it's not my thing, ya!"*

Mother: *"Sven still wets the bed frequently. He just acts tough. He's really a good kid."*

Chapter 2 – The Svengster at the dealer

Svengster: *"Hey, dude! I'm the Svengster! A real gangster..."*

Dealer: *"Oh, close your trap! Come on in my pad. What do you need?"*

Svengster: *"A fat one!"*

Dealer: *"Here are my selling rooms. Sit down in the beanbag! Do you want speed, coke, heroine, hash, or rather a flavored limonade?"*

Svengster: *"A flavored lemonade? Do you have Fanta as well?"*

Dealer: *"Back there is my lab. We make crystal meth here. Over there is the bath. You can really pinch it there. And the room over there is our arsenal."*

Svengster: *"Wow! You sell arms? Do you also have a flame thrower and some mashine guns?*

Dealer: *"Sure. We also have some awesome liquid explosives."*

Svengster: *"And who's that on the poster up there?"*

Dealer: *"They're the No Angels. Whenever I sniff a line and see this poster, then I jerk off..."*

Svengster: *"Oh yeah... It's alright. I'm a fan of Bushido. Do you know him?"*

Dealer: *"Is that the gangster from Berlin Tempelhof? From the skyline to the gutter? All good comes from behind, right? Is that the one with the autobiography?*

Svengster: *"Exactly! That's him!"*

Dealer: *"Nah. I don't know him."*

Chapter 3 – The Svengster at school

Sven, the Svengster, goes to school. Here he meets He-Man Müller, She-Do and MC Fire-alarm. None of the three like the Svengster very much.

Svengster: *"Hey guys! Should we battle a bit?"*

He-Man: *"Ah, shut up, Svengster! Go beg on your own!"*

She-Do: *"I'll punch you in the face if you like?"*

MC Fire-alarm: *"How often do we have to tell you that we don't like you!"*

Svengster: *"You shouldn't be so mean all the time! We could at least talk a bit. I also bought drugs!"*

She-Do: *"We aren't allowed to take drugs anymore."*

MC Fire-alarm: *"It's off-limits for us at school."*

Svengster: *"And now you don't do drugs anymore?"*

He-Man: *"No! We're now against drugs. For drugs are misleading! Despite this, can you give me some after school?"*

Svengster: *"I can sell you drugs."*

He-Man, She-Do and MC Fire-alarm: *"Sell?! Let us speak very clearly to you: Give us all your drugs! Now!"*

Svengster: *"No! Only for money!"*

He-man and his friends don't want to wait nor pay and beat-up the Svengster together. She-Do kicks the Svengster in the balls, He-Man beats the Svengster "in his stupid mouth" and MC- Fire-alarm stabs the Svengster with a knife through the kneecap. Then they take his drugs.

Svengster: *"Ah, crap! They say: Three against one is unfair!"*

He-Man: *"I only know 'Three times is just in Bremen'."*

MC Fire-alarm: *"Whoever makes out three times with the same one, already belongs to the establishment!"*

She-Do: *"And I always say 3 and 3 is 9!"*

Svengster wants to contradict them, but the ambulance is already there. The paramedics bring him to hospital.

Chapter 4 – A day in the life of Helmut Schmidt

11 a.m.: Helmut awakes and gets up. First, he drinks a wake-up beer. He goes to the kitchen and lights himself a cigarette. Then he looks out of the window and yells out insults against foreigners.

Helmut: *"The Russian is an all-round danger and eats kids! The Chinaman is yellow and stinks! The Iranian is right. Italians are cowards. The American is completely out of his mind and absolutely dumb. The Somalian isn't any better. The Spaniard is a paella-eater..."*

2 p.m.: Helmut is tired of ranting. He lights his 30th cigarette and lays down in bed.

2:15 p.m.: The doorbell rings. Helmut is pissed-off and opens the door. It's Ivo. Ivo is a drug buddy of the Svengster. He wants to sell newspaper subscriptions.

Ivo: *"Hello! I'm Ivo and I'm from Kosovo."*

Helmut: *"Don't lie! You are from the slammer, Ivo. Aggravated assault!"*

Ivo: *"Yeah, it's okay. I need money. Would you like a newspaper subscription?"*

Helmut: *"No. I have a subscription to the BILD and the Nationalzeitung."*

Ivo: *"Perhaps your wife would like a Brigitte?"*

Helmut: *"No. She can't read. But I'll give you some money if you go to Kosovo, Switzerland or Iraq."*

Ivo: *"Thanks Mr. Schmidt."*

Helmut gives Ivo 10,000 euros and closes the door. He then says to himself: *"Foreigners! If you know one, you know them all. The foreigner is lazy, accomplishes nothing and steals our money. Work-avoiding swindlers. That is what they are!"* Helmut sits down on the couch, gets some hard liquor from the kitchen and watches "Judge Alexander Holt". He doesn't want to shower today.

5 p.m.: It's cold. Helmut notices that he's only wearing underpants.

5:35 p.m.: Helmut drinks booze and smokes. He's now wearing a jogging suit.

9:17 p.m.: Helmut wakes up. His family is sitting together in the living room watching "Germany seeks a Superstar." Helmut is happy. He lights a cigarette and gives his wife Eve and the children a couple of puffs. They finish off the booze together.

1:10 a.m.: Helmut falls asleep to the "sexy-clips" on the German Sports Channel.

Chapter 5 – Eve buys and sells

Eve owns a snack bar. She sells Ket sausage here. Ket sausage is made of Ket and sausage. Nobody knows exactly what Ket is and nobody knows what the sausage is made of. But it doesn't matter because there is glutamate. Today, Eve is buying at the city's central market. There's everything there, however sometimes she has to go to Poland to buy things on the black market. Eve has 500 euros in small, unmarked bills with her. She took the money from the Svengster. Now she's at the Ket sausage stand talking with the main seller at the Ket sausage stand.

Eve: *"How much does the bulk pack of light-green colored Ket sausage cost?"*

Seller: *"57 euros and 12 Cents."*

Eve: *"But they're already moldy!"*

Seller: *"It's good for the Ket sausage aroma."*

Eve: *"I'll give you 56 euros and 87 Cents."*

Seller: *"But I also have to make a living!"*

Eve: *"I have 2 kids, a husband and debt up to my nose from the nail studio. Please!"*

Seller: *"Maybe I can do something with the price. But you have a little to budge, too."*

Eve: "Anything! Anything that you want!"

10 minutes later. Eve leaves the central market. Besides the bulk pack, she also got a dime bag of powdered milk which was produced in Minsk (Ukraine), 27 hand-counted bread powdered rolls and 2 free tickets for a musical from Michael Flatley about the Turkish genoicide of the Armenians. Eve is happy and drives to her Ket sausage-stand.

She peels the nastiest of the mold from the sausages, warms them up in old fat, puts on her apron and starts selling.

Customer: *"Hi. I don't want any Ket sausage. I want a coke and exchange money!"*

Eve: *"Do I look like a bank?"*

Customer: *"No, more like a tall, wide stool. Or a fat, comfortable leather chair."*

Eve: *"Aw, a comedian. How much money do you want to change?"*

Customer: *"This 300 euro bill here. Sorry, I don't have anything smaller."*

Eve: *"It's okay. 300 Ocken ... so Euronen minus the coke that makes 292.50 euros!"*

Customer: *"But isn't that a bit expensive for a coke, 7.50 euro!"*

Eve: *"That includes sales tax and average service! I also have to make a living!"*

Customer: *"I have 2 kids, a husband and debts from the nail studio!"*

Eve: *"Are you gay?"*

Customer: *"No. My husband is gay. I was completely surprised, when he told me – having been together for 3 years. But we saw one another seldomly, because he's blind and I'm a truck driver."*

Eve: *"I love trucks!"*

Customer: *"I think, this is the beginning of a beautiful friendship."*

Chapter 6 – Doreen and the casting

Doreen and her best friend Schacklihn are 13 years old and want to be superstars. Unfortunately, Doreen and Schacklihn don't look like superstars. But, this is something that they want to change. Together they're saving for a boob job. They're just not sure, who of them will enlarge one of their breasts.

Doreen and Schacklihn are going shopping today. They want to look good for the "superstar"-casting in the huge discotheque at the city limits. There are great clothes at "Restposten aus Birmingham – Mode aus Brest" ("Remnants from Birmingham – Style from Brest") at Kottbusser Damm.

Doreen: *"I love R.A.B.M.A.B.! There's awesome rags here. Don't you think?"*

Schacklin: *"Ya, I love gold miniskirts and also rose, and also pink."*

Doreen: *"And then the great stuff from Et Hertie!"*

Schacklihn: *"Ya, Et Hertie really has taste and style..."*

Doreen: *"Let's go to the Et Hertie Department, Schacklihn."*

Sales assistant to sales assistant: *"If only I would have stayed a federal judge!"*

Schacklin: *"Hi sales lady! Do you also have this t-shirt in double XL? The XL somehow feels a bit too small!"*

Sales assistant: *"Buy two of them and sew them together. With a bit of luck, it'll fit then."*

Doreen: *"I'm always telling you Schacklihn. Since you're no longer addicted to eating and puking but rather addicted to eating only, you should do more sports."*

Schacklin: *"That's not true. The color is unbelievably nice. Pink and gold! And with this glittery print on top. And the skull and crossbones are also fantastic."*

Doreen: *"Then I'll take this skirt here! It's perfect, giving a nice and tight stretch across my intimite area. Besides, it adorns my belly-button piercing."*

Schacklin: *"I'm not sure..."*

Doreen: *"Aw! That's also from Et Hertie!"*

Saleswoman: *"This skirt is only a belt, girls!"*

Doreen: *"You're only jealous, because you can't wear stuff like this anymore."*

Schacklihn: *"Right on! You shouldn't even go out on the street anymore!"*

Doreen: *"Naw! You should stay home and lock yourself in."*

Saleswoman: *"Please, stop! The register is on the ground floor."*

Schacklihn to Doreen: *"As if we wanted to pay!"*

Doreen and Schacklihn run, with their highheeled pumps, out of "Restposten aus Birmingham". They stumble and fall on their faces. The store detective catches both and prohibits them from entering the store again. Doreen and Schacklihn are sad. Now they can't buy any more clothes from Et Hertie.

Doreen: *"Shoot! How am I supposed to become a superstar now?"*

Schacklihn: *"Why 'I'? Didn't we both want to become superstars?"*

Doreen: *"When I say 'I', I mean 'we'!"*

Schacklin: *"Sometimes your're really philosophical."*

Chapter 7 – Breakfast at the Schmidt's

The Schmidt family got up at 10 a.m. this morning. They are all sitting at the breakfast table together when Helmut asks Eve something:

Helmut to Eve: *"What is there to eat, Eve?"*

Eve: *"What? What should there be? Strawberries with shit!"*

Svengster: *"Yummy! Strawberries! I love strawberries!"*

Helmut: *"Please don't talk to me like that, Eve. I do love you though. I'll also bring you something from the kiosk later."*

Eve: *"Aw Helmut! Really? I'm sorry! Then please get me a Nordhäuser Doppelkorn schnapps! A magnum bottle."*

Svengster: *"Dad! Mom! Doreen! I have something to tell you, guys."*

Doreen: *"Take a look at that. My brother has something important to share!"*

Eve: *"Aw Svenny! You don't have to tell us again that you wetted your bed. You'll grow out of it."*

Svengster: *"But that's not it..."*

Helmut: *"And so what's there to eat?"*

Eve: *"I'll get you a beer."*

Doreen: *"I also want a beer."*

Svengster: *"I..."*

Eve: *"Do you also want a beer, Svenny?"*

Svengster: *"No, I only want..."*

Eve: *"A coke?"*

Helmut: *"That's my boy! He wants a Coke Light and then after that a gay straw."*

Doreen: *"Totally gay, hey. You, Sven! Do you know what I'm going to call you from now on? Svenja!"*

Eve: *"Why are you guys so mean to my little Svenny!"*

Helmut: *"And so what's there to eat?"*

Eve: *"Wait a minute, Helmut."* To Svengster: *"Svenny, didn't you want to share something important with us?"*

Svengster: *"Oh, it's not so important."*

Doreen: *"Hey, please! First you make a big fuss and then you pull your tail between your legs like a sissy!"*

Helmut: *"I still want a beer, Eve! Beer is the best meal! Don't you kids agree?"*

Eve: *"Crap! The frozen pizza just burned in the oven."*

Doreen: *"Aw sucks, mom!"*

Svengster: *"It's not so bad. Doreen weighs too much anyway."*

Doreen: *"Shut up, Svenja!"*

Recipe: Strawberries with shit
Ingredients for 4 people:

500 grams of fresh or old strawberries, sugar and salt, 2 spoons of cow excrement (at the butcher's), 2/3 lemon (full of pesticides) Preparation: Put a few drops of lemon on the cow excrement. Then mash up everything with a butcher until it becomes lightly fluffly. Pour equal measures in small glass bowls, quarter the strawberries, rinse and carefully press in the lemon-shit-slosh. At the end sprinkle according to taste with sugar and/or salt. Done.

Chapter 8 – Svengster on the run

Svengster is at a hip-hop event. He meets a pair of enemy rappers here with whom he had some beef. The situation escalates as the bad gangster rapper Hard Sack tips a beer over on Svengster's head. Svengster is peepingly mad and yells at Hard Sack.

Svengster: *"Hey, Hard Sack! Fuck your mother!"*

Hard Sack: *"Fuck YOUR mother!"*

Svengster: *"Hey, buddy! What did you say?! Fuck your mother?!"*

Hard Sack: *"Hey, what did YOU say?! Fuck your mother?!"*

Svengster: *"Is there an echo?! Fuck your father! Fuck your sister! Fuck your dog, son of a bitch!"*

Hard Sack: *"I'll fuck your TV! I'll fuck your sister and I'll fuck your fuck!"*

Svengster: *"Fuck yourself, fuckface!"*

Hard Sack has had enough and pulls his butterflyknife out of his fanny pack. He want's to stab Svengster, but the Svengster runs away. Hard Sack runs after him and loses his hiphop pants. Steamingly mad, he takes his pants off and continues to pursue the Svengster. Svengster runs straight outside, and hides amongst a group of pensioners from the city of Hanau. Hard Sack stands at the top of the stairs and looks for Svengster: *"Where is he? The other people say he ran out. When I see him again, there'll be a kasalla. I really want to finish him off!"*

Svengster crawls under a bus. *"Maybe I can hold on tight here and get away? I don't want to die yet. Crap! Today's really not my day. This fucking son of a dog whore's mother!"*

Svengster pissed himself again. The bus driver is perplexed about the puddle under his vehicle and discovers the scared Svengster under his bus.

Bus driver: *"What are you doing there? Rise from under there immediately!"*

Svengster: *"Sorry! My name is Sven Schmidt. The Hard Sack wants me knocked-off, the stupid fuckface!"*

Bus driver: *"Hey young man! Don't say that! That's not nice, do you understand!"*

Svengster: *"Yeah, don't you also use swear words once in a while?"*

Bus driver: *"No! Never! Come on. I'll drive you home with my bus. It smells like pee here all day."*

The bus driver, the pensioners and the Svengster get on the bus. Hard Sack doesn't find the Svengster and goes back inside. Svengster sits in the front next to the bus driver. The bus driver speaks into his microphone: *"Dear passengers from Runter-Reisen. We're going to take a shortcut and take this young gentleman home. Please take note: Don't eat any food on this bus!"* The bus drives over a red light and runs over a small vehicle with 8 people inside.

"Damn filth! Fucking shit! Now I have to go to the traffic test for idiots again and can't drink anymore alcohol when I drive!" The bus driver cries. Svengster wants to console him. The pensioners ask themselves if there'll be anything for dinner later on.

Chapter 9 – Girl talk

Eve and Doreen meet in the kitchen. Lately Doreen finds herself ugly and wants to know if Eve thinks so, too.

Doreen: *"Mom, I find myself so ugly. Do you also think that I'm ugly?"*

Eve: *"But Doreen! I'll answer you very sincerely: You are not ugly. Take a look at dad or the Svengster. Next to both of those hut faces, you look like a beautiful swan!"*

Doreen: *"You're saying that I look better than two hut faces. This compliment doesn't make things any better."*

Eve: *"You have my looks! I gave them to you. Trust me Doreen and believe your mother. I'll tell you all you need to know or wish that you'll be just as pretty as me..."*

Doreen: *"So you don't think that I'm pretty."*

Eve: *"But of course! When I see you and Schacklihn, I always think: two graces."*

Doreen: *"Graces! "*

Eve: *"Graces! Two good-looking women, one of them beeing of course too fat."*

Doreen: *"Schacklihn, right? After eating, she always orders 5 scoops of ice-cream with whipped cream at the creamery across the disco. She's been doing it for 3 years."*

Eve: *"Don't you do that! Ice cream is unhealthy! Remember kid!"*

Doreen: *"Does dad eat a lot of ice-cream?"*

Eve: *"Why?"*

Doreen: *"Today dad ran naked through the apartment to the shower and under his first belly I discovered a second and then a third one."*

Eve: *"There's something going on with your father. When I lie underneath him in bed and we have sex, I always hope that there's no one else in the apartment beneath us."*

Doreen: *"Why then?"*

Eve: *"Naw, when your father with his 100 kilos gets at it and the ceiling begins to crack..."*

Doreen: *"Then someday I'll buy the flat below on the ground floor for you guys."*

Eve: *"You're so cute Doreen."*

Doreen: *"Cute but not fat ... right?"*

Eve: *"No, only cute."*

Doreen: *"My teacher also finds me cute!"*

Eve: *"Then tell your teacher sometime that it's illegal and that you also have a cute mommy."*

Doreen: *"In the bible it says: thou shall not lie!"*

Eve is very sour. She takes a wooden spoon and swings it towards her daughter. Then she bellows loudly: *"Get out of here you fat pig! I'll help you for once! I'll listen to you only one more time!"*

Doreen: *"Thanks! Finally you're being honest with me. I know that I'm too fat, but do you have to always tell me so directly?"*

Doreen cries a lot, because her mother just doesn't understand her. Out of frustration she orders a maxi-menu at McDonalds.

Chapter 11 – Grandpa's visit

Today, Eve, Doreen and the Svengster are very excited. Grandpa Dolfi announced his visit. Grandaddy Dolfi actually lives somewhere in Brasil. In his letters from Brasil, he always writes that a small German village is still bitterly resisting enemy attacks. Nobody knows for sure what he exactly means, and those that do, aren't too excited of talking about it. Right, Eve, born Braun?

Helmut picks up grandpa Dolfi, the "old sack", at the airport. He recognizes him from a distance due to his bright red suitcase on which emblazons an interesting suitcase sticker: a black and weird cross on a white background. At first Helmut just thought it was an issue of taste; then however he hastens the old guy to quickly leave the El-Al-airline-counter, where he has just started an argument. The security guards keep looking at him strangely, but that doesn't bother grandpa Dolfi.

In the car grandpa is furious about his son-in-law. *"Helmut! You're no patriot! I mean, you belong to the Third Reich's elite, I mean, Germany's elite naturally! Why did you drag me away from the El-Al-counter?"* Helmut drives on ignoring the grandpa, leaving him to rant slogans and blither like an idiot. Luckily grandpa landed via a special permit in Tempelhof – no idea, whether or not he had to sleep with Klaus Wowereit for that.

Helmut and Grandpa Dolfi arrive at the Schmidt's house. Eve tied extra braids for herself and Doreen. Both are wearing long pleated skirts and the Svengster is stuck in funny "Lederhosen". *"Hopefully my rapper buddies don't see me like this!"*, wishes the Svengster but too late. MC Fire-alarm just comes around the corner and sees how the Svengster in "Lederhosen" kisses an old man with an odd upper-lip mustache. *"What luck!"* thinks MC Fire-alarm to himself! *"Lucky that I have my camera cellphone with me! I'm going to send the picture to the Bild newspaper or youtube tomorrow."*

Doreen drops a curtsey before grandpa Dolfi and all go together inside the house. There's a black forest cherry cake and spaghetti, because according to Guido Knopp grandpa always liked to eat it. Everything is a huge mess, because grandpa Dolfi's Parkinson hasn't gotten any better in the last 60 years. Luckily everyone has special red napkins that are only taken out when grandpa Dolfi is there. They look just like his suitcase with the sticker on it. The Svengster wouldn't mind having such a napkin as t-shirt, but Eve tells him that that's not possible. *"Copyright problems, you know."*

Grandpa Dolfi talks of his village. *"There's a wolf entrenchment, a Führer-headquarter and everything according to plans from Speer."* None of the Schmidts understand what exactly a wolf entrenchment could be. A ski jump okay but a wolf entrenchment? In the rain forest? And what is a Führer-headquarter, please? And who or what are spear-plans? Does grandpa Dolfi live with wild indians? The Schmidts ignore everything, while grandpa Dolfi is talking about his friends, Heinrich, Heydrich and Heini from the post office, of the grave bathing accident of his old friend Jupp: *"Slipped, wham! Crashed on his head, a wave came and then he was gone. Almost like how we dissappeared from here back then in the 40s!"*

Svengster *(wakes up): "Grandpa, are you from Berlin?"*

Grandpa: *"Yeah, ah, um not exactly. I'm really from a small place on the Inn."*

Svengster: *"On the Inn? On the Rhine? That means on the Rhine?"*

Grandpa: *"No, my boy! On the Inn. That's a river in the Ostmark!"*

Svengster: *"There are no more East marks anymore!"*

Grandpa: *"Ostmark, that's Austria..."*

Svengster: *"No. They also have euros in Austria since 2000."*

Grandpa: *"Yeh, no. Ostmarkwww's a term that means an area..."*

Svengster: *"It's okay grandpa ... so were you on vacation in Berlin?"*

Grandpa: *"Sort of. One could say so. A 1000-year vacation ... was planned, but then it didn't turn out so well. You can't always get what you want, my boy!"*

Svengster: *"I also want a 1000-year vacation!"*

Grandpa: *"Don't worry. It'll come again. That's for sure."*

Svengster: *"And when's that? And, why are you in Brasil now?"*

Grandpa: *"I say only the flight panes from New Schwaben country. In eternal ice! The South pole!!!!"*

Svengster: *"Grandpa? Is everything alright? Do you want some water?*

Grandpa: *"In Brasil I'm sort of professionally re-oriented. My job was hard and I was totally exhausted. So-to-say burn-out syndrome just like in Dresden. Fortunately, not only to the final stage. Burning gasoline and even that doesn't want to burn..."*

The Svengster ignores grandpa again and grandpa Dolfi talks the whole night through with his screechy, snoring voice. But we really don't want to listen to him, because now there's grammar exercises to do and questions to answer.

Chapter 12 – Helmut and the police

Helmut is an enthusiastic driver. Unfortunately, the police aren't so excited about Helmut, because he reves up his car and speeds on like an idiot and doesn't obey any traffic regulations. Over the last three weeks Helmut has already collected 27 points on his card of traffic offenses. He drove into a slow-traffic-street turning at 120 km per hour, he ignored at least five red lights, insulted multiple officials, called with his cellphone while driving at 200 km/hour, rampaged on the highway and spat out exhaust. Today Helmut is driving without beeing buckled up in his lowered bright yellow Ford Capri on a bike path and slightly clips a guy that is blocking the way with his wheel chair.

Meanwhile, Helmut is observed by a patrol car. When Helmut fails to stop, a steet-blockade is set-up and nails are strewn over the street so that Helmut's tires pop. 15 police cars encircle Helmut in his car and Helmut is furious and fried because his tires are now trashed and that goes also for his aluminium rims that he got as a present for his last birthday from Eve. He jumps out of the car and brawls at the police. They take out their guns, but that doesn't bother Helmut.

Helmut: *"You stupid idiot jack-offs! What did you do with my beautiful car? Are you guys crazy? I can also trash your cars, you cop pigs!"*

Helmut runs full blast to a police car, and with an out-stretched leg, he kicks in the front windshield. Then, with his bare hands, he punches and breaks the headlights and throws a burning pack of matches in the gas tank. Suddenly a blow nails him down and Helmut turns unconscious.

When he awakes, he's lying with a ton of blue bruises, a broken nose and two broken arms in a roadside ditch. His Ford Capri is still charring a bit. He finds a letter from the police in his jacket pocket.

Dear Mr. Schmidt,

It's enough. Due to your unmeasured driving habits, we were forced to destroy your car. It was also a lot of fun breaking your arms so that you won't be able to drive a car anytime in the near future. We've confiscated your driver's license and we took a blood sample from the gaping wound on your left cheek. The analysis shows that you were drunk driving. Your alcohol level was 2.3‰, 1.5‰ above limit. Please understand our dealing with the situation, for we simply can't put up with your driving any more. Your driver's license is now suspended and if you'll go on pestering us, then it'll be gone even longer.

Sincerely,
Your police, or as you call us, your "cop pigs"

Helmut is now even more enraged than before. His beautiful car is torched, his driver's license is gone and his arms are broken. Regrettfully he tries to call home, but he can't touch his cellphone buttons. He has to walk home. Helmut starts to cry because he doesn't like to walk.

When Helmut gets home, Eve and the kids are already asleep. Helmut is sad, but luckily there's still something to drink. After four hours with grain liquour and schnapps, Helmut is a bit happier. Satisfied, he lights a cigarette and falls asleep on the couch.

Chapter 13 – Helmut's politics in beer heaven

Helmut loves his favorite bar, the Beer Heaven. He's here as often as possible and meets up with his friends. Then they all drink a bunch of liters of beer and schnapps and they're happy. But today, Helmut is not in a good mood, because back in time everything was better, he thinks.

Helmut: *"The beer used to taste better. It was more yellow and the head was much foamier. Alltogether the Beer Heaven used to be nicer. The people here looked better than the ones nowadays, the lady behind the counter was definitely 20 years younger and also much more entertaining. Also you guys, my buddies, were more fun and also had much more hair on your heads."*

Erich *(a friend of Helmut's): "And now the politicians!"*

Helmut: *And now the politicians! Back in the day we had Willy Brandt, Franz-Josef Strauß and Herbert Wehner! Today we have Merkel and this secret service guy Steinmeier! That guy stole my driver's license! The politicians are the worst they've ever been. The whole political system. Democracy is ok, but I find a dictatorship much more effective. With me as dictator! "*
Erich: *"Cheers, Helmut! To you as the best dictator of all-time, the all-time greatest dictator, the GreatDicTioaT!"*

Helmut: *"Thanks Erich. But take a look at the whole political system! The Rus-*

sian, Putin has gas. The exchancellor Schröder belongs to Putin and the gas mafia. The gas mafia blackmails the West. Merkel belongs to the industry just as the CDU, the FDP and the SPD. The industry blackmails Merkel. Merkel works for the industry and the banks. The banks own the houses and cars. People still live in the houses, but Merkel and the banks and the industry make sure that the Germans are blackmailed and then will soon have to sleep in their cars. And if they don't have a car, then they'll be on the street. The Green Party have become the FDP, the Left is the opposition. The auto industry is drowning, but German cars also aren't better than American or Indian cars."

Erich: *"Drink something Helmut. You have to conserve your voice! Cheers!"*

Helmut: *"It's just that way. Everything's going down hill. Exactly as we do and the little guy on the street."*

Erich: "*Which little guy on the street?"*

Helmut: *"Aw, people like you and me. Everyone blackmails the little man on the street. And also the little woman. I just have to think of Eve. The amount she has to pay for fees and taxes and crap! From her take-home cash I can live, at best, a week!"*

Erich: *"Tell me, Helmut! Can you paint me a picture of how the political system in Germany looks like and functions? Then I can explain it tomorrow to my kids. At the moment they're learning about this at school."*

Helmut: *"Rosi! Service! I desperately need a pen and a bit of paper."*

Rosi: *"Here is the paper!"*

Helmut: *"No! Not Zewa wipe & gone paper! Noone did any eating here! A note pad, please."*

Rosi: *"Ah, okay. Just a minute."*

Chapter 14 – The Schmidts buy Mielke

Doreen is on her way home from school… No! She's on her way home from shopping and still has 25 euros in her purse. All of a sudden she sees a dog dealer standing on the street. He's got a small cute dog for sale and Doreen's heart is melting.

Doreen: *"Hello dog seller! How much for the dog there?"*

Dog seller: *"40 euros."*

Doreen: *"I'll give you 10!"*

Dog seller: *"No, never, not for that price. Are you nuts? 30 euros!"*

Doreen: *"22 euros, and that's my final offer."*

Dog seller: *"24.50 is my last offer. It's a real pitbull! Raised, with full service history, biting machine, orphan. He ate his parents."*

Doreen: *"It's a deal. Sold! What does he have there in front of his mouth?"*

Dog seller: *"That's a little basket for collecting mushrooms! No! Nonsense! It's a muzzle of course. You have to leave this thing on him so that nothing happens."*

Doreen takes the pitbull that she endearingly names Cocky and goes home with him to her parents. Eve and Helmut are not too happy. They've never permitted their kids to have pets. Already when they had lice Helmut and Eve were horrified. Now, there is a heavy 80 kg pitbull in their living room and evily blinking at them with his piggy eyes. Doreen begs and pleads and cries, but Eve stays firm.

Eve: *"Never ever does this beast enter my house! If we're lucky, he'll only eat the hair from our head! If we're unlucky, then he'll bite through our throats!"*

Doreen: *"But he's got a muzzle, of course! We'll simply feed him his whole diet with a straw! Schacklin's grandma has been living like that for years, although she doesn't have a muzzle but rather a hole in her stomach."*

Helmut (only half paying attention): *"Was she aggressive, her grandma?"*

Eve: "*Helmut! Now you say something too! That won't fly with the dog!"*

Helmut: *"Alright. So a dog could be of some worth. And here in the neighborhood there was a break-in not long ago. If a burglar ran into a pitbull like him, he'd think twice and break in somewhere else."*

Doreen: *"Exactly! Exactly!"*

Eve: *"But that was Svenny with his buddies. They're the ones that broke in."*
Helmut: *"And so it is. I decide that the dog is kept as protection. I'll take care of it."*

Eve: *"You don't take care of anything! You don't do anything! I've never seen you working! You're a complete good-for-nothing!"*

Helmut: *"Now the dog only needs a name."*

Doreen: *"Ya! Cocky! He's called Cocky!"*

Helmut: *"What? No! Why don't we just call him 'Penis'! He's got to have a German name, a name that inspires respect that sounds bad and at the same time unpredictable. Leader? Hatey? I've got it! Mielke! I baptize you 'Mielke', Cocky!"*

Helmut takes Mielke and goes with him to the park. Mielke shall become a real watch dog. So that Mielke doesn't take off, Helmut trains him in the caged-in street soccer field. There are a couple of boys playing soccer there at the moment, but that doesn't bother Helmut at all. Mielke plays along, but Helmut doesn't want him to. He hits and kicks Mielke who continually chases the ball or a player and thereby yowls and whines. Suddenly Helmut wants to know if Mielke is bitey. He picks up a thick stick and stands in front of the field's caged fencing. From here he distances the muzzle through the cage and spurs him on with the stick. Mielke snaps to and almost pulls Helmut through the caged fence-wall towards himself. Then he loses interest and looks for new sticks. The nicest are the moving sticks under the soccer players that support them. Mielke doesn't know that these are legs. But the most important thing is that they taste good.

Helmut knows that Mielke is bitey. Actually, Helmut now knows that Mielke is a murdering beast, although he doesn't want to find this out. He calls the police from a phone booth and tells them that a pitbull-gone-mad has killed two whole teams of 5 at the soccer field in Görlitzer park. He tells Doreen and Eve that Mielke simply disappeared. No idea where he went off to. Animals are often just strange.

Chapter 15 – Helmut at the employment office

Whenever Helmut needs money, he goes to the job center in order to create a ruckus. Today he goes in at 1 p.m. He didn't bother to dress up at all and his hair hasn't been washed for 5 days. The woman at the counter honks meaningless to him in order to calm him down, but Helmut only shows her his middle finger. The woman hasn't met his finger yet because she's only been working there for a couple of days. Shocked, she calls the security services, but they already know Helmut and don't do anything to him.

Whenever Helmut is at the employment office, the security fuzzes don't need to come right away. In the meantime Helmut is on his way to his staffer Mr. Koleps. In most cases the staffer knows less than a rubber tree that stands in his room. The only thing that Helmut has to do: he has to browbeat him a bit. He has to threaten him and then, in emergencies, he has to get loud. The staffer is afraid of Helmut and is off today. Helmut makes an effort to open the door to the staffer's room. Suddenly he kicks the door in to look around and see if Mr. Koleps didn't just hide somewhere in the office.

Mr. Koleps is really not there, but Helmut likes the desk lamp quite a bit. He thinks, *"I'll take that with me"*, and puts it under his joggingsuit top. *"If they don't give me any money, then I am allowed to pay myself in kind – taking things away, right?"* Helmut just leaves the room as he crosses paths with another staffer, Mr. Dschango. *"Hey, my favorite client! What are you doing here?"*

Helmut: *"I need money and am not getting anything from you guys!"*

Mr. Dschango: *"Come on with me and we'll collect something for you in the cafeteria."*

Helmut: *"Really?"*

Mr. Dschango: *"Am I the welfare services or what? If you kick in doors, then you'll get nothing from us. In order to get dough, you have to be friendly!"*

Mr. Dschango leads Helmut into his office and there shows him a picture in a golden frame.

Mr. Dschango: *"Here! This is our favorite client, 'Mr. Tobstarr!' At the end of the year he was elected friendliest unemployed person of 2008 he won first place by a lot. Mr. Tobstarr isn't only friendly but also good-looking, musically-inclined, intelligent and funny. Ya. Concerning 'humor,' he could improve a bit, but we also weren't looking for the most-comical unemployed person, rather the friendliest."*

Helmut takes a look at the picture of Mr. Tobstarr and just then doesn't want to be friendly anymore. He thinks to himself: *"I know this guy from somewhere. He's only friendly in order to get his money! However, I've always got my lot of money, until now, whenever I've staged a rampage."* Helmut wants to turn over Mr. Dschango's desk with both hands just as he is laid flat by Mr. Dschango's fist. Through the fog he hears him speaking with another man. *"That was clearly self-defense! Right, Mr. Tobstarr?"*

"Obviously, Mr. Dschango! You did well. Oh, did you go to the barbers? Looks good... "Mr. Tobstarr and Mr. Dschango contemplate whether or not they should take back the stolen desk lamp from Helmut in order to give it back to Mr. Koleps. Mr. Dschango can't have a share of it anyway. *"And if he notices something, he shouldn't be so upset!"*

Helmut asks friendly for an early pay-out of his monthly heating bill support and for once Mr. Dschango doesn't want to be this way and gives him a pay slip. *"And if you cause problems here again, Schmidt, we really will let the beating begin! Do you understand me?"*

Helmut nods, gets paid in another room and leaves the employment office. He definitely won't go there in the near future. First and foremost not to Mr. Dschango.

Chapter 16 – Eve cheats

Eve has already been working in her Ket sausage stand for 7 hours today. She worked straight through and couldn't even take 5 minutes to sit down, lay down or simply hang out. Continually, someone kept coming to the snack bar and ordered a Ket sausage or Grilletta. Eve ist very tired and frustrated. She has already eaten 12 Ket sausages herself – not because she was hungry but rather out of frustration.

"Back home Helmut is lounging again on the sofa – drunk. The kids are also living on me asking for money every day. How much I'd like to just leave everything behind!" she murmurs in her lady's beard as suddenly a young man perks her interest. He is just getting out of his 30-ton truck and heads in the direction of Eve's Ket sausage stand.

Man: *"Hello! I'm Mobutu and I'd like a Ket sausage."*

Eve: (following every step of Mobutu and blushing) *"... why ... why this then?!"*

Man: *"I'm hungry. I've been sitting behind the wheel for 8 hours, listening to Truckstop and Tom Astor the whole time."*

Eve: *"Ah! Uh huh. Then a Ket sausage for you, Mr. Mobutu?"*

Man: *"Mobutu is my first name. If you call me 'Mr. Mobutu', then I'll call you 'Mrs. Eve' ... or perhaps 'Ms.'?"*

Eve: (blushes even more): *"No, Mrs., so Ms., yah it doesn't matter. Simply call me Eve."*

Mobutu blushes likewise and grins: *"Gladly, Eve!"*

Eve shoots an orderly load of ketchup in the Ket sausage sandwich. Then she stuffs a Ket sausage of Trioland in the Ket sausage sandwich opening and smears the ketchup evenly on the inner edges of the sandwhich. Highly interested, Mobutu watches everything. He sees how gently and sweet Eve prepares the food for him. Every movement flows, every handhold appropriate and Eve's whole body seems to resonate with every twitch. Mobutu falls in love immediately. Surely, he's already seen a lot of women, but definitely no one like Eve. There were some that were cute and some that were ugly but none like Eve. Eve is one like no other before.

Eve: *"Mr. Mob... Mobutu, what's up with you? Everything okay? Your Ket sausage is ready."*

Mobutu: (awakes as from a nice dream): *"What? How? Who am I? Eve... I don't know how I should say it. I love you. I've loved you from the first moment. Your smile, your body, your charm, your Ket sausage... Excuse me, but I can't help myself."*

Mobutu and Eve clash faces together and stick their tongues in each other's mouths. Then they get undressed and lay down behind the stand's counter. Eve is afraid that other clients will catch her and Mobutu having sex. Therefore she opens up the big door to the storage closet under the counter and puts all the frozen fries as well as other supplies and rat poison in the foot room. Then Mobutu and her crawl into the storage closet and sleep together.

It's 6 o'clock in the evening. Helmut is awake once again and hungry. He decides to go to Eve and her food stand and eat up the rest of her Ket sausages. He makes his way to the snack bar.

Around 5 after 6 pm. Eve and Mobutu are done with sex. Both Eve and Mobutu contemplate playing a funny joke of Ket sausage and penis, but both refrain from this. They kiss one another briefly and Mobutu goes back to his truck. He turns around one more time and calls to Eve: *"I won't forget you, dear! And if your lying in bed in the next days and suddenly are very hot... then we'll have long-distance traffic, hahahahah!"*

Eve laughs but not for long because just then Helmut comes around the corner. Did he see any of that? Helmut appears upset. Upset and hungry. He rips the door open, sits himself on a stool and begins to rant:

Helmut: *"Did you see that nigger? Such people are taking jobs away from me!"*

Eve: *"But you don't have a job?"*

Helmut: *"It doesn't matter! If he wasn't driving the truck, then I could drive it!"*

Eve: *"But you don't have a driver's license anymore."*

Helmut: *"I could have one! And he doesn't even know German!"*

Eve: *"So what?"*

Helmut: *"Didn't you hear what he just yelled out?"*

Eve doesn't feel well, she has to sit down. But Helmut talks on.

Helmut: *"He wanted to make fun of me! Sounded like "Do we have TVs!" What the hell's that? Do I look like that? I don't have a job, but I DO have a TV!"*

Eve is happy. Neither Helmut nor any of the customers noticed how she and Mobutu had sex under the Ket sausage backburner counter. She passes Helmut the last six sausages and asks herself if Mobutu will ever come again.

Chapter 17 – The Svengster becomes gay

Svengster and Doreen are watching TV together when all of a sudden Bruce (the former supermodel coach) appears on the screen. Svengster suddenly becomes very queasy and of course Doreen notices it.

Doreen: *"What's up with you, Sven?"*

Sven: *"I don't know. Somehow I don't feel good."*

Doreen: *"Weird. It's like that since Bruce appeared."*

Sven: *"Bruce, Bruce, Bruce! What should he have to do with it!"*
Doreen: *"Ya, he's black, he's thin, he's totally buff, he's bald, he can move and..."*

Sven: *"...and he's got a totally sweet accent!"*

Doreen thinks that she didn't quite here that right. Has her brother suddenly become gay? Her brother, a gay gangster-rapper and bed-wetter! With eyes wide-open she turns around to Svengster, takes a glance at his crotch (is there a bulge?) and then at his face.

Doreen: *"Svengster!"*

Sven: *"Yah? What... what's up?"*

Doreen: *"You just said that you think Bruce is sweet... Are you also gay now?"*

Sven: *"I'd know that wouldn't I! Just because I find Bruce sweet, adore his subtleness and worship his body like a Nubian temple, I am not necessarily gay!"*

Doreen observes her brother. Svengster has sweat on his forehead, his face is bright red, his tongue runs continually over his lips; confused he tries to hide the erection. Doreen has got enough and switches the channel to RTL 2 Action News.

Two weeks later.

It's 10 p.m. In front of the Schmidt house stands a dark-haired man with his face deep in a hooded sweatshirt. He presses the door bell and after a short wait the door opens. The man disappears in the house entrance.

Today Helmut comes home from his local bar a bit earlier than usual. The wife of the owner was found this morning dismembered and now the owner has to take care of the burial. Helmut isn't really in a good mood because he hasn't drunken enough yet. In a mean mood, he pees on the neighbor's car before he enters the house. He staggers home, opens up, opens the fridge and is horrified. Yesterday there were still 3 beers there!

Steaming mad he starts looking for the missing beers. He looks in the parents' bedroom, in the hobby basement, in Doreen's room, Helmut even looks in the bath and in the toilet bowl. *"Of course they're all gone whenever someone is looking for them! If only Eve was here! She would go get me some more beers!"*

But Helmut doesn't give up and continues to search. He hasn't checked the balcony yet. As he is standing there, he hears some strange noises. There's rubbing, squeaking and in between he thinks he might hear the Sengster moaning. Helmut is confused. There! That scream! That was the Svengster! Surely he must have some problems with some other rappers.

Worn-out, Helmut storms into Svengster's room and freezes. His beer! Two beer bottles are standing on the floor, empty. Svengster is lying on his belly in bed, a black man inside Svengster's backside and in the backside of the black man there's a full bottle of beer. Helmut takes immediate action. With zip he luckily pulls the full bottle of beer out of the backside of the black guy.

Just now the Svengster and the black man notice Helmut. Helmut wipes the bottle's neck briefly with a little spit and his undershirt and then leaves the room. A short while later Eve comes home. Just as she hangs her purp-le patent leather jacKet on the coatrack, a young black man comes out of Svengster's room. Eve and the young man are shocked for they know one another well. Helmut calls from the living room: *"Hey, Eve! Our son is now gay! First a gangster rapper, now gay! I could always see it coming!"*

Mobutu's face turns light red and he is very embarrassed. Before Helmut co-mes staggering out of the living-room, he gives Eve a quick french kiss. Then he leaves the place. Eve is crying in the corridor, Svengster is crying in his room, Helmut has tears of joy in his eyes because he DID find a last beer.

Vocabulary

Chapter 1

sich vorstellen	*to introduce oneself*
sein	*to be*
typisch	*typical*
deutsch	*German*
die Familie	*family*
hallo	*hello*
die Fresse halten	*to shut the fuck up*
kommen	*to come*
Deutschland	*Germany*
woher	*where from*
sonst	*else*
der Mond	*moon*
arbeitslos	*jobless*
die Ausbildung	*education*
der Fallschirmspringer	*airborne ranger*
der inoffizielle Mitarbeiter = I.M.	*Homeland security guard in the GDR*
trinken	*to drink*
sehr	*very*
viel	*much / many*
der Alkohol	*alcohol*
Prost!	*Cheers!*
alt	*old*
gehen	*to go*
nicht	*not*
die Schule	*school*
doof	*stupid*
Schule ist doof.	*School sucks.*
egal	*It doesn't matter.*
der Name	*name*
arbeiten	*to work*
der Imbiss	*snack-bar*
die Ketwurst	*German sausage speciality*
der Mann	*man / male husband*
die Frau	*woman / female husband*
das Leben	*life*
leben	*to live*
wo?	*where?*
der Sohn	*son*
hier	*here*
groß	*big*
der Gangster	*gangster*
wenn, falls	*if*
hart	*hard*
mein	*my*
der Prozess	*lawsuit*
nachts	*at night*
sich einnässen	*to wet oneself*
böse	*evil*
die Wirklichkeit	*reality*
ein ganz Lieber	*a really good kid*

Chapter 2

der Dealer	*dealer*
Mahlzeit!	*Greeting line suitable for mornings, noons, afternoons and evenings – original translation: Meal!*
Hoschi	*buddy*
reinkommen	*to come inside*
gut	*good*
die Stube	*room*
brauchen	*to need*
dick	*fat, obese*
danke	*thank you*
Dickes Danke!	*modern German term for saying thank you*
die Verkaufsräume	*shopping rooms*
sich setzen	*to sit down*
der Sitzsack	*beanbag*
mögen	*to like*
ich möchte	*I would like*

das Speed	*speed*
das Koks	*cocaine*
das Heroin	*heroin*
das Hasch	*pot*
oder	*or*
lieb	*dear*
die Fassbrause	*draught soda pop*
haben	*to have*
die Fanta	*Fanta*
da hinten	*there in the back*
das Labor	*lab*
herstellen	*to produce*
das Crystal Meth	*crytsal meth*
das Bad	*bathroom*
können	*can, be able to*
gern	*feel free to*
sich etwas drücken (Drogen)	*to push oneself something*
das Zimmer	*the room*
das Waffenlager	*arsenal*
Wow!	*Wow!*
verkaufen	*to sell*
der Flammenwerfer	*flame-thrower*
das Maschinengewehr	*machine-gun*
sicher doch	*for sure*
der Flüssigsprengstoff	*liquid explosive*
wer?	*who?*
da oben	*up there*
auf	*on*
das Poster	*poster*
die No Angels	*formerly succesful German girl group*
eine Line ziehen	*to sniff a line*
wichsen	*to wank off*
ach so	*I see*
schon gut	*well fine*
auf jemanden / etwas stehen	*to be fan of someone / something*
total	*completely*
der Bushido	*succesful German Gangsta rapper*
kennen	*to know*
Tempelhof	*local quarter of Berlin, which is quite middle class, former airport*
die Skyline	*skyline*
der Bordstein	*kerbstone*
Alles Gute kommt von hinten	*homosexual saying: everything good comes from behind.*
die Autobiografie	*autobiography*
genau	*exactly*
neeee	*no*

Chapter 3

fahren	*to drive*
treffen	*to meet*
Müller	*common German family name*
der Feuermelder	*fire alarm*
He-Man Müller, She-Do, MC Feuermelder	*German wannabe-rapper-names*
alle	*all*
drei	*three*
jemanden nicht gerne mögen	*to like someone not so well*
die Leute	*people*
sollen	*shall*
ein wenig	*a little bit*
batteln	*to battle (rhyme)*
betteln	*to beg*
selber	*yourself*
auch	*too*
das Gesicht	*face*
schlagen	*to beat*
wie oft?	*how many times?*
noch	*again*
sagen	*to say*
immer	*all the time*
gemein	*nasty*
uns	*us*
sich unterhalten	*to have a chat*

die Drogen	*drugs*
kaufen	*to buy*
dürfen	*to be allowed to*
nicht mehr	*no more*
nehmen	*to take*
man	*one*
verbieten	*to forbid*
jetzt	*now*
wir	*we*
gegen	*against*
verlogen sein	*to be a liar*
Drogen sind verlogen!	*German anti-drug slogan of the mid 90s*
nach	*after*
trotzdem	*nonetheless*
welche	*some*
geben	*to give*
sprechen	*to speak*
der Klartext	*clear text*
Klartext sprechen	*in (the) clear*
sofort	*at once*
gegen Geld	*for money*
der Freund	*friend*
warten	*to wait*
zahlen	*to pay*
und	*and*
jemanden zusammenschlagen	*to beat someone up*
treten	*to kick*
das Ei	*usually "egg" but in common Germany also often used as an equivalent of testicles, then in plural "die Eier"*
hauen	*to slap*
stechen	*to stab*
das Messer	*knife*
durch	*through*
die Kniescheibe	*knee-cap*
jemandem etwas abnehmen	*to take away something from someone*
aua	*ouch*
Menno!	*Fuck it!*
unfair	*unfair*
Drei gegen einen ist unfair	*saying: Three against one is not fair*
kennen	*to know*
Dreimal ist Bremer Recht	*saying: Three times is right in Bremen.*
Wer dreimal mit derselben pennt, gehört schon zum Establishment!	*saying: Whoever fucks the same girl three times in a row is part of the establishment.*
3 und 3 ist 9	*saying: 3 and 3 makes 9.*
widersprechen	*to contradict*
aber	*but*
der Krankenwagen	*ambulance*
schon	*already*
da	*there*
der Sanitäter	*ambulance man*
bringen	*to bring, take, get, fetch*
das Krankenhaus	*hospital*

Chapter 4

der Tag	*day*
die Uhr	*watch / o' clock*
erwachen	*to wake up*
aufstehen	*to stand up, get up*
zuerst	*first*
das Aufwach-Bier	*wake-up-beer*
die Küche	*kitchen*
anzünden	*to light*
die Zigarette	*cigarette*
schauen	*to watch*
das Fenster	*window*
dann	*then*
gegen jemanden hetzen	*agitate against someone*
der Ausländer	*foreigner, stranger*
der Russe	*the Russian*
gemeingefährlich	*dangerous to the public*
fressen	*devour, gorge*
das Kind	*the child*

der Chinese	*the Chinese*
gelb	*yellow*
riechen	*to smell*
streng riechen	*to stink*
streng	*strong*
der Iraner	*the Iranian*
Recht haben	*to be right*
der Italiener	*the Italian*
feige	*coward*
der Ami	*short form of "der Amerikaner": citizen of the USA*
sie nicht mehr alle haben	*to be completely out of one's mind*
der Somalier	*the Somalian*
besser	*better*
der Spanier	*Spaniard*
der Paellafresser	*Paella gorger*
müde	*tired*
sich ins Bett legen	*to lay down in bed*
klingeln	*to ring*
die Tür	*door*
stinkwütend	*angry as hell*
der Drogenfreund	*drug buddy*
das Zeitungsabo	*subscription to a paper*
ich komme aus	*I come from*
der Kosovo	*Kosovo*
lügen	*to lie, to tell lies*
kommen	*to come*
der Knast	*jail*
schwer	*serious, severe, grievous*
die Körperverletzung	*bodily harm*
ja	*yes*
ist ja gut	*fine*
besitzen	*to possess, have*
die BILD	*Germany's biggest newspaper*
die Nationalzeitung	*German nazi-newspaper*
vielleicht	*maybe*
die Brigitte	*German woman's magazine*
lesen	*to read*
das Geld	*money*
die Schweiz	*Switzerland*
der Irak	*Iraq*
schließen	*to shut*
kennen	*to know*
faul	*lazy*
schaffen	*to work*
klauen	*steal*
arbeitsscheu	*work-shy*
das Gesindel	*rabble, riff-raff*
das Sofa	*sofa, couch*
holen	*go and take*
der Schnaps	*schnapps*
der Richter	*judge*
duschen	*to take a shower*
kalt	*cold*
bemerken	*to notice*
nur	*only*
die Unterhose	*underpants*
tragen	*to wear, to carry*
rauchen	*to smoke*
die Jogginghose	*training trousers*
seine	*his*
„Deutschland sucht den Superstar"	*German equivalent of Pop Idol / American Idol*
glücklich	*happy*
anzünden	*to burn, light*
schenken	*to donate, make a gift / present*
die Kippe	*other word for cigarette*
die Sexy Clips (Pl.)	*German equivalent of the David Letterman Late Show*
das Deutsche Sport Fernsehen	*German Sport TV*
austrinken	*to drink out*
einschlafen	*to fall asleep*
während	*while*

Chapter 5

das Ket	*probably the beginning of the word "Ketchup"*
die Wurst	*sausage*
niemand	*no one, nobody*
wissen	*to know*
woraus	*out of what*
aber	*but*
denn	*because*
es gibt	*there exists, there is*
das Glutamat	*Glutamate*
der Großmarkt	*wholesaler*
vor	*in front of*
die Stadt	*city*
manchmal	*sometimes*
müssen	*must*
Polen	*Poland*
der Schwarzmarkt	*Black market*
der Euro	*German equivalent of the Dollar*
klein	*small*
unmarkiert	*not marked*
jemandem etwas abnehmen	*to take something away from someone*
stehen	*to stand*
das Ketwurst-Regal	*Ketwurst-shelf*
der Fachverkäufer	salesman
leicht	*slightly*
grünlich	*slightly green*
die Großpackung	*big pack*
der Cent	*German equivalent of the Cent*
schimmlig	*moldy, musty*
das Ketwurst-Aroma	*Ket sausage aroma / flavour*
gut sein für etwas	*to be good for something*
was = etwas	*something / anything*
zwei	*two*
die Kinder (Pl.)	*children*
die Schulden (Pl.)	*debts*
das Nagelstudio	*nail saloon*
der Hals	*neck, throat*
etwas am Hals haben	*to have something on one's back*
Bitte!	*Please!*
der Verkäufer	*seller, retailer*
etwas am Preis machen	*to negotiate the price of something / someone*
jemandem entgegenkommen	*to come to meet with someone*
alles	*everything*
später	*later*
etwas verlassen	*to leave something*
zusätzlich	*additionally*
der Zentnersack	*hundredweight sack*
das Milchpulver	*milk powder*
Minsk	*Minsk = White Russian or Ukrainian equivalent of Baltimore or Cleveland or Birmingham*
die Produktion	*production*
von Hand abgezählt	*counted by hand*
das Brötchenpulverbrötchen	*rollpowder roll*
die Freikarte	*free ticket*
das Musical	*musical*
der Michael Flatley	*German equivalent of Michael Flatley*
der Genozid	*genocide*
der Türke	*the Turkishman*
der Armenier	*the Armenian*
schaben	*to scrape, rasp*
grob	*coarse, rough, rude*
etwas erwärmen	*to heat*
alt	*old*
fett	*fat*
sich etwas anziehen	*to dress oneself in something*
beginnen	*to begin*
der Kunde	*customer*
kein/e	*no*
die Cola	*coke, cola*
umtauschen	*to change, exchange*
aussehen wie	*to look like...*
die Bank	*bank*

eher	*more*
breit	*broad, wide*
der Hocker	*stool*
bequem	*comfortable*
der Ledersessel	*leather chair*
der Komiker	*comedian*
wie viel	*how much*
tut mir leid	*I am sorry*
kleiner	*smaller*
die Ocken (Pl.)	*other word for any amount of money*
die Euronen (Pl.)	*see Ocken*
ein bisschen	*a little bit*
teuer	*expensive*
fuffzich = fünfzig	*slang expression usually used in Germany for "fifty"*
inklusive	*inclusive*
die Umsatzsteuer	*turnover tax*
die Service-Pauschale	*service flat rate*
schwul	*gay*
völlig	*extremely*
überrascht	*surprised, astonished*
die Beziehung	*relationship*
sich sehen	*to see each other*
selten	*seldom*
blind	*blind*
der LKW-Fahrer	*truck driver*
der LKW	*truck*
glauben	*to believe, think*
der Beginn	*beginning, start*
wunderbar	*wonderful*
die Freundschaft	*friendship*

Chapter 6

das Casting	*casting*
der, die, das Beste	*best*
der Superstar	*superstar*
leider	*unfortunately*
aussehen wie	*to look like*
wollen	*to want*
jetzt	*now*
ändern	*to change*
gemeinsam	*together*
sparen	*to save money*
die Brust-Operation	*breast augmentation*
sich einig sein	*to be at one, to agree*
vergrößern	*to enlarge*
wer von beiden	*who of them*
einkaufen gehen	*to go shopping*
hübsch	*pretty*
die Großraumdiskothek	*open plan discotheque, club*
das Ende der Stadt	*the end of the city*
toll	*fantastic*
das Kleid	*dress*
der Restposten	*remnants, remainder*
aus	*from*
Mode	*fashion*
der Kottbusser Damm	*The Kottbus Blvd (nice little road in Berlin)*
geil	*horny, rank*
die Klamotten (Pl.)	*things, rags*
Findest Du auch?	*Don't you think so?*
golden	*golden*
der Minirock	*mini skirts*
rosa, pink	*pink*
die Sachen (Pl.)	*stuff*
Et Hertie	*German equivalent of...*
der Geschmack	*taste*
der Style	*style*
die Abteilung	*department*
die Verkäuferin	*female seller*
gucken	*to look*
schon wieder	*once again*
ein paar	*some*
die Gangstarapvideo-babystricherinnen	*gangstarapvideobabywhores*
wäre ich geblieben	*I should have stayed (in my old job)*

der Bundesverfassungs-richter	*judge at the federal constitutional court*
haben	*have*
das T-Shirt	*t-shirt*
XXL	*XL*
klein ausfallen	*to be too small*
XL	*L*
kaufen	*to buy*
zusammennähen	*to sew, to stitch together*
das Glück	*luck, fortune*
etwas passt	*something fits*
sagen	*to tell*
seit	*since*
ess-brech-süchtig	*bulimic*
essüchtig	*gluttonic*
Sport treiben	*to do sport*
stimmt doch gar nicht	*that's not true*
die Farbe	*colour*
unglaublich	*unbelievable*
schön	*beautiful*
glitzern	*to twinkle*
die Applikation	*application*
drauf	*on something*
der Totenkopf	*skull head*
fantastisch	*fantastic*
nehmen	*to take*
der Rock	*the skirt*
richtig	*right*
spannen	*to sit tight, stretch*
eng	*tight*
der Intimbereich	*private parts*
schmücken	*to adorn, decorate*
das Bauchnabelpiercing	*belly piercing*
der Gürtel	*belt, girdle*
neidisch	*envious*
etwas tragen	*to wear*
stimmt	*that's right*
überhaupt nicht mehr	*not any longer at all*
raus	*out*
die Straße	*street*
bleiben	*to stay*
daheim	*at home*
sich einschließen	*to lock oneself*
aufhören	*to stop*
die Kasse	*cash register*
das Erdgeschoss	*ground floor*
als ob	*as if*
laufen	*to run*
die Pumps (Pl.)	*high heels*
stolpern	*to stumble*
fallen	*to fall*
der Ladendetektiv	*shop detective*
jemanden festnehmen	*to arrest*
das Hausverbot	*ban to enter a store*
jemandem etwas erteilen	*to give something to someone*
beide	*both*
traurig	*sad*
wie?	*how?*
warum?	*why?*
zusammen	*together*
meinen	*to think*
manchmal	*sometimes*
echt	*really, real*
philosophisch	*philosophical*

Chapter 7

das Frühstück	*breakfast*
bei	*at*
sich outen	*to come out*
heute	*today*
früh	*early*
gemeinsam	*alltogether*
um	*around, about*
der Frühstückstisch	*breakfast table*
als	*when*

fragen	*to ask*
zu	*to*
was?	*what?*
essen	*to eat*
Bitte?	*I beg your pardon?*
es gibt...	*we'll have..., there is / are*
die Erdbeere	*strawberry*
die Scheiße	*shit*
lecker	*delicious*
lieben	*to love*
reden	*to talk*
mit mir	*with me*
nachher	*later*
der Kiosk	*kiosk*
wirklich	*really*
die Entschuldigung	excuse
etwas mitbringen	*to bring along something*
der Nordhäuser Doppelkorn	*German schnapps speciality*
die Magnumflasche	*magnum bottle*
der Vater	*father*
die Mutter	*mother*
Sieh mal einer an	*Look who's talking*
mein	*my*
der Bruder	*brother*
wichtig	*important*
mitteilen	*to announce*
erzählen	*to tell, to narrate*
nicht wieder	*not again*
das Bett	*bed*
irgendwann	*some time (or other)*
sich auswachsen	*to grow out*
rüberreichen	*to pass (across)*
das Bier	*beer*
Svennie	*diminuitive name for Sven*
gleich	*soon*
Cola Light	*Coke Light*
der Strohhalm	*straw*
Svenja	*female version of Sven's male name*

warten	*to wait*
kurz	*short*
warte noch kurz	*wait a second*
nicht wahr?	*isn't it? don't you?*
groß tun	*to try to impress*
den Schwanz einziehen	*to show the white feather*
das Mädchen	*girl*
Bier ist die beste Mahlzeit!	*German saying: Beer ist the best meal*
Mist!	*Fuck!*
die Tiefkühlpizza	*frozen pizza*
der Backofen	*oven*
verbrennen	*to burn*
schlimm	*bad*
wiegen	*to weigh*
zu viel	*too much*
Halt dein Maul!	*Shut the fuck up!*
das Rezept	*recipe*
die Zutaten	*ingredients*
die Person	*person*
das Gramm	*gram*
frisch	*fresh*
der Zucker	*sugar*
das Salz	*salt*
der Löffel	*spoon*
der Rinderkot	*cow shit*
der Metzger	*butcher*
die Zitrone	*lemon*
ungespritzt	*organic*
die Zubereitung	*preparation*
beträufeln	*to sprinkle with some liquid*
der Fleischhauer	*butcher*
zermatschen	*to crush*
fluffig	*fluffy*
die Masse	*substance*
gleichmäßig	*even*
die Glasschale	*glas bowl*
aufteilen	*to divide*

etwas vierteln	*to divide in fourths*
abwaschen	*wash off*
vorsichtig	*cautious*
die Matsche	*pulp, slush*
drücken	*to push*
zum Schluss	*finally*
nach Gefühl	*just like you feel it is right*
etwas bestreuen	*to besprinkle something with*
fertig	*ready*
der Supermarkt	*supermarket*
die Tiefkühltruhe	*freezer*
entweder ... oder	*neither ... nor*
die Pizza	*pizza (plural: die Pizzen)*
unter	*under*
der Pullover	*pullover*
verstecken	*to hide*
einfach so	*just plain and simple*
herausgehen	*to walk out*
vorheizen	*pre-heat*
das Ofenblech	*baking tray*
der Ofenrost	*furnace grate*
legen	*to put*
abwarten	*to wait for*

Chapter 8

die Flucht	*escape, getaway*
der Hiphop-Event	*Hiphop event*
auf	*on*
treffen	*to meet, see*
ein paar	*some*
feindlich	*hostile*
der Rapper	*rapper*
das Rindfleisch	*beef*
die Lage	*situation, condition*
eskalieren	*to escalate*
böse	*evil*
der Gangstarapper	*gangsta rapper*
der Sack	*sack, balls*
etwas über jmd. kippen	*to pour something over someone*
jemanden beschimpfen	*to insult someone*
stinkewütend	*bloody angry*
ficken	*to fuck, bang*
Alter (Person)	*dude*
der Hund	*dog*
der Hurensohn	*son of a bitch*
der Fernseher	*TV*
das Fickgesicht	*fuck face*
genug haben	*to have enough, to be fed up*
das Butterflymesser	*butterfly knife*
die Gürteltasche	*fanny bag, bum bag*
jemanden erstechen	*to knife / to stab someone to death*
wegrennen	*to run away*
hinterher rennen	*to pursuit, to track*
etwas verlieren	*to lose something*
die Hiphophose	*baggy pant*
ausziehen	*to undress*
jemanden verfolgen	*to pursuit, to track*
laufen	*to run*
nach	*to*
draußen	*outside*
sich verstecken	*to hide oneself*
mitten in	*in the middle of*
die Gruppe	*group*
der Rentner	*retired person, senior citizen*
Hanau	*ugly city in Germany*
oben	*on top of*
die Treppe	*stairs*
suchen	*to search*
wohin?	*where to?*
hinaus	*onto, out*
jemanden wieder sehen	*to see someone again*
die Kasalla	*aggro*
jemanden fertig machen	*to mob someone,* *to wear someone down*
krabbeln	*to crawl*

unter	*under*
der Bus	*bus*
vielleicht	*maybe*
sich festhalten	*to grab hold of something, to hold tight on something*
entkommen	*to escape, to get away*
noch nicht	*not yet*
sterben	*to die*
Mist!	*Fuck! Shit!*
heute	*today*
der Glückstag	*lucky day*
verfickt	*fucking*
die Hundehurenmutter	*dog whore mother*
sich wundern	*to be astonished*
die Pfütze	*puddle, slop*
entdecken	*discover*
verängstigt	*scared, frightened*
der Busfahrer	*bus driver*
dort	*there*
raus	*out*
sich entschuldigen	*to say sorry, to excuse oneself*
jemanden verkloppen	*to beat someone up*
jung	*young*
nett	*nice*
das Wort	*word*
verstehen	*to understand*
etwas benutzen	*to use something*
manchmal	*sometimes*
das Schimpfwort	*curse*
niemals	*never*
mit	*with*
nach Hause	*back home*
nach etwas riechen	*to smell, stink*
der Urin	*urine*
in etwas steigen	*to enter*
finden	*to find*
reingehen	*to go back into*
sprechen	*to speak*
das Mikrofon	*the mic*
verehrter	*dear, honoured*
das Reisen	*travelling*
der Umweg	*detour, indirection*
bringen	*to bring*
der Herr	*Sir*
etwas beachten	*take care of*
kein	*no*
die Lebensmittel (Pl.)	*eatables*
etwas überfahren	*to run over*
etwas überrollen	*to roll over*
der Kleinwagen	*compact / small car*
die Leute (Pl.)	*people*
drin	*in, inside*
verdammt	*damned*
der Dreck	*dirt*
der Idiotentest	*Medical Psychological Assessment to get a driving license*
zu	*to*
dürfen	*to be allowed, may*
weinen	*to cry*
jemanden trösten	*to comfort, to console someone*
das Abendessen	*dinner*
sich etwas fragen	*to wonder*

Chapter 9

das Frauengespräch	*women's talk*
sich hässlich finden	*to think one is ugly*
etwas wissen möchten	*to want to know something*
ob	*whether, if*
es stimmt	*it is right*
die Mama	*mum*
jemandem gefallen	*to please someone*
antworten	*to answer*
ehrlich	*honest*
jemanden anschauen	*to look at*
der Vati	*daddy*

neben	*next to, compared to*
die Gesichtsbaracke	*ugly face*
schön	*beautiful*
der Schwan	*the swan*
also	*also*
besser	*better*
das Kompliment	*compliment, flattery*
es wird nicht besser	*it doesn't get better*
das Aussehen	*the looks*
jemandem etwas empfehlen	*to advise something to someone*
glauben an	*to believe in*
der Tipp	*advice*
jemandem etwas wünschen	*to wish someone something*
doch	*however, still*
wenn	*when, if*
denken	*to think*
die Grazie	*grace*
die Gratziege	*a fine line goat*
etwas	*a little, something*
dick	*fat*
sicherlich	*for sure*
sich etwas bestellen	*to order something for oneself*
das Bällchen	*scoop*
das Eis	*ice*
die Sahne	*cream*
die Eisdiele	*ice cream parlour*
gegenüber	*across, adverse from*
machen	*to do, to make*
das Eisfressen	*ice cream gorging*
ungesund	*unhealthy*
sich etwas merken	*to keep something in mind*
nach	*after*
duschen	*to take a shower*
nackt	*naked*
die Wohnung	*the apartment*
der Bauch	*belly*
der erste	*the first*
der zweite	*the second*
der dritte	*the third*
einiges	*to a considerable degree*
etwas ist dran an jemandem	*there's something about someone*
unter	*below*
Sex haben	*to have sex*
hoffen	*to hope*
zufällig	*by chance, at random, accidentally*
das Kilo(gramm)	*kilogram*
rummachen	*to make out*
die Decke	*ceiling*
einkrachen	*to crash down*
irgendwann	*someday, sometime*
das Erdgeschoss	*first floor, ground floor*
süß	*sweet*
der Lehrer	*teacher*
illegal	*illegal*
die Bibel	*the bible*
Du darfst nicht lügen	*Thou shall not lie*
sauer sein	*to be pissed*
der Holzlöffel	*wooden spoon*
brüllen	*shout*
die Sau	*swine, pig*
helfen	*to help*
jemandem zuhören	*to listen to someone*
danken	*to thank*
zu	*too*
deutlich	*clearly, explicit*
einfach	*just, simple*
der Frust	*the blahs, frustration*
das Maxi-Menü	*XXL-Menu*

Chapter 10

der Onkel	*uncle*
der M.C.-Escher	*famous German painter*
Wendeltreppe	*corkscrew stairs / spiral stair*
die Batik	*batik*
die Hose	*trousers*

der Swankster	*compound: wanking Svengster*
der Sado	*Sado (1st open gay German gangstarapper)*
der Starschnitt	*star cut*
die Bong	*bong, shisha*
die Borderline	*borderline*
die Barbie	*Barbie*
der Teddy	*teddybear*
das Münchhausensyndrom	*factitious disorder*
das Schlüsselloch	*key lock*
der Baseballschläger	*compound: bad ball bat*
der Oberschenkel	*thigh*
der Hals	*neck*
der Oberschenkelhals	*neck of femur*
der Knochen	*bone*
die Strickleiter	*rope-ladder*
gemütlich	*cozy*
der Nebenerwerb	*side job*
der Puff	*brothel*
die Ratte	*rat*
die Candy	*female name (often used in Eastern Germany)*
die Fucka-Palme	*special kind of palmtree*
die Schöpfkelle	*dipper*
der Zorro	*Zorro*
die Maske	*mask*
die Kerze	*candle*
die Riesenketwurst	*huge Ket sausage*
der Lokus	*old word for toilet (latin)*
der Chefsessel	*executive chair*
die NVA	*Nationale Volksarmee (army of the GDR)*
der Wimpel	*pennant*
die Trophäensammlung	*collection of trophies*
der Siebenender	*seven pointer*
das Klopapier	*toilet paper*
das große X	*big X*
Stinknase	*stink nose (disease)*

Chapter 11

der Besuch	*visit*
aufgeregt sein	*to be excited*
sich ankündigen	*to announce oneself*
der Opa	*grandfather*
irgendwo	*somewhere*
Brasilien	*Brasil*
der Brief	*letter*
schreiben	*to write*
immer	*always*
deutsch	*German*
das Dorf	*village*
der Übergriff	*assault, violation*
erbittert	*grim, acrimonious*
der Widerstand	*resistance, opposition*
Widerstand leisten	*to resist someone / something*
meinen	*to mean, think*
die, die	*those, who*
die Lust	*lust*
Braun	*Eve's maiden name*
Nicht wahr?	*Am I right?*
abholen	*to pick up*
der alte Sack	*common German nickname for an old man*
jemanden erkennen	*to recognize*
der Flughafen	*airport*
von Weitem	*afar, from a distance*
knallrot	*bright red*
der Koffer	*suitcase*
interessant	*interesting*
der Kofferaufkleber	*suitcase sticker, suitcase label*
prangen	*to be resplendent*
schwarz	*black*
seltsam	*strange, weird*
das Kreuz	*cross*
weiß	*white*
der Grund	*ground*

die Geschmackssache	*a matter of taste*
zusehen, dass	*to be in a hurry to avoid something*
der El-Al-Schalter	*El-Al-counter (El Al is Israel's famous airline)*
jemanden wegbekommen	*to get someone away from somewhere*
gerade	*just when*
das Streitgespräch	*argument*
jemanden stört etwas nicht	*someone does not care about something*
der Sicherheitsbeamte	*security guard*
der Schwiegersohn	*son-in-law*
empört sein über	*to be outraged, to be shocked*
der Patriot	*patriot*
zu etwas gehören	*to belong to something*
die Elite	*elite*
das Deutsche Reich	*The German Empire, The Third Empire*
jemanden von etwas wegziehen	*to pull away someone from something*
auf Durchzug stellen	*to ignore someone / something*
Parolen dreschen	*to bellow jibber jabber*
dummschwätzen	*to talk rubbish*
per	*per, via*
die Sondergenehmigung	*special permit*
Tempelhof	*great airport in Berlin that was shut down in 2008*
mit jemandem schlafen	*to sleep with someone*
keine Ahnung	*no idea*
das Haus	*house*
ankommen	*arrive*
sich Zöpfe binden	*to make oneself braids, to braid*
der Faltenrock	*pleated skirt*
in etwas stecken	*to be stuck in something*
lustig	*funny*
die Lederhose	*leather trousers*
hoffentlich	*hopefully*
der Rapperkumpel	*rapper buddy*
zu spät	*too late*
um die Ecke kommen	*to walk around the corner*
der Oberlippenbart	*moustache, mustache*
küssen	to *kiss*
das Glück	*luck, fortune*
das Foto-Handy	*mobile phone including a camera*
das Bild	*picture*
der Knicks	*curtesy*
die Schwarzwälder Kirschtorte	Black Forest cake
Spaghetti (Pl.)	*Spaghetti*
Guido Knopp	*Germany's biggest and funniest historian*
die Riesensauerei	*huge mess*
der Parkinson	*Parkinson illness alias shake the disease*
der, die, das letzte	*the last*
nicht besser werden	*not become better*
dieser, diese, dieses	*that, this, Pl.: these*
die Spezialserviette	*special napkin*
herausholen	*to fetch*
das T-Shirt	*t-shirt*
nicht gehen	*to be impossible*
die Wolfsschanze	*Wolf's Lair – one of Hitler's head quarters*
das Führerhauptquartier	*Hitler's head quarter*
der Plan	*plan*
Speer	*spear, but also Germany's biggest architect right after S.-M. Ranzenberger*
die Sprungschanze	*ski jump*
der Regenwald	*rain forrest*
wild	*wild*
der Indianer	*Native American*
der Freund	*friend*
treu	*faithful, loyal*
Heinrich	*probably Heinrich Himmler concerning "The Downfall"*
Heydrich	*probably Reinhard Heydrich*
Heini von der Post	*probably Heini from the Post office*
schlimm	*bad*
der Badeunfall	*bathing accident*
Jupp	*probably Josef Mengele, evil Nazi-doctor in Auschwitz*
der Kumpel	*buddy*

ausrutschen	*to slip*
peng	*bang*
auf etwas knallen	*to bang on something*
der Kopf	*head*
die Welle	*wave*
weg war er	*there he went*
fast so	*merely the same as*
damals	*once upon a time*
verschwinden	*to disappear*
äh …	*err …*
der Ort	*place*
der Inn	*small river in Austria*
der Rhein / Rhin	*the river Rhine*
der Junge	*boy*
die Ostmark	*geographically: former name of Austria / economically: former currency of the GDR*
die Ferien (Pl.)	*holidays*
auf Ferien	*on holidays*
kann man so sagen	*you can say so*
1000-jährige	*1000-years*
planen	*to plan*
nicht so laufen	*not everything went as planned*
das Wunschkonzert	*musical request programme*
Das Leben ist kein Wunschkonzert	*Life is not a bowl of cherries / a picnic*
keine Bange	*don't worry, no fear*
wieder kommen	*to return, to come back*
ganz bestimmt	*for sure*
die Flugscheibe	*UFO*
Neuschwabenland	*area in the Antarctica, where there are rumours that the Nazi elite had to escape to*
ewig	*forever, eternal*
der Südpol	*South pole*
in Ordnung	*okay, allright*
das Wasser	*water*
quasi	*quasi*
berufliche Neuorientierung	*professional re-orientation*
der Job	*job*
ausgepowert sein	*to have a burnout*
das Burn-Out-Syndrom	*burn-out syndrome*
sozusagen	*so to speak, sort of*
die Endstufe	*final stage*
brennen	*to burn*
das Benzin	*gas, petrol, fuel*
krächzen	*to cark, croak, caw*
schnarren	*to snarl, vibrate*
rollen	*to roll*
die Stimme	*voice*
grammatisch	*grammar*
die Aufgabe	*task*
erfüllen	*to achieve something*
die Frage	*question*

Chapter 12

die Polizei	*police*
der Autofahrer	*driver, car driver*
leider	*sadly, unfortunately*
begeistert sein	*to be ardent, enthusiastic*
heizen	*to drive like a maniac*
der Idiot	*idiot*
die Verkehrsregel	*international traffic rule*
der Punkt	*point*
die Verkehrssünderkartei	*traffic offender list*
sammeln	*to collect*
die Spielstraße	*play street*
die Schrittgeschwindigkeit	*walking pace, walking speed*
Km/h	*hilometers per hour / 1 mile per hour = 1,6 kilometers per hour*
etwas missachten	*to ignore*
der Beamte	*the officer*
beleidigen	*to libel, to insult, to dis*
das Steuer	*steering wheel*
das Fahrzeug	*car*
das Tempo	*speed*
die Autobahn	*highway, interstate*

drängeln	*to shove, to swarm*
der Auspuff	*tail pipe, exhaust pipe*
abbauen	*to decompose*
unangeschnallt	*without using the safety belt*
tiefer legen	*to lower, to lower down*
knallgelb	*bright yellow*
der Ford Capri	*German Ford muscle car from the 80s*
der Fahrradweg	*bike path, cycle way*
anstupsen	*to nudge someone*
der Krankenfahrstuhl	*invalid car*
den Weg versperren	*to barricade, to block*
der Streifenwagen	*police patrol car*
beobachten	*to monitor, to observe*
anhalten	*to stop*
die Straßensperre	*road barrier, road block*
etwas errichten	*to build*
der Nagel	*nail*
die Straße	*street*
etwas verstreuen	*to litter, to scatter*
der Reifen	*wheel*
platzen	*to explode*
der Polizeiwagen	*police car*
jemanden oder etwas einkreisen	*to circle someone or something*
angefressen sein	*to be pissed*
kaputt	*out of order, smashed, trashed*
die Leichtmetallfelge	*light alloy rim / wheel*
der Geburtstag	*birthday*
springen	*to jump*
die Pistole	*pistol*
die Pistole zücken	*to pull out the pistol*
der Idiotenwichser	*idiot-wanker*
Habt Ihr sie noch alle?	*Are you completely out of your mind?*
kaputtmachen	*to smash*
das Bullenschwein	*cop swine*
mit Schwung	*in full swing*
gestreckt	*stretched*
das Bein	*leg*
die Frontscheibe	*front window, windscreen*
bloße Hände	*bare hands*
der Scheinwerfer	*headlamp, headlight*
die Packung	*box*
das Streichholz	*match*
der Tank	*tank*
plötzlich	*suddenly*
die Ohnmacht	*unconsciousness*
in Ohnmacht fallen	*to fall unconsciousness*
der blaue Fleck	*bruise*
gebrochen	*broken*
die Nase	*nose*
der Arm	*arm*
der Straßengraben	*roadside ditch*
kokeln	*to char*
die Jackentasche	*pocket*
sehr geehrte / r	*formal letter opening: Dear Mr. / Mrs.*
es reicht	*it's enough*
angemessen	*adequate, appropriate*
die Fahrweise	*manner of driving*
zu etwas gezwungen sein	*to be forced to do something*
zerstören	*to destroy*
Spaß machen	*to make fun*
erst recht	*even more, more than ever*
der Führerschein	*driving license*
konfiszieren	*to conficate*
klaffende Wunde	*gaping wound, wide open wound*
die Blutprobe	*blood test*
jemandem etwas entnehmen	*to take a sample from someone, to extract something*
der, die, das linke	*left*
die Wange	*cheek*
die Analyse	*analysis, dissection*
etwas ergibt etwas	*something proves something*
betrunken	*drunk*
der Alkoholspiegel	*alcohol level*
das Verständnis	*appreciation, comprehension*

das Handeln	*act, action*
etwas tolerieren	*to tolerate*
Mit freundliche Grüßen	*formal letter end line (best wishes)*
jemanden nennen	*to call someone something*
vorher	*before*
abfackeln	*to torch / bleed something*
hinüber sein	*to be trashed*
vergeblich	*unsuccessfull*
anrufen	*to call on the phone*
die Tastatur	*keyboard*
zu Fuß	*by foot*

Chapter 13

Politik machen	*to talk about politics*
der Bierhimmel	*beer heaven*
die Lieblingskneipe	*most favourite bar*
möglich	*possible*
der Liter	*liter = 0,26 gal (US), 0,22 gal (UK)*
die Laune	*mood*
früher	*in former times*
schmecken	*to taste*
gelber	*more yellow*
schaumig	*foamy*
gut aussehend	*good looking*
die Bardame	*barmaid*
unterhaltsam	*entertaining*
das Haar	*hair*
der Politiker	*politician*
Willy Brandt	*famous chancellor from the Social Democratic Party*
Franz-Josef Strauß	*famous + infamous politician from a small Bavarian party*
Herbert Wehner	*other famous Social Democratic Party politician*
Die Merkel	*first female chancellor of Germany*
Der Steinmeier	*foreign department secretary, former spy coordinator*
klauen	*to steal*
die schlimmsten	*the worst*
je	*ever*
überhaupt	*generally*
das politische System	*the political system*
die Demokratie	*democracy*
die Diktatur	*dictatorship*
effektiv	*effective*
der Diktator	*dictator*
der größte Diktator aller Zeiten (GröDiZ)	*biggest dictator of all times (BDoaT)*
das Gas	*gas*
der Exkanzler	*former chancellor*
Schröder	*former chancellor, now working for Russia*
die Gasmafia	*the gas mafia*
jemanden erpressen	*to blackmail someone*
der Westen	*west*
jemandem gehören	*to belong to someone*
die Industrie	*industry*
CDU, FDP, SPD	*German right wing parties*
die Bank	*the bank*
wohnen	*to live*
die Grünen, die Linke	*German left wing parties*
werden	*to become*
die Opposition	*opposition*
die Autoindustrie	*the car industry*
indisch	*Indian*
die Stimme	*voice*
Prost!	*Cheers!*
Ist doch so	*That's the way it is*
den Bach runter gehen	*to go down the tube*
der kleine Mann von der Straße	*Little John from the street*
die kleine Frau von der Straße	*Little woman from the street*
die Abgaben (Pl.)	*taxes and stuff*
die Steuern (Pl.)	*taxes*
der Gewinn	*benefit, gain*
bestenfalls	*at (the) best*
aufmalen	*to scribble*
funktionieren	*to work*

morgen	*tomorrow*
jemandem etwas erklären	*to explain something to someone*
etwas durchnehmen	*to go through something*
die Bedienung	*waiter, waitress*
der Kuli	*ballpoint pen, underling*
das Papier	*paper*
Zewawischundweg	*kitchen roll*
andersrum essen	*puke (eat the other way around)*
der Block	*block*
der Moment	*moment*
zeichnen	*to draw*
die Skizze	*draft, sketch*
nachfolgend	*subsequent, consecutively*
die Seite	*page*
grafisch	*graphically*
darstellen	*to demonstrate, to describe*

Chapter 14

der Heimweg	*the way home*
die Handtasche	*handbag, purse*
der Hundehändler	*dog trader*
schmelzen	*to melt*
das Herz	*heart*
das Angebot	*offer*
wie viel	*how much*
nein, niemals nicht	*no, never ever*
spinnen	*to be nuts*
der Pitbull	*pit bull*
ausgewachsen	*grown up*
scheckheftgepflegt	*with full service history*
die Beißmaschine	*biting machine*
die Vollwaise	*absolute orphan*
die Eltern	*parents*
abgemacht!	*deal!*
der Mund	*mouth*
das Körbchen	*little basket*
Pilze sammeln	*to pick up mushrooms*
der Quatsch	*nonsense*
der Maulkorb	*muzzle*
unbedingt	*necessarily*
etwas passiert	*something happens*
passieren	*to happen*
liebevoll	*affectionate, loving*
jemandem etwas erlauben	*to allow something to someone*
das Haustier	*pet*
die Laus, Läuse	*louse, lice*
entsetzt sein	*to be shocked*
schwer	*difficult, weighty*
das Wohnzimmer	*living room*
blinzeln	*to blink, to wink*
die Schweinsäuglein (Pl.)	*piggy eyes*
nie und nimmer	*never ever*
die Bestie	*beast*
Glück haben	*to be lucky*
Pech haben	*to be unlucky*
durchbeißen	*to bite through*
der Strohhalm	*straw*
die Sondennahrung	*enteral tube feeding*
das Loch	*hole*
aggressiv	*aggressive*
naja	*well*
etwas her machen	*to represent something*
die Nachbarschaft	*neighbourhood*
einbrechen	*to break in*
der Einbrecher	*burglar*
sich etwas zweimal überlegen	*to think twice*
woanders	*somewhere else*
und wenn schon	*who cares*
dafür sein	*to be for*
der Schutz	*security*
sich um etwas kümmern	*to take care of something*
total	*total*
der Nichtsnutz	*goodfornothing*
jemanden rufen	*to call someone*

der Penis	*penis*
der Respekt	*respect*
unberechenbar	*erratic, incalculable*
der Führer	*the leader*
jemanden taufen	*to baptize*
Mielke	*former boss of the GDR Homeland security office called STASI*
der Park	*park*
der Wachhund	*watchdog, guard dog*
abhauen	*to run away*
jemanden / etwas trainieren	*to coach, to train*
vergittert	*barred, grilled*
das Street-Soccer-Feld	*street soccer field*
Fußball spielen	*to play football*
der Fußball	*the football*
hinterher hetzen	*to run after*
jaulen	*to yelp*
wimmern	*to whimper, to whine*
bissig	*snappy, bitchy, acid-tongued*
dick	*thick, bulky*
der Stock	*cane, stick*
das Gitter	*fence, grill*
das Spielfeld	*playing field*
entfernen	*to remove*
zuschnappen	*to close with a snap*
ziehen	*to pull*
das Interesse	*interest*
suchen	*to look for*
beweglich	*moving, moveable*
die Mörderbestie	*murder beast*
obwohl	*although*
etwas herausfinden	*to detect something*
die Telefonzelle	*phone booth / box*
wildgeworden	*crazed*
das Fußballfeld	*football field*
der Görlitzer Park	*eautiful park in Berlin where you can buy any drug*
komplett	*complete*
der Spieler	*player*

Chapter 15

die Arbeitsagentur	*job center*
die Agentur für Arbeit	*see above*
ärger machen	*to act up, to make waves*
eintreffen	*to arrive*
sich schick machen	*to dress up*
extra	*especially*
sich waschen	*to wash oneself*
der Tresen	*counter*
jemanden anschnauzen	*to bawl someone out, to snub someone*
jemanden einschüchtern	*to awe someone, to buffalo someone*
der Mittelfinger	*middle finger*
geschockt	*shocked*
der Sicherheitsdienst	*security firm*
jemandem nichts tun	*not harm someone*
der Sicherheitsfuzzi	*security ass*
mittlerweile	*in the meantime, meanwhile*
der Sachbearbeiter	*administrator, clerk*
meistens	*in most times*
der Gummibaum	*rubber tree*
das Zimmer	*room*
der, die, das einzige	*the only thing*
jemandem drohen	*to menace, to threaten so.*
notfalls	*in case of need, at a push*
laut werden	*to become loud*
die Angst	*angst, fear*
frei haben	*to have one's free day*
etwas eintreten	*to kick in something*
nachschauen	*to check up*
jemandem gefällt etwas	*someone likes something*
die Schreibtischlampe	*desk lamp*
stecken	*to pocket, to rake*
die Trainingsjacke	*tracksuit top*
die Naturalien (Pl.)	*natural products*
Oder etwa nicht?	*Am I right?*
jemandem über den Weg laufen	*to run into someone*

der Kunde	*customer*
etwas kriegen	*to get something*
die Kantine	*canteen, lunch room*
die Wohlfahrt	*(social) welfare*
die Kohle	*other word for money (= Geld)*
freundlich	*nice, friendly*
das Büro	*office*
jemandem etwas zeigen	*to show something to someone*
der Rahmen	*frame*
der Lieblingskunde	*favourite customer*
das Jahresendvoting	*final voting of the year*
der Arbeitslose	*male jobless person*
der Abstand	*distance*
der erste Platz	*first place*
musikalisch	*musical*
intelligent	*intelligent*
humorvoll	*full of humour*
das Thema	*issue, subject, theme*
an etwas arbeiten	*to work on something*
witzig	*funny*
jemanden kennen	*to know someone*
randalieren	*to rampage, to riot*
der Schreibtisch	*desk*
etwas umstoßen	*to knock over, to overturn*
niederstrecken	*to knock down*
der Nebel	*fog*
mit jemandem sprechen	*to talk to someone*
eindeutig	*clearly*
die Notwehr	*self-defence*
selbstverständlich	*naturally, self-evident*
etwas gut machen	*to do something well*
der Friseur	*hairdresser*
etwas überlegen	*to think about something*
jemandem etwas abnehmen	*to take away something from someone*
etwas merken	*to notice, to realize*
jemandem etwas zurückgeben	*to give something back to someone*
jemanden nicht ab haben können	*to dislike someone extremely*
sich nicht so anstellen	*not act as if, not be a pussy*
vorzeitig	*ahead of schedule / time*
die Auszahlung	*payback, payment*
monatlich	*monthly*
der Heizkostenzuschuss	*heating costs subvention*
ausnahmsweise	*for once, exceptional*
mal nicht so sein	*to be not overly precise*
der Zahlzettel	*receipt*
es setzt richtig Haue	*you will get a real hard spanking*
nicken	*to nod*

Chapter 16

fremdgehen	*to be unfaithful, to cheat on one's partner*
die Stunde	*hour*
arbeiten	*to work*
schuften	*to drudge, to graft, to toil*
sich hinsetzen	*to sit down*
sich hinlegen	*to lie down*
rumhängen	*to hang around*
ständig	*all along, constantly*
Grilletta	*some kind of burger*
bestellen	*to order*
müde	*tired, sleepy*
sie selbst	*she herself, personally*
besoffen	*drunk*
die Couch	*couch*
jemandem auf der Tasche liegen	*to sponge off someone, to live off someone*
jeder Tag	*every day*
alles stehen und liegen lassen	*to drop everything*
murmeln	*to murmur*
der Damenbart	*ladybeard*
das Interesse erregen	*to quicken interest, to arouse interest*
aussteigen	*to exit, to get out*
der 30-Tonner-LKW	*30 tons truck*

der LKW = Last Kraft Wagen	*lorry, truck*
in Richtung	*in direction of*
Mobutu	*African name*
ich hätte gerne	*I would like to have*
der Schritt	*crotch*
erröten	*to turn red*
auf dem Bock sitzen	*to sit on the driver's seat of a truck*
hören	*to listen to, hear*
Truckstop	*Famous German Country Band, equivalent of Johnny Cash*
Tom Astor	*Famous German Country singer, comparable to Billy Ray Cyrus*
der Vorname	*first name*
das Fräulein	*miss*
noch mehr	*even more*
nennen	*to call*
ebenfalls	*also, as well, ditto*
grinsen	*to grin*
gerne	*it's a pleasure*
ordentlich	*neat, fair*
der Ketchup	*ketchup*
die Stulle	*sandwich*
stopfen	*to plug, to stuff*
die Ketwurststullen-öffnung	*the opening of the Ketwurst-sandwich*
etwas verreiben	*to rub in, to levigate*
gleichmäßig	*even*
der Innenrand	*inner border*
zuschauen	*to watch*
zärtlich	*affectionate, endearing*
das Essen zubereiten	*to prepare the meal*
die Bewegung	*movement*
der Handgriff	*grip, knack*
das Zucken	*twitch, tremor*
mitschwingen	*to resonate*
sich verlieben	*to fall in love*
hübsch	*pretty*
hässlich	*ugly*
was ist los?	*what is up with you?*

eine wie keine	*movie title "She's all that" = There is no other girl like her*
alles okay?	*Everything allright?*
fertig sein	*to be ready*
der Traum	*dream*
was?	*what?*
wie?	*how?*
wo?	*where?*
jemanden lieben	*to love somebody*
das Lächeln	*smile*
der Körper	*body*
der Anmut	*charme, sweetness*
jemandem etwas verzeihen	*to forgive someone something*
aufeinanderklatschen	*to slap on top of each other*
die Zunge	*tongue*
der Mund	*mouth*
sich ausziehen	*to undress*
die Ladentheke	*counter*
der Sex	*sex*
jemanden bei etwas erwischen	*to catch someone flat-footed*
das Staufach	*storage locker*
die Tiefkühlpommes	*frozen french fries*
die Vorräte	*stock, supply*
das Rattengift	*rat poison, rodenticide*
der Fußraum	*leg room, leg area*
miteinander schlafen	*to sleep with one another*
etwas beschließen	*to conclude, to determine*
restlich	*remaining, residual*
wegessen	*to eat away*
sich auf den Weg machen	*to hit the road, to set off*
schlecht	*bad*
der Witz	*joke*
der Penis	*penis*
sich etwas verkneifen	*to deny oneself something*
sich umdrehen	*to turn around*
jemandem etwas zurufen	*to call out to someone*
jemanden vergessen	*to forget someone*
Schatz	*sweetheart*

das Bett	*bed*
erregt sein	*to be arroused / excited*
der Fernverkehr	*long distance traffic / intercourse*
hahahahaha	*hahahahaha*
um die Ecke biegen	*to turn around the corner*
etwas mitbekommen	*to get / to notice something*
etwas aufreißen	*to rip something, to tear something open*
der Hocker	*stool*
der Neger	*politically incorrect for African German*
so Leute	*these people*
jemandem etwas wegnehmen	*to take away something from someone*
der Arbeitsplatz	*employment, job, position*
ich könnte	*I could*
jemandem wird es von etwas schlecht	*someone nauseates something*
sich über jemanden lustig machen	*to mock at someone, to make fun of someone*
froh sein	*to be glad*
irgendwelche	*any other*
die Warmhalteplatte	*hot / heating plate*
übrig bleiben	*to be left over, to remain*

Chapter 17

schwul werden	*to turn gay*
fernsehen	*to watch TV*
Bruce Darnell	*former German TV celebrity supermodel coach*
der Coach	*coach*
jemandem wird es mulmig	*someone feels queasy*
jemandem ist nicht so gut	*someone doesn't feel fine*
an jemandem ist etwas dran	*there is something about someone*
schwarz	*black*
dünn	*thin*
austrainiert sein	*to be trained / fit*
die Glatze	*skinhead, bold head*
sich bewegen können	*to know how to move*
der Akzent	*accent*
mit großen Augen	*with eyes wide open*
die Beule	*bruise*
das Gesicht	*face*
jemanden süß finden	*to think someone is hot*
die Geschmeidigkeit	*suppleness, softness*
etwas anbeten	*to adore something*
etwas verehren	*to admire / idolize something*
nubisch	*nubian*
der Tempel	*temple*
der Schweiß	*sweat*
jemandem steht Schweiß auf der Stirn	*to have sweat on one's forehead*
die Lippen	*lips*
verzweifelt	*desperate*
die Erektion	*erection*
umschalten	*to redirect, to commutate*
etwas verbergen	*to hide / bury something*
RTL 2 Action News	*biggest German news show*
später	*later*
dunkelhäutig	*dark skinned*
tief	*deep*
sich etw. ins Gesicht ziehen	*to pull sth. in your face*
der Kapuzenpulli	*hoody*
die Klingel	*bell*
der Hauseingang	*entrance, front door*
verschwinden	*to disappear*
ausnahmsweise	*as an exception, exceptional*
die Stammkneipe	*local*
zerstückelt aufgefunden werden	*to be found fragmented*
der Wirt	*innkeeper, host*
die Beerdigung	*burial, funeral*
sich um etwas kümmern	*to take care of something*
pinkeln	*to piss, to pee*
wanken	*to stagger, to dodder*
aufschließen	*to open, to unlock*
der Kühlschrank	*fridge, refrigerator*
entsetzt sein	*to be aghast / horror-stricken*

die Bierflasche	*bottle of beer*
das Elternschlafzimmer	*parent's bedroom*
der Hobbykeller	*garage, hobby room*
das Bad	*bath*
der Spülkasten	*cistern, flushing tank*
die Toilette	*toilet*
wenigstens	*at least*
der Balkon	*balcony*
nachschauen	*to check up*
das Geräusch	*noise*
schaben	*to scrape something, to scratch*
qietschen	*to squeak*
zwischendrin	*in between*
der Schrei	*scream*
erstarren	*to be awestruck, to freeze*
austrinken	*to drink up*
der Boden	*the bottom*
der Hintern	*the bottom*
abwischen	*to wipe something*
der Flaschenhals	*bottleneck*
die Spucke	*spit, spittle*
das Unterhemd	*undershirt, wife beater's shirt*
lila	*lilac, mauve*
der Lackmantel	*lace coat*
die Garderobe	*coat rack*
sich erschrecken	*to be scared*
etwas kommen sehen	*to see something coming*
verlegen sein	*to be embarrassed*
der Zungenkuss	*french kiss*
Freudentränen (Pl.)	*tears of joy*

Alles geht vorbei

DER GROSSKONZERN mischt auch das Internet auf: der-grosskonzern.de

Deutsch für den Ausländer ist eine Originalausgabe von
DER GROSSKONZERN Der kleine Verlag

Idee und Konzept: Florian Lamp / Heldrich Johannes
Text, Einbandgestaltung, Layout, Illustration und Fotografie: Heldrich Johannes
Text und Fotografie: Florian Lamp
Übersetzung der Kapitel ins Englische: Lisa Hüther / Paul Nissler
Lektorat und Korrektorat: Lisa Hüther, M. Lamp, Frau Dr. H.

ISBN-Nummer: 978-3-941934-00-9
Gedruckt bei Druckpunkt Berlin

Die Deutsche Bibliothek verzeichnet diese Publikation in der Deutschen Nationalbibliothek; detailierte Daten sind im Internet über dnb.ddb.de abrufbar.

Erscheint bestimmt bald in 175 Sprachen. Afrikaans, Albanisch, Amharisch, Ancash-Quechua, Arabisch, Armenisch Armenisch (Westarmensich), Aserbaidschanisch, Aserbaidschanisch (kyrillische Schrift), Ayacucho-Quechua, Aymará, Baule, Bemba, Bengali, Bikol, Birmanisch, Bislama, Bulgarisch, Cebuano, Chewa, Chinesisch (Tonaufnahmen nur in Hochchinesisch), Chinesisch (vereinfachte Schriftzeichen), Cuzco-Quechua, Dänisch, Deutsch, Deutschschweizer Gebärdensprache (auf Wunsch gerne auch in Zürcher-, Berner-, Basler-, Luzerner- und St. Galler Dialekt), Efik, Elliceanisch (Tuvalu), Englisch (auch in Breilleschrift), Estnisch, Ewe, Fitschi, Finnisch, Französisch, Ga, Ganda, Georgisch, Gilberthesisch, Griechisch, Grönländisch, Gun, Guaraní, Gujarati, Haussa, Hebräisch, Hiligaynon, Hindi, Hiri Motu, Ibo, Ilokano, Indonesisch, Isländisch, Italienisch, Japanisch, Kannada, Kaonde, Kasachisch, Khmer, Kinyaruanda, Kirgisisch, Kongo, Kongo (Monokutuba), Koreanisch, Kosraeanisch, Kreolisch (Haiti), Kroatisch, Kwangali, Kwanyama, Lettisch, Lingala, Litauisch, Lozi (Rotse), Luba-Kasai, Luba-Katanga, Luena, Lunda, Luo, Makedonisch, Malagassi, Malayala, Maltesisch, Marathi, Marshalesisch, Mauritius (Kreolisch), Maya, Mizo, Mossi, Ndonga, Nepali, Niederländisch, Niue, Norwegisch, Nyaneka, Oromo, Ossetisch, Palau, Panchabi, Pangasinan, Papiamento (Curaçao), Pedi, Persisch, Polnisch, Punapeanisch, Portugisisch, Rarotonganisch, Rumänisch, Rundi, Russisch, Ruund, Salomonen (Pidgin), Samoanisch, Sango, Schwedisch, Serbisch, Serbisch (latainische Schrift), Seychellen-Kreolisch, Shona, Singhalesisch, Slowakisch, Slowenisch, Soko, Sotho (Süd), Spanisch, Sranantongo, Suaheli, Südbolivianisches Quechua, Tagalog, Thaitisch, Tamil, Tatarisch, Telugu, Tetela, Thai, Tikrinja, Tiv, Tok Pisin, Tonga (Sambia), Tongaisch, Trukesisch, Tchechisch, Tsonga, Tswana, Tumbuka, Türkisch, Twi, Tzotzil, Ukrainisch, Umbundu, Ungarisch, Urdu, Usbekisch, Venda, Vietnamesisch, Wallisianisch, Waray, Xhosa, Yapesisch, Yoruba, Zande, Zapoteco (Istmo), Zulu